READING STORIES FOR COMPREHENSION SUCCESS:

Primary Level

BY

KATHERINE L. HALL

45 High-Interest Lessons with Reproducible Selections and Questions That Make Kids Think

Library of Congress Cataloging-in-Publication Data

Hall, Katherine L. (Katherine Louise).
     Reading stories for comprehension success : primary level (grades
1-3) : 45 high-interest lessons with reproducible selections &
questions that make kids think / by Katherine L. Hall.
          p.   cm.
     Includes bibliographical references (p.   ).
     ISBN 0-87628-755-0 (pbk. : spiral-wire).—ISBN 0-87628-888-3
(pbk. : adhesive)
     1. Reading (Primary)—Problems, exercises, etc.   2. Reading
comprehension—Problems, exercises, etc.   I. Title.
LB1525.7.H35   1996   96-32585
372.41—dc20   CIP

Printed in the United States of America

10   9   8   7   6   5   4   3   2   (paper)

10   9   8   7   6   5   (spiral)

ISBN 0-87628-888-3 (PAPER)

ISBN 0-87628-755-0 (SPIRAL)

DEDICATION

To my Mother, Doris L. Hall
Thank you always for your love, support, patience, and confidence,
not only during the writing of this book, but through all the
ups, downs, pains, and joys of our lives.

ABOUT THE AUTHOR

Katherine Hall attended the University of Texas at El Paso and earned her Bachelor's degree in elementary education and special education in 1982. She has worked with students at the elementary school level for many years as a teacher for the first grade, English as a Second Language program, and resource room as well as a private tutor.

An interest in reading comprehension was first sparked by her experience in elementary school resource rooms. Disillusioned by her students' lack of progress, she found that the multiple-choice question format often became monotonous and did not excite students or offer opportunities for self expression. The challenge of opening up the world of literature to her students, including learning disabled, prompted the creation of a new format for teaching comprehension skills. Katherine developed *Reading Stories for Comprehension Success* to increase students' confidence, interest, and involvement in learning. She found that by using high-interest, nonfiction stories, her students' curiosity about learning began to grow. From her own experience, she has found that *Reading Stories for Comprehension Success* also creates a rewarding teaching experience that can be implemented in schools, homes, and tutoring centers.

For over ten years, Ms. Hall was an active member of the Texas State Council of the International Reading Association and of a Parent Teacher Association. She has presented in-services for teachers and was published in several magazines. In addition to reading and teaching, she also enjoys music and is an avid performer of the harp, flute, and piccolo. She resides in Hurst, Texas, where she continues to tutor students at the elementary to college level.

ACKNOWLEDGEMENTS

We wish to thank the following for permitting us to use their photographs and artwork:

READING LEVEL 1

Training Sam: Susan Rosenberg

The Frog: Mark Bolster/International Stock

In the Deep Sea: Marine Studios

Reading Tracks: PH College Archives

"Little Peter" the Clown: Laima E. Druskis/Simon & Schuster/PH College

Mary Read: Lady Pirate: Katherine Hall

John Rock: PH College Archives

Brer Rabbit and Anansi the Spider: Katherine Hall

The Caldecott Medal: The Caldecott Medal and the name Caldecott Medal are property of the American Library Association and are used with permission.

The Color Wheel: Katherine Hall

To Fly Over the Ocean: The National Portrait Gallery, no. NPG.80.243

Superfast Trains: Japanese Air Lines

Thomas Edison's Newspaper: Fred R. Conrad/New York Times Pictures

Sequoyah and the Cherokee Alphabet: Courtesy of the Cherokee National Historic Society, Cherokee Heritage Center, Willis Road, Tahlequah, OK 74465, (918) 456-6007.

Piñatas: Ken Frick/International Stock

READING LEVEL 2

Fast-Food Computers: Randy Masser/International Stock

How Much Do You Weigh: National Aeronautics and Space Administration, no. AS11-40-5942

Stories in the Stars: National Aeronautics and Space Administration, no. S96-01095

Set a World's Record: Tony Demin/International Stock

Glenn Cunningham: National Archives, no. 306-NT-27553V

Home for the Summer: Ron Sanford/ International Stock

Japan's Kites: Eric Stanford/International Stock

Tramp's Code: Katherine Hall

The Stanley Steamer: Smithsonian Institution, Transportation, photo no. 11017

Albino: Phillip Gendreau, N.Y./PH College Archives

White Buffalo Calf Woman: Simon & Schuster/PH College

The Hubble Space Telescope: National Aeronautics and Space Administration, no. S96-01094

Jules Verne: Wilson North/ International Stock

Teamwork: Peter Langone/International Stock

Jackie Torrence: Irene Young [For bookings contact: John Ullman, Traditional Arts Services, 16045 36th Ave. NE, Seattle WA 98155, (206) 367-9044.]

READING LEVEL 3

Big, Bigger Biggest: Stanford/Agliolo/International Stock

Climbing High: Peter Krinninger/International Stock

Secrets in the Wings: Bob Firth/International Stock

The First Cartoons: The Museum of Modern Art, Film Stills Archives

Edwin Land: Al Lock/ International Stock

Harp Medicine: Rae Russel/International Stock

Signals on the Sea: Tom and Michelle Grimm/International Stock

Your Time Machine: National Aeronautics and Space Administration, no. S96-01092

For the Love of Patty Cake: AP/Wide World Photos

Fish for Pets: John Bechtold/International Stock

Rockets: National Aeronautics and Space Administration, no. 572-55070

The Snowshoe Rabbit Changes Its Fur: Mark Newman/International Stock

Before the Dinosaurs: George Ancona/International Stock

The Pupfish of Devil's Hole: Michelle and Tom Grimm/International Stock

The First Astronaut: National Aeronautics and Space Administration, no. G60-2615

INTRODUCTION

USING READING STORIES FOR COMPREHENSION SUCCESS

Reading Stories for Comprehension Success includes an entire week or more of activities for each story lesson. Turn to the beginning of any of the three reading levels, and you'll see that they all follow this format:

Contents

The Contents page lists all the story titles, along with the reading grade level of each story and the story's page number. The reading grade level tells the teacher the story reading difficulty within the reading grade level.

About the Story

A brief description of the story introduces the teacher to the topic.

Preview Words

The Preview Words are *not* words that the teacher drills before the lesson. These words allow the teacher to expose the students to words they may not know or are unable to pronounce. Young students should prepare for unknown words before reading in public.

Choose all or only a few of the words, based on your students' needs. Write the Preview Words on chart paper or on overhead projector transparencies before the day of the story lesson.

Throughout the Week or Prior to the Lesson

Some of the stories include these topics. *Throughout the Week* presents such activities as reading from chapter books or decorating the classroom on a theme. *Prior to the Lesson* tells you about any important preparations you must make before the week begins.

Books to Read

A list of books that relate to the subject of each story lesson is provided. These books are at many levels, from picture books to chapter books to books found in the adult section of the library. Your librarian can provide you with additional sources.

*Important—Always review any books, videos, and other materials before introducing them to your students, whether they are on the Books to Read *list or suggested by a librarian. What is considered appropriate for the students varies from state to state, or from school district to school district.*

Videos

This section lists videos on the story lesson subject. Many public libraries lend videos without charge.

*Use caution, however, when showing videos to your class. Make sure your situation does not require special fees to show the film. Avoid violating copyright laws!

CDs, Records, and Cassettes

Here you'll find other materials that coordinate with the story lesson.

Introductory Activities

Introductory Activities introduce the student to the story lesson. In Reading Level 2, Fast-Food Computers, the Introductory Activities begin with play-acting. The students take on the roles of the manager, employees, and customers of a fast-food restaurant. These experiences encourage more logical, well thought out answers to interpretive questions.

Story Lesson

The stories—each with an accompanying photograph—are the foundation of *Reading Stories for Comprehension Success*. Prior to the lesson, make a copy of the black-line master for each student. If you choose question 11, "Write a title for the story" (Identification of Main Idea), make one copy of the story. Erase the title of the story with correction fluid, then make the number of copies needed for your class.

The design of the story meets the needs of the learning-disabled and students with lower reading skills. The story is only one page long, about 150 words. The margins are wide to reduce the clutter on the story page, and there are no pictures, questions, or decorations on it. This helps students with perceptual problems, attention deficits, short attention spans, or other disabilities to see the text more clearly.

If a student has an extremely short attention span, cut the stories apart between paragraphs. Present only one paragraph at a time. When the student masters reading one paragraph without losing attention, increase the page length to two paragraphs. Continue in this way until the student reads an entire story at one sitting.

Following the lesson plan, choose the questions the students will answer. Make one copy of the black-line master of the Questions Sheet and cut out only the questions you wish to present in the lesson. Mount the questions on plain white paper. Erase the numbers with correction fluid, then renumber the questions and make your copies.

For students with short attention spans, run one question per page to reduce distractions. Place one question in front of the student at a time.

Follow the *Presenting the Story Lesson* instructions (p. 00) for each story. Every story follows the same presentation procedure. The consistent format is important for learning-disabled students.

The nonfiction, multicultural stories of *Reading Stories for Comprehension Success* are high-interest, and encourage the students to learn more. The biographies tell about such people as Glenn Cunningham and Jackie Torrence, who reached beyond themselves and their circumstances to achieve their dreams.

Extension Activities

Each story includes a list of *Extension Activities,* which allow the students to experience the subject beyond the story. Art projects, plays, and special activities for the whole school are offered.

Questions

The question format of *Reading Stories for Comprehension Success* requires students to answer in complete, well thought out sentences. There is no answer key because students create their own answers. Count any answer within reason as correct.

When presenting the Questions Sheet, encourage the students to debate possible answers to the interpretive questions. For example, the Drawing Conclusion question in the story about Edwin H. Land reads, "What one word best describes Edwin H. Land?" Many words describe Edwin H. Land; the word I believe is best may not be the word you choose. Discuss the choices made by the students. Each student's opinion is valuable, and they must know this every time they choose an answer to an interpretive question.

One exercise the students enjoy is a discussion group. The students play-act a television discussion group. The teacher acts as moderator and the students discuss ideas presented in the story. Ask individual students interpretive questions about the story; encourage them to state their own opinions, and to back up their opinions with evidence.

This exercise helps students to realize that not all questions have the same answer. After using *Reading Stories for Comprehension Success,* students can better evaluate the choices presented in a multiple-choice test.

Unlike many other reading comprehension programs, *Reading Stories for Comprehension Success* bases all of the comprehension questions on the text of the story. You choose the number and difficulty of the questions, based on the needs of your students.

Comprehension exercises include literal and interpretive questions, using the following format:

I. *Literal questions:* The students find and retrieve answers directly from the text.

    A. *Description* (questions 1-4 on the Questions sheet): literal questions in which the student takes exact answers from the text.

    B. *Sequence* (questions 5-6): ask the students to demonstrate an understanding of the sequence of events in the story.

II. *Interpretive questions:* The students are asked to draw logical conclusions, based on the information presented in the text. Answers to these questions might vary from student to student.

    A. *Conclusion* (question 7): These questions ask students to look at the facts of the text, then draw a conclusion based on these facts.

    B. *Inference* (question 8): Here, students must look beyond the stated text to what is inferred by the author.

    C. *Prediction* (question 9): To answer questions dealing with prediction, the students must imagine a future influenced by the events described in the text.

    D. *Identification of Cause* (question 10): The students speculate on the cause of an event or someone's actions.

    E. *Identification of Main Idea* (question 11): This seems to be a difficult concept for many children, with or without learning disabilities. One of the best ways to teach this concept is to ask students to write a title for the story. The title must state the topic or main idea of the story in only a few words.

        1. Throughout *Reading Stories for Comprehension Success,* the question for main idea is basically the same, "Write a title for the story. Use as few words as possible."

        2. First, remove the title from the story page with correction fluid, then make the number of copies needed for your class.

    F. *Comparison* (question 12): Students must compare subjects, concepts, and events found within the story.

    G. *Summarize* (question 13): These questions ask the students to summarize an event in their own words.

    H. *Effect* (question 14): The questions ask students to consider the effects of the events presented in the story.

    I. *Fact and Opinion* (question 15): Students determine if a statement from the story is a fact or an opinion. The question also asks the students if they can prove their answers. For example, can they find sources in reference books to back up their answers?

III. *Teacher-Created Question* (question 16): In this section, you can create your own question. Add your question to a copy of the Questions sheet. Inject the students' own experiences into the questions. The questions must relate to the text.

Student Data Sheet

■ Students track their progress on the Student Data Sheet.

■ All students record their time on task. Those with attention deficits see concrete evidence of their improvement.

Reading Ability Guidelines

■ *Reading Stories for Comprehension Success* provides a chart enabling teachers to follow a lesson procedure that matches a student's reading ability.

■ Routines for Poor Readers, Average Readers, and Upper Level Readers further allow you to tailor the lesson to the student's abilities. As the student improves, move to the next level of the Guidelines.

WHO CAN USE *READING STORIES FOR COMPREHENSION SUCCESS?*

TO TEACHERS

While working in the public schools as a Resource teacher, I saw more of the educational responsibility for students with learning disabilities fall on the shoulders of the regular classroom teacher. Some of these teachers had important and valid concerns:

■ "Tommy's attention span is so short. What can I do when I have twenty other students in the classroom?"

■ "Julia reads two years below grade level. How can I modify my lessons to include her in a subject dependent on reading?"

I could give the teachers only the same list of modifications: Reduce distractions. Seat Tommy close to your desk. Underline the important information in Julia's books. These modifications, however, only emphasize the special students' disabilities in front of their peers.

Reading Stories for Comprehension Success has all the modifications built into the program. The entire class works on the same lesson without singling out the learning-disabled student. This book works well for students in a variety of settings, including the following:

1. Public schools
2. Private schools (both regular and special education)
3. Classes for the learning disabled
4. Behavior disorders classes
5. Bilingual education classes
6. Tutoring centers
7. Home schools
8. Adult education classes

According to the U.S. Department of Education, the population of students with attention deficit disorder (ADD), dyslexia, and other learning disabilities is rising faster than any other educational group. *The Fifteenth Annual Report to Congress on the Implementation of Individuals With Disabilities Education Act (1993)* states:

> ... Since 1976–77 ... the number of students with specific learning disabilities has increased by more than 1.4 million (183 percent).

As the number of students with specific learning disabilities has increased, so has the percentage of learning-disabled students served in the regular classroom. Over the past several years, *The U.S. Department of Education's Annual Report to Congress on the Implementation of The Individuals With Disabilities Education Act* showed a steady increase in the percentage of learning-disabled students served within the regular classroom setting.

Percentage of Children Age 6-21 with
Specific Learning Disabilities Served
in Regular Classes Throughout the U.S.

1989–90	*1990–91*	*1992–93*
20.70%	33.75%	34.83%

Percentage of Students with Specific Learning
Disabilities Exiting the Educational
System Across the United States[1]

During the 1990–91 School Year

Age Group	*Graduated With Diploma*	*Graduated With Certificate*	*Reached Maximum Age*	*Dropped Out*	*Other*
14–21+	51.67%	10.80%	0.69%	22.16%	14.67%

Note that while this population grows, nearly 50% of learning-disabled students fail to graduate with a diploma.

TO TUTORS

Students in tutoring centers can benefit from the use of *Reading Stories for Comprehension Success.* As a tutor, you can tailor the lessons to the individual student's needs.

The week before the story lesson, give the student a list of books, videos, and activities to which the parent should expose the student. At the end of the list, add activity suggestions from the *Introductory Activities* and the *Extension Activities,* which the parents can do with the child.

TO PARENTS

Parents can use *Reading Stories for Comprehension Success* to supplement a child's education. When using this program with your child, follow the instructions for the teacher. Ask your child's teacher to administer an Individual Reading Inventory and inform you of your child's independent reading level. Many teachers already have this information in your child's file.

---

[1]Current (1995) figures are not available.

Remember to be consistent. Use complete sentences whenever you talk to your child. For example, your child might ask, "Where are we going?" Answer in the complete sentence, "We are going to the store." Do not answer with the sentence fragment, "to the store." Reduce visual distractions and clutter around the home and use natural light whenever possible.

Read one story a week with your child. Before reading the story, complete the *Introductory Activities,* and take your child to the library to check out books on the story subject.

Follow the *Presenting the Story Lesson* instructions on the day you read the story. If your child has a very short attention span, begin with only one paragraph of the story, and only one question from the Questions sheet. Note the length of time the child stays on task on the Lesson Plan (Objective 3 on p. xvii), and monitor progress on the Student Data Sheet. Over time, slowly increase the length of the story read, and the number of questions on the Questions sheet.

After reading the story, complete the *Extension Activities.* All the activities are great family projects, and a parent has more freedom than a classroom teacher to expose students to a variety of learning experiences.

CLASSROOM ENVIRONMENT

When creating a classroom environment, keep the distractions to a minimum. The classroom decorations don't have to be plain and dull — just not too busy. Some suggestions are:

1. Hang the same color of bulletin board paper throughout the room. White paper does not fade, so the same paper will last all year.
2. Use bulletin board borders that are not busy. Even plain borders can be attractive.
3. Play soft instrumental music as the students enter the room or while they are doing seat work. The music masks such random noises as dropped pencils and squeaky chairs.
4. Use natural light whenever possible; students seem more at ease without fluorescent lights.
5. If you store your materials in open bookcases, put them in boxes. Cover them with shelf paper without a busy design. Use the same design on *every* box.
6. Keep a few plants in the room. They add beauty and act as living air filters.

"IF YOU DO IT FOR ONE, DO IT FOR ALL"

The most important rule a teacher can follow is: "If you do it for one, you do it for all." Too often, teachers make modifications for special education students that are visible to the entire class. These modifications, which are put in place to help the student educationally, can destroy the student's morale. You *must* use modifications for learning-disabled students; however, modifications should be subtly implemented. Publicly announcing a student's special needs in front of her or his peers embarrasses and demoralizes a child already struggling for acceptance. These students will withdraw in shame or act out to find approval from their peers.

Watch your special education student throughout the day; note how many times you make special allowances or modifications of which the entire class is aware. For example:

■ Seating the student in an isolated area, even when there is no disruptive behavior involved.
■ Stating the modifications when giving an assignment. Avoid statements like these:

"Read Chapter One and answer questions one through ten. Frank, you need to do only questions one through five," or "Everyone read Chapter Six. Susan, I'll underline the parts you need to read after *everyone* begins working."

Later, look over your notes. Are there modifications that the entire class can participate in? If you do it for one, can you do it for all? For example, students with learning disabilities have difficulty keeping their work organized. If one modification is to set up a notebook with individual folders for each subject area and homework, all the students should have such a notebook.

Sometimes you cannot use modifications with the entire class. It is best to meet with the student privately to discuss these modifications. When you meet with the student, write down all the modifications she or he can expect and how you will implement them. Remember to make the implementation as private and subtle as possible. After the student understands and agrees to these modifications, sign a contract. File it in the student's file; it will be invaluable as proof of modifications if school district or other officials ask for it.

ATTENTION DEFICIT DISORDER

Aside from the recent surge in drug therapy, few programs offer innovative teaching aids for learning-disabled students, including those with ADD. Focus on strategies that go beyond medication, and remember to use these strategies with the entire class whenever possible. For example, the rate at which the teacher reads a story affects the student's comprehension levels during auditory presentation. According to one study, hyperactive students were less active and stayed on task when the teacher read the story fast "without added nonrelevant detail." Comprehension improved, however, when the teacher read the story slowly without added detail.[2]

According to Fiore, Becker, and Nero, the following techniques are most likely to be effective in academic areas:

Positive Reinforcement

1. Social praise
2. Group reward contingencies
3. Parent rewards
4. Token economies

Punishment ("a contingency that reduces the frequency of behavior")

1. Hyperactive students remained on task longer using negative feedback. However, errors increased significantly.
2. Short, strong, and consistent reprimands reduced disruptive behaviors.

In her book *When Children Don't Learn,* Diane McGuinness states that educators must meet the following three needs before hyperactive students can change their behaviors and begin to improve their academic performance.[3] We should apply these needs to all students, with or without learning disabilities.

1. *ACHIEVABLE GOALS: Reading Stories for Comprehension Success* allows the teacher to determine "achievable goals" for each student on an individual basis. The teacher chooses the type and number of questions used. As the students achieve success, the teacher gradually increases the number of questions.

---

[2]Thoms A. Fiore, Elizabeth A. Becker, and Rebecca C. Nero, "Educational Interventions for Students With Attention Deficit Disorder," *Exceptional Children,* v 60 (Oct.–Nov. 1993), 163 (II).

[3]Diane McGuinness, *When Children Don't Learn: Understanding the Biology and Psychology of Learning Disabilities* (New York: Basic Books, 1985).

2. *GOALS BASED ON ACADEMIC SUBJECT AREAS: Reading Stories for Comprehension Success* incorporates the needs of learning-disabled students in an academic subject (reading comprehension) in a format that benefits every student in the class. Students can develop reading comprehension skills at any reading level.

The teacher chooses a reading level based on the learning-disabled reading skills, and uses this level for the entire class. The high-interest, factual stories mask the true reading level. Everyone in the class, learning disabled or not, learns comprehension skills with modifications built into the program, without being aware of special provisions for learning-disabled students.

3. *FREQUENT PRAISE:* As the students progress through *Reading Stories for Comprehension Success,* they complete their assignments without undue stress. They participate in making the Data Sheets, proving to themselves that they can succeed. The factual, fascinating content of the stories inspires students to learn more, and possibly to set goals based on newly found interests.

TEACHING STRATEGIES

Teachers can use several teaching strategies with the entire class to improve the reading comprehension skills of students with or without learning disabilities. *Reading Stories for Comprehension Success* begins with one to two days of introductory activities before the story lesson. From these experiences, the students develop a better understanding of the story. The Extension Activities build on the students' comprehension; with them, you create a "total sensory experience."

Students with learning disabilities have difficulty remembering what they learned even minutes after reading the story. Use this activity presented by Jerome Rosner in his book *Helping Children Overcome Learning Difficulties: A Step-by-Step Guide for Parents and Teachers* with the entire class. (Note: This skill also prepares all students for achievement tests, which require strong short-term memory.)

Give each student a paragraph written at the child's independent reading level. The students copy as much of the paragraph as they can in two minutes. Set a timer for two minutes and say, "Go." The students stop when the timer rings.

At the bottom of the page, the students write "number of words copied = _____" and "number of spelling errors and omissions = _____." On a separate page, the students copy the following chart:

Day	Number of Words Copied in Two Minutes	Number of Errors and Omissions
1		
2		
3		
4		
5		

The chart can be kept for the number of days needed. The goal is to increase the number in column 1 while decreasing the number in column 2. Tell the students to try to keep larger sections of the story in their memory while they write; it will increase the number of words they copy. It is also helpful to say the words to themselves as they write. According to Rosner, repeating the information to themselves will improve short-term memory. Keeping larger pieces of the paragraph in their heads will improve reading speed.

Language Development

The Preview Words of *Reading Stories for Comprehension Success* introduce the students to new vocabulary words without drill. The students not only hear the words in the story, but continue to use them in speech and writing during the Introductory and Extension Activities. Encourage the students to find new words based on the concepts presented in the story. Remember to model the use of these words in your own speech.

Team Learning

Throughout *Reading Stories for Comprehension Success,* students work in groups or teams. This allows the learning-disabled students to participate in an activity without depending solely on their own abilities. Break the class into groups of two to three students. Subtly assigning a higher level reader to each group helps the others in the group with difficult words or passages, and learning-disabled students don't feel singled out when other students in the group also ask for help.

Set up a permanent book center in the classroom. Encourage the students to read books that interest them.

Read to the Class

Chapter books supplement several stories in *Reading Stories for Comprehension Success.* Look for these titles in the *Throughout the Week* section. Read chapters from these books each day. Soon students will ask the librarian for books on the same topic or by the same author. An active interest in reading quickly improves a student's reading comprehension skills.

Reading Stories for Comprehension Success aims to improve reading comprehension by introducing and reinforcing basic concepts of the subject matter through multisensory Introductory and Extension Activities. With the high-interest, factual stories, students expand their vocabulary, reinforcing the Preview Words.

READING ABILITY GUIDELINES[4]

The guidelines suggest teaching procedures, based on the students' reading comprehension skills. As poor readers improve, move to the next level.

A student's answers to interpretive questions may not be logically sound. Conduct a short, open discussion about other possibilities. Consider the answer correct, however, if the student arrived at the conclusion based on his or her best effort. Remember that the purpose of *Reading Stories for Comprehension Success* is to create joy in learning and expressing oneself.

*Note: Do not include interpretive questions in your question list until the student demonstrates mastery of literal questions. Then introduce only one interpretive question until the student shows confidence.

---

[4]Based on information from: Durkin, Dolores, *Teaching Them to Read,* 3d ed., p. 442 (Boston: Allyn and Bacon, 1979).

Poor Readers

1. Read the literal questions orally.
2. Read the story silently.
3. Discuss the answers to the literal questions. (Encourage students to speak in complete, understandable sentences.)
4. Read the interpretive questions orally.
5. Read the story silently (second reading).
6. Discuss the answers to the interpretive questions.
7. The students complete the Questions sheet independently, writing all the answers in complete sentences.

Average Readers

1. Read the literal and interpretive questions orally.
2. Read the story silently.
3. Discuss the answers to the interpretive questions.
4. The students complete the Questions sheet independently, writing all the answers in complete sentences.

Upper Level Readers

1. Read the interpretive questions orally.
2. Read the story silently.
3. Conduct a discussion based on the questions. (Guide the students in the use of complete, well thought out sentences.)
4. The students complete the Questions sheet independently, writing all the answers in complete sentences.

PRESENTING THE STORY LESSON

*Important: Remove all extra stimulation from the students' view or reach. The work area must be clear of distractions.

1. Review the Introductory Activities. Discuss what the students did and learned.
2. Display and discuss the Preview Words, then remove the words from the children's sight.
3. Display the story picture. Engage the students in a discussion about the illustration. Focus on the topic of the story and guide the students in such a way as to focus their attention on the subject.
4. Read the quote found in the Story Lesson section of each story. This question prepares them for the content of the story. For example, "The title of the story we're reading today is *The First Astronaut.* What do you think the story is about? What do you already know about astronauts?"
5. Hand out the story pages.

6. Choose the lesson format from the guidelines that suits your students' reading ability. Remember to remove the story from the students' view when they work on their question sheets to avoid distractions. They can refer to the story if needed; however, remove the story from the students' view as soon as possible.

7. Grade the questions in front of the students when they complete their work. Because you monitor the work closely, there should be few errors.

8. Students record their scores on the Student Data Sheets.

SENTENCE WRITING LESSONS

MATERIALS

■ photographs or drawings with simple subjects

Do not use complicated, busy photographs. Calendars provide a good source for photographs and drawings because they usually focus on a single subject (e.g., a dog in a simple pose).

PROCEDURE

Week One

1. Display a calendar picture in front of the class.

2. Teacher:

Every picture has a subject. A subject is the most important figure in the picture. Look at this picture. The subject of this picture is a dog. What is the subject of this picture? (Answer: The subject of the picture is a dog.)

3. Show five more pictures. Display the pictures one at a time. Ask the students the subject of the picture. Model a complete sentence for the answer whenever the students answer in sentence fragments.

4. Repeat the exercise with five photographs each day for a week, or until the students demonstrate mastery of the skill.

Week Two

1. Display the same dog picture used in Week One, step 1.

2. Teacher:

Each subject in a picture is doing something. What is the subject in this picture? (Answer: The subject in the picture is a dog.) What is the dog doing? (Answer: The dog is sitting in a basket.)

The part of a sentence that tells us the subject of the picture is the subject. The part of the sentence that tells us what the subject is doing is the predicate. What is the part of the sentence that tells us what the subject is doing? (Answer: The part of the sentence that tells us what the subject is doing is the predicate.)

If we were to tell about this picture in a complete sentence, we would say, "The dog is sitting in a basket." (Write the sentence on the board.)

What is the subject of this sentence? (Answer: The subject of this sentence is "The dog." Underline the words "The dog.")

What is the predicate of this sentence? (Answer: The predicate of this sentence is "is sitting in a basket." Draw two lines under the words "is sitting in a basket.")

The sentence "The dog is sitting in a basket" is a complete sentence. It has a subject and a predicate. What must a complete sentence have? (Answer: A complete sentence must have a subject and a predicate.)

3. Remove the dog picture and display another picture. Follow the procedure outlined in step 1.
4. Erase the sentence and remove the picture from the students' view.
5. Repeat the procedure for three more photographs.
6. Do this exercise with five photographs each day of the week, or until the students demonstrate mastery of the skill.

Week Three

Students who have difficulty writing can do these exercises orally. Remember, if one student does the exercise orally, everyone does the exercise orally.

1. Display one picture.
2. Ask the students to write or state a complete sentence about the picture. If the students answer orally, write the sentence on the board.
3. The students will underline the subject of the sentence. They will draw two lines under the predicate. If this is an oral exercise, ask students to come to the board. They will underline the subject and draw two lines under the predicate. If the students write their answers, call on individuals to read their sentences. Ask them to tell the subject and the predicate.
4. Erase the sentence on the board and remove the picture.
5. Repeat the exercise with four more pictures. Show only one picture at a time.
6. Practice this exercise with five pictures each day of the week, or until the students demonstrate mastery of the skill.

Supplemental Lessons

Repeat Week Three throughout the year to refresh the students' skill. Remember to model complete sentences at all times. Ask the students to speak in complete sentences all day in *every* subject.

PRETEST

Determine the reading grade level of each student in the class. Survey each student's reading grade level using your favorite Individual Reading Inventory (IRI). You are looking for the student's independent reading level, *not* the instructional level. *Reading Stories for Comprehension Success* aims to improve comprehension skills only. If you begin the program at the student's instructional level, the reading of individual words becomes the focus of his or her efforts; if you present the stories at the student's independent reading level, he or she comfortably reads the text and concentration is on the content.

Look over the IRI scores. Which score is the lowest? Begin *Reading Stories for Comprehension Success* one level below this score, unless the lowest score is grade 1. In this case, begin on Reading Level 1. For example, if your students are fifth-graders, look at the lowest IRI score. If the lowest independent reading level is grade level 3, begin *Reading Stories for Comprehension Success* at Reading Level 2.

This procedure ensures that the student with the lowest reading level will feel comfortable reading with the rest of the class. Never tell the students the reading level they are working on; because of the factual, high-interest nature of the stories, they will not realize that they are reading at a lower reading level. You can teach any reading comprehension skill at any reading grade level.

TEACHER LESSON PLAN

The Lesson Plan form in *Reading Stories for Comprehension Success* saves valuable teacher time. First, choose the type and number of questions you will ask the students. Begin with only literal questions on the first lesson, presenting one to no more than five questions in one lesson. The number of questions asked depends on the students' ability and attention span.

LESSON PLAN FORM

1. *Basic Information*

   ■ fill in the class information at the top of the page.

2. *Objectives*

   ■ The lesson format of *Reading Stories for Comprehension Success* is consistent and predictable throughout the series. Therefore, each lesson teaches and reinforces the same basic objectives.

   Objective 1

   ■ Circle if the student is to read orally or silently.

   Objective 2

   ■ Circle if the student is to answer the questions orally or in writing.

   Objective 3

   ■ Fill in the number of minutes the student will stay on task. Use this objective to monitor students with short attention spans. By beginning with a short question list and increasing the number of questions over time, you can actually help the student to increase his or her time on task.

3. *Comprehension Skills Taught in This Lesson*

   ■ Check off the comprehension skills you will present in the lesson.

4. *Materials*

   ■ Every lesson uses all the materials listed.

LESSON PLAN

Date: _____   **Teacher Edition page ____**

Class Period: _____   **Student page ____**

Student: _____

Reading Group: _____

Story: _____

Objectives:

(circle one)
1. The student(s) will read the story orally/silently.

(circle one)
2. The student(s) will orally state/write the answers to the following comprehension skills in complete, understandable sentences.

3. The student(s) will complete the given assignment in _____ minutes.

Comprehension Skills Taught in This Lesson:
(Check the skill to be taught.)

I. Literal questions

   A. Description _____

   B. Sequence _____

II. Interpretive questions

   A. Conclusion _____

   B. Interference _____

   C. Prediction _____

   D. Identification of Cause _____

   E. Identification of Main Idea _____

   F. Comparisons _____

   G. Summarize _____

   H. Effect _____

   I. Fact and Opinion _____

III. Teacher-created question _____

Materials:
__ Story page   __ Questions Sheet   __ Student Data Sheet

STUDENT DATA SHEET

STUDENT DATA SHEET (Example)   Student: ___Frank_____

Story	1
Date	4/6/97
Description	2
Sequence	1
Conclusion	1
Inference	0
Prediction	
Cause	
Main Idea	
Comparison	
Summarize	
Effect	
Fact/Opinion	
Score	4/5
Percentage	80%
Time on Task	6 min.

Consider a comprehension skill mastered when the student has five correct answers in a row. Move on to the next skill; however, intermittently include the mastered skills in the Questions Sheet as review.

STUDENT DATA SHEET   Student: _____

	Story	1	2	3	4	5	6	7	8	9	10	11	12	13	14	15	AVERAGE
L I T E R A L	Date																
	Description																
	Sequence																
I N T E R P R E T I V E	Conclusion																
	Inference																
	Prediction																
	Cause																
	Main Idea																
	Comparison																
	Summarize																
	Effect																
	Fact/Opinion																
	Score																
	Percentage																
	Time on Task																

© 1997 by The Center for Applied Research in Education

Purpose of Student Data Sheet

The easy-to-use Student Data Sheet helps both teacher and students track their progress through *Reading Stories for Comprehension Success*. The Data Sheet serves several purposes:

1. The students track their own performance, which serves also as a motivational reward system.
2. The students track their time on task, and thus see tangible evidence of their efforts. This is also a powerful, yet often overlooked, reward system.
3. You can use the Data Sheet to monitor the student's mastery of comprehension skills.
4. School districts require teachers to keep a written record of any provisions made for students who qualify as learning disabled. The Data Sheet is a good record to keep in your files.

Using the Student Data Sheet

1. After the students complete their Questions sheets, grade the answers in front of each student. At the top of the page write:

   The Number of Correct Answers
   The Total Number of Questions

   For example, if a student answered four out of five questions correctly, write the following at the top of the page:

   $$\frac{4}{5}$$

2. Give the student her or his Student Data Sheet.
3. Write the date under the number of the story read.
4. Look at the list of reading comprehension question styles listed down the sheet. In front of the student, enter the number of correct responses to each question style. Because of the presentation of the material, there should be few errors.
5. The student enters the score from the Questions sheet into the space marked Score.
6. Using the score numbers, enter the percentage into the Percentage box. If the student has the skills to calculate the percentage, he or she will enter the number into the Data Sheet; otherwise, you must calculate and enter the percentage. (You can also use this number as the grade for the lesson.)
7. The student enters the time in minutes that he or she stayed on task in the Time on Task space.
8. At the end of the reading level, average the percentage scores and enter the total score under the Average box. For example, Frank's Questions sheet contained two description questions, one sequence question, one comprehension question, and one inference question on Story 1. He answered every question except the inference question correctly. The score on his paper would read: 4/5. His time on task was 6 minutes.

IN CONCLUSION

The aim of *Reading Stories for Comprehension Success* is to incorporate modifications for learning-disabled students into one program. This program gives teachers maximum flexibility in lesson presentation. Unlike other reading comprehension programs, this book gives you the freedom to base a lesson on your students' needs. Always keep in mind the following:

1. Keep the room and work area as distraction free as possible.
2. If you do it for one, do it for all.
3. Always model complete sentences in your own speech.
4. Encourage the students to speak in complete, well thought out sentences.
5. Create an environment in which students feel free to develop and communicate their unique ideas. Allow them to debate the interpretive questions, and to learn from the variety of backgrounds each student brings to the class.

Katherine L. Hall

CONTENTS

BRER RABBIT AND ANANSI THE SPIDER 59

THE CALDECOTT MEDAL 69

THE COLOR WHEEL 79

TO FLY OVER THE OCEAN 88

SUPER-FAST TRAINS 95

THOMAS EDISON'S NEWSPAPER 102

SEQUOYAH AND THE CHEROKEE ALPHABET 112

PIÑATAS 119

BIBLIOGRAPHY 129

READING LEVEL 2

READING LEVEL 3

THE FIRST ASTRONAUT 373

BIBLIOGRAPHY 382

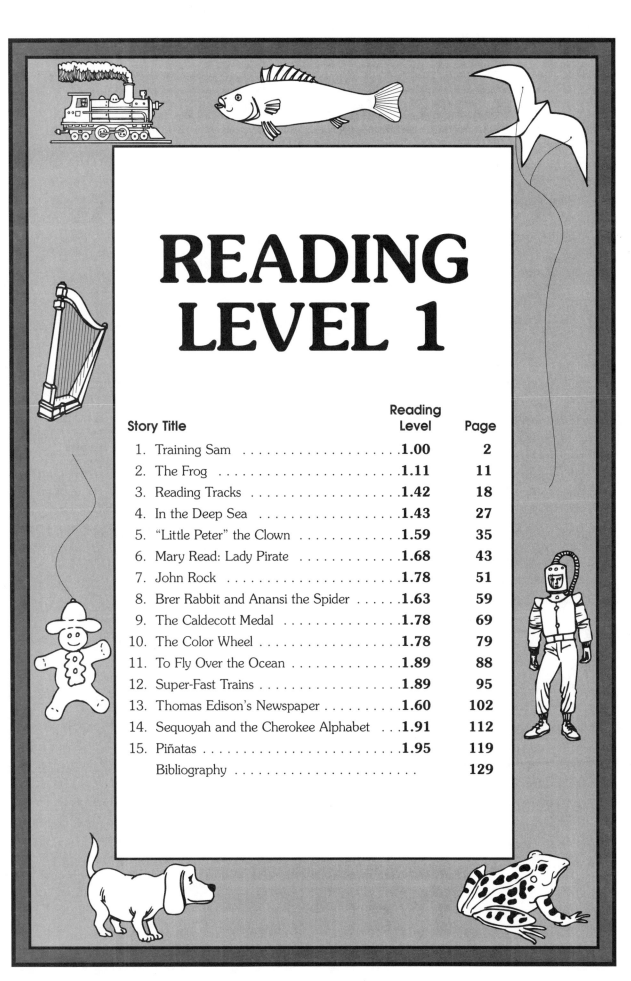

READING LEVEL 1

TRAINING SAM

ABOUT THE STORY

This story tells how to train a dog. The author emphasizes patience and gentleness.

PREVIEW WORDS

training	Sam	hungry
pet	first	next
last	leash	learn
gently	angry	always

THROUGHOUT THE WEEK—Read these books to the class:

Mush, a Dog From Space by Daniel Manus Pinkwater (New York: Atheneum Books for Young Readers, 1995)

Buffy's Orange Leash by Stephen Golder and Lise Memling (Washington, D.C.: Kendall Green Publications, 1988)

Dog Breath!: The Horrible Terrible Trouble With Hally Tosis by Dav Pilky (New York: Blue Sky Press, 1994).

BOOKS TO READ

Maggie by My Side, Beverly Butler (Dodd, Mead, 1987).

Snow On Snow On Snow, Cheryl Chapman (Dial Books for Young Readers, 1994).

Making Friends: Training Your Dog Positively, Linda Colflesh (Howell Book House, 1990).

Buffy's Orange Leash, Stephen Golder and Lise Memling (Kendall Green Publications, 1988).

My First Puppy, Rosemarie Hausherr (Four Winds Press, 1986).

Dreaming, Bobette McCarthy (Candlewick Press, 1994).

Dog Breath!: The Horrible Terrible Trouble With Hally Tosis, Dav Pilky (Blue Sky Press, 1994).

Mush, a Dog From Space, Daniel Manus Pinkwater (Atheneum Books For Young Readers, 1995).

Make It Yourself: Animals, consultant Caroline Pitcher (Franklin Watts, 1983).

Companion Dogs: More Than Best Friends, Elizabeth Ring (The Millbrook Press, 1994).

Speak!: Children's Book Illustrators Brag About Their Dogs, edited by Michael J. Rosen (Harcourt Brace & Jovanovich, 1993).

All About Dogs As Pets, Louis Sabin (Julian Messner, 1983).

Woe Is Moe, Diane Stanley (Putnam's, 1995).

Understanding Dogs, Su Swallow (Usborne Publishing Ltd., 1978).

The New Dog Handbook, Hans-J. Ullmann with Evamaria Ullmann (Barron's Education Series, Inc., 1985).

Puppies at Play: A 101 Dalmatians Word Book, Samantha Walker (Disney, 1995).

Walkies: Dog Training and Care the Woodhouse Way, Barbara Woodhouse (Summit Books, 1982).

VIDEO

A Dozen Dizzy Dogs, based on a book by William H. Hooks. A Read Along Bank Street Story Video. Great Neck, NY: Best Film & Video Corp., 1990. Length: 30 minutes.

CDS, RECORDS, AND CASSETTES

The Case of the Double Bumblebee Sting (Cassette), John R. Erickson (Texas Monthly Press, 1994).

INTRODUCTORY ACTIVITIES

DAY ONE

Objective: The students will listen to a speaker talk about training and caring for dogs.
Curriculum subject: Language Arts or Science

Ask a speaker to visit your class. The speaker might be a member of the police department with a trained dog, a disabled person who uses a guide dog, or a trainer from a local dog obedience school. The speaker should demonstrate some of the things the dog is trained to do. Discuss how to care for the dog with patience and gentleness. Why should a dog be trained with kindness? What can the students do at home to train their own dogs?

After the speaker leaves, the students will write thank-you notes and draw pictures to send to the speaker. The students should tell what they enjoyed about the visit.

DAY TWO

Objective: The students will write about how people use trained dogs.
Curriculum subject: Language Arts
Teacher: Yesterday we saw how to train a dog to do special things. What were these special things?

Today we'll break into groups of three to four students. I'll give each group the name of a job a dog might have. You'll write about what the dog does. After you finish, draw a picture of a dog doing that job.

Assign each group one of the following topics:

◆ Guard dogs
◆ Police dogs
◆ Guide dogs for the blind
◆ Dogs trained to find people trapped by earthquakes
◆ Dogs trained to find people trapped in avalanches
◆ Dogs trained to help the deaf
◆ Circus dogs
◆ Dogs who act in movies—Lassie, for example
◆ Sled dogs

Younger students make lists of what the dog does. Older students will write a short description of the dog's job by answering the following questions:

1. Who uses the dog?
2. What does the dog do?
3. When does the dog do his or her job?
4. Where does the dog work?
5. Why do people use dogs to do the job?

Display the pictures and lists or descriptions in the classroom.

DAY THREE

Story Lesson
Follow the *Presenting the Story Lesson* instructions in the Introduction. Each story lesson follows the same procedure; however, say the following in step 4:
"The title of the story we're reading today is *Training Sam*. What do you think the story is about?" If the students' answers include training dogs, ask, "What do you already know about training dogs?"

EXTENSION ACTIVITIES

1. Several days before the lesson, ask students to bring in pictures of their dogs. Their parents must give permission to use the photos in an art project. Also, ask them to bring in any item for a dog that they no longer need. (See materials list for suggestions.)

Dog Collage
Materials

◆ dog pictures—suggestions: drawings of dogs, photographs of the students' pets, pictures from dog magazines (ask your local veterinarian for donations), pictures from dog calendars
◆ glue
◆ poster boards of various colors
◆ dog "things"—suggestions: old dog tags; old dog collars; dog biscuits shaped like bones, to be painted with clear paint
◆ clear paint for dog biscuits
◆ construction paper dog shapes made by tracing around cookie cutters
◆ glitter paints and poster paints to highlight pictures
◆ names of breeds of dogs and names of their own dogs cut out of magazines or written on paper

Procedure

◆ Give each student a poster board. If there are not enough pictures to make a collage for each student, break the class into groups to work on the collages together.

◆ The students glue the items listed in the materials randomly on the poster board. Encourage the students to cover the entire poster board in a creative way.

◆ Display the completed collages in the school library, cafeteria, or other prominent location. Entitle the display "Gone to the Dogs!"

2. The students will decorate clothes using sponge art and a dog motif.

Sponge Art Clothes
Materials

◆ Students bring a plain clothes items from home. (Examples include T-shirts, sweat shirts or suits, skirts, jackets, pants, etc.) Be sure to have signed permission from the parents to decorate the shirt. If the students cannot afford to buy these items, ask local department stores for donations.

> **Important:** The clothes must be washed before the students paint them. New clothes do not hold the paint.

◆ compressed sponges found in arts and crafts stores in clothes painting section

◆ dog-shaped cookie cutters

◆ fabric paint

◆ bone-shaped dog biscuits

◆ clear paint

◆ glue

◆ small pin backings found in craft stores or safety pins

◆ cardboard to slide into clothing

Procedure

◆ Slide cardboard into clothing. This prevents the paint from bleeding through.

◆ Choose a cookie cutter shape. Trace the shape onto a compressed sponge. Cut out the shape and dip it into water. Wring out the water after the sponge expands. (Note: Students can share their dog sponges to vary the shapes on their clothes.)

◆ Dip the sponge into fabric paint and press the sponge onto the clothing.

◆ The students decorate the dogs. Suggestions: Sew ribbon bows at the neck, sew on bead eyes, paint on leashes.

◆ To make dog paw prints walking around the shirt, use finger prints. Paint your thumb and press it onto the shirt. Paint your little finger and press it four times over the thumb print. Example:

◆ Paint bone-shaped dog biscuits with clear paint. Allow the front to dry completely, then turn it over and paint the back.

◆ Emphasize to your students that the painted bones cannot be eaten.

◆ The teacher should paint the bones before class for the younger students. After the paint dries, glue a pin backing on the back of the bone. Let dry, then pin the bone onto the clothing.

3. Ask the students to bring pictures of their pets to school. The pictures can be photographs or the students' drawings. A student who does not have a pet can draw a picture of a pet he or she would like to have. Encourage them to be creative—maybe drawing a dinosaur pet, so these students feel special, too. The students share their pictures with the rest of the class, then display them around the room.

4. Discuss which animals make good pets, and which animals do not (i.e., wild animals versus domestic animals). Hand out magazines and ask the students to cut out pictures of animals. Display a poster board chart at the front of the room, divided in half and labeled *Pets/Not Pets*. Show the students the pictures from the magazines, then after discussing each picture, tape the picture under the appropriate title.

<u>Pets</u>	<u>Not Pets</u>

5. Bring a stuffed dog or cat to class. Begin by telling the students not to touch an animal they do not know or an animal unaccompanied by its owner. Discuss how to care for an animal, and why we should treat animals with kindness. Let the children practice petting the stuffed animal gently. What does an animal need from its owner (food, water, shots, veterinarian checkups). Write the list as the children dictate on the board.

6. For the younger students, show the video *A Dozen Dizzy Dogs* during math class. The video counts dogs as they play with a bone.

TRAINING SAM

This is Sam. Sam is a dog. He is a happy pet. I feed Sam when he is hungry. I play with Sam. I like Sam and Sam likes me. If I want Sam to be a good pet, I must train him.

First, I teach Sam to come. I put Sam on a long rope. Sam walks around, and is soon far away. I clap my hands, and say, "Sam, come!" Slowly, I pull the rope until Sam is with me. I do not pull hard. I do not want to hurt Sam. Every day I work with Sam. Now Sam comes when I call him.

Next, I teach Sam to walk on a leash. I hold most of the leash in my hand. I want Sam to learn to walk next to me. Gently, I tug on the leash and say, "Sam, walk!" Sam learns to walk next to me.

Last, I teach Sam to sit. I wave my hand down and say, "Sam, sit!" I gently push Sam down until he sits. Soon, Sam learns to sit.

I never hit Sam. I tell him when I am angry, and I pet him when he does well. I know that if I take good care of Sam, he will always be my friend.

QUESTIONS FOR TRAINING SAM

1. What is the name of the dog in the story?

   _____

   _____

2. What must the person do to make Sam a good pet?

   _____

   _____

3. What three things does Sam learn to do in the story?

   _____

   _____

4. What does the person do to Sam when he does well?

   _____

   _____

5. What does Sam learn <u>first</u>?

   _____

   _____

6. What does Sam learn <u>last</u>?

   _____

   _____

7. The story tells us that Sam likes the person in the story. Name two reasons why Sam likes the person.

   _____

   _____

8. Do you think it took one day to teach Sam to come, to walk on a leash, and to sit? Why do you think so?

   _____

   _____

9. The person in the story wants to teach Sam more. Name three other things she or he might teach Sam.

_____

_____

10. How does training a dog make it a good pet?

_____

_____

11. Write a title for the story. Use as few words as possible.

_____

_____

12. How is training a dog to come like training it to walk on a leash? How is it different?

_____

_____

13. In your own words, tell how to teach a dog to sit.

_____

_____

14. What would happen if the person teaching Sam yelled at the dog? Would Sam learn more quickly, or would he learn more slowly? Why do you think so?

_____

_____

15. The story says, "If I train Sam, he will be a good pet." Is this a fact, or is it an opinion? Why do you think this way?

_____

_____

16. _____

_____

Name _____ Date _____

THE FROG

ABOUT THE STORY

This story is about how a frog's body allows it to live in its environment. The students look for ways a frog's body helps it to live in a pond.

PREVIEW WORDS

bumpy	pond	around
strong	back feet	carefully
next	picture	body

THROUGHOUT THE WEEK—Read *Frog and Toad* stories by Arnold Lobel (New York: HarperCollins), including *Frog and Toad All Year* (1976), *Frog and Toad Are Friends* (1970), *Frog and Toad Pop-Up Book* (1986), and *Frog and Toad Together* (1971).

BOOKS TO READ

The Toad Hunt, Janet Chenery (Harper & Row, 1967).

Find the Hidden Insect, Joanna Cole and Jerome Wexler (Morrow, 1979).

Froggie Went A-Courting (folk song) illustrated by Chris Conover (Farrar, Straus & Giroux, 1986).

The Frog Princess: A Russian Tale Retold, Elizabeth Isele (Harper, 1984).

Frogs and Toads, Bobbie Kalman and Tammy Everts (Crabtree Publishing Company, 1994).

The Frog, Margaret Lane (Dial Press, 1981).

Frog and Toad All Year, Arnold Lobel (Harper & Row, 1976), and *Frog and Toad Are Friends* (1970), *Frog and Toad Pop-Up Book* (1986) and *Frog and Toad Together* (1971).

Frog, Where Are You?, Mercer Mayer (Dial Press, 1973).

The Frog Who Drank the Waters of the World, Patricia Montgomery Newton (Atheneum, 1983).

The Frog Alphabet Book and Other Awesome Amphibians, Jerry Pallotta (Charlesbridge Publishing, 1990).

Sprig the Tree Frog, Margaret Sanford Pursell (Carolrhoda Books, 1976).

Walt Disney's The Adventures of Mr. Toad, Walt Disney Productions (Random House, 1981).

VIDEO

Frog and Toad Together: Friends Forever, Arnold Lobel (Golden Book Video, 1985).

CDS, RECORDS, AND CASSETTES

Picasso the Green Tree Frog (filmstrip/cassette), Amanda Graham (Gareth Stevens Media, 1988).

The Frog (cassette and book set), Paula Z. Hogan (Raintree Publishers, 1985).

Mark Twain Stories, Mark Twain (Caedmon, 1956).

Days With Frog and Toad (cassette and book set), Arnold Lobel (HarperCollins, 1985).

Frog and Toad (cassette and 4 book set), Arnold Lobel (Listening Library, 1990).

Frog and Toad All Year (cassette and book set), Arnold Lobel (Listening Library, 1985).

INTRODUCTORY ACTIVITIES

DAY ONE

Objective: The students will keep a tadpole in the class and record its growth.
Curriculum subject: Science

Obtain a tadpole, tank, and food from the school district's science department. If this is not possible, Three Rivers Amphibian's *Grow a Frog* is a kit including a tank and food, plus a coupon for a tadpole. *Grow a Frog* is distributed (not exclusively) by Insect Lore. It is recommended for children ages 6 to 10.

Set up the tank as the students take notes or draw pictures. The students will keep a diary of the tadpole's development. On each page of the diary the students will record the date, draw a picture of the tadpole, then write a brief description of the changes they see. Discuss the tadpole's growth until it become a frog.

DAY TWO

Objective: The students will listen to the book *Frogs and Toads* by Bobbie Kalman and Tammy Everts. They will discuss vocabulary words about frogs.
Curriculum subject: Science

Before this lesson, write the words and their definitions (p. 31 of *Frogs and Toads*) on a chart. Review the words with the students.
Teacher: Yesterday, we set up a tank to watch a tadpole grow. Today, we'll listen to a story about frogs. As I read the story, think about the ways a frog's body helps it to live in a pond.

Read the story *Frogs and Toads*. After the story, tell the students they will read a story tomorrow about how a frog's body helps it to live in a pond.

DAY THREE

First, read the story *The Frog Alphabet Book and Other Awesome Amphibians* by Jerry Pallotta to the class.

Story Lesson
Follow the *Presenting the Story Lesson* instructions in the Introduction. Each story lesson follows the same procedure; however, say the following in step 4:
"The title of the story we're reading today is *The Frog*. What do you think this story is about? What do you already know about frogs?"

EXTENSION ACTIVITIES

1. Discuss how the frog's body helps it to live in ponds. Display pictures of animals. Ask the children to list ways that the animal's body helps it to live in its environment. Write the list on the board next to the corresponding pictures.

Some suggested animals are: giraffe, polar bear, monkey, and dolphin.

2. Invite a representative from the zoo to come to class to discuss how animals' bodies help them to live in their environment.

3. Show the video *Frog and Toad Together: Friends Forever.* Ask the children: "Is the story real or make-believe (fiction or nonfiction)? How can you prove your answer?"

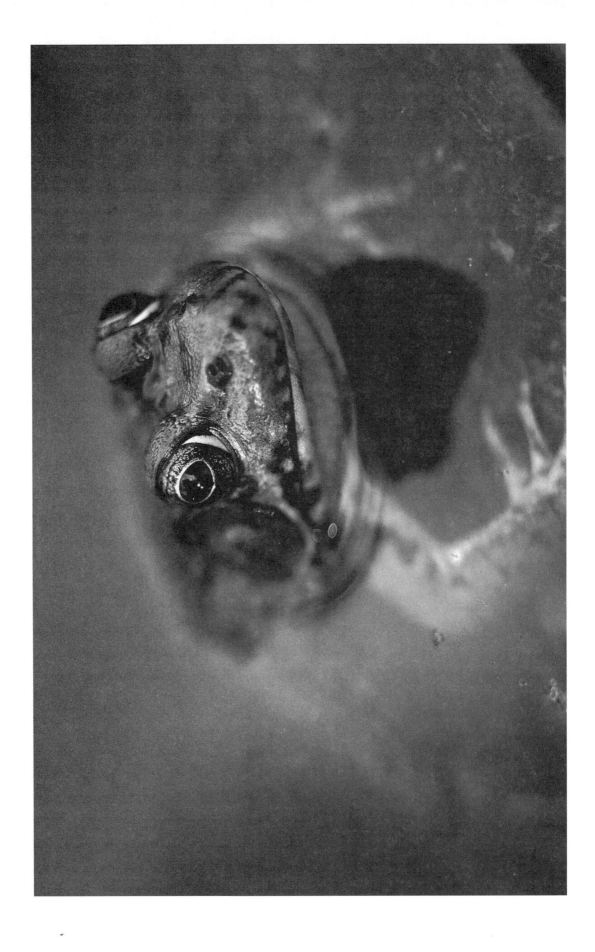

THE FROG

Look at the picture of a frog. A frog's body helps it to live in a pond.

A frog's skin is bumpy. The color of a frog can be green or brown. It looks like a rock when it sits still.

A frog has eyes on top of its head. It can sit under water, but keep its eyes above the water. The frog can see what is around it.

The back legs of a frog are very long. With strong back legs, the frog can jump far.

Look at the frog's back feet. There is skin going from toe to toe. The back feet help the frog swim.

Next time you see a frog, look at it carefully. Can you find other ways its body helps the frog to live in a pond?

QUESTIONS FOR THE FROG

1. What does a frog's body help it to do?

   _____

   _____

2. What makes a frog look like a rock?

   _____

   _____

3. What do the frog's back legs help it to do?

   _____

   _____

4. What helps the frog to swim?

   _____

   _____

5. What part of a frog does the story tell about first?

   _____

   _____

6. What part of a frog does the story tell about last?

   _____

   _____

7. The story tells us that the skin of a frog makes it look like a rock. How can this help a frog to live in a pond?

   _____

   _____

8. Look at the picture of the frog. Can you find another body part that helps the frog to live in a pond?

   _____

   _____

9. Would a frog be able to live in a dry, sandy desert? Why do you think so?

_____

_____

10. The story tells us that frogs sit under water, but they keep their eyes above the water. Why does a frog do this?

_____

_____

11. Write a title for the story. Use as few words as possible.

_____

_____

12. How are frogs and lizards alike? How are they different?

_____

_____

13. In your own words, tell how a frog's skin helps it to live in a pond.

_____

_____

14. Imagine a frog living in a pond. What would happen if the frog were bright red, not green or brown?

_____

_____

15. The story says, "With strong back legs, the frog can jump far." Is this a fact, or someone's opinion? How do you know?

_____

_____

16.

_____

_____

Name _____ Date _____

READING TRACKS

ABOUT THE STORY
This story tells about the types of tracks left by birds. The author describes how bird tracks change when the bird hops or walks.

PREVIEW WORDS

tracks	special	sparrows
robins	starlings	dinosaurs
together		

THROUGHOUT THE WEEK—For younger students, read a book from the Nature's Footprints series by Q.L. Pearce and W.J. Pearce each day of the week.

Pearce, Q.L., and W.J. Pearce. *Nature's Footprints in the African Grasslands.* Englewood Cliffs, NJ: Silver Press, Simon & Schuster, Inc., 1990.

and, *Nature's Footprints in the Barnyard, Nature's Footprints in the Forest, Nature's Footprints in the Desert.*

Read *The Case of the Fantastic Footprints: A McGurk Mystery,* by E.W. Hildick, throughout the week for older students (New York: Macmillan, 1994).

BOOKS TO READ

Tracks in the Wild, Betsy Bowen (Little, Brown, 1993).

Footprints in the Refrigerator, Selma and Pauline Boyd (Franklin Watts, 1982).

Big Tracks, Little Tracks, Franklyn M. Branley (Crowell, 1986).

Keepers of the Animals: Native American Stories and Wildlife Activities for Children, Michael J. Caduto and Joseph Bruchac (Fulcrum Publishing, 1991).

Whose Footprints?, Molly Coxe (Crowell, 1990).

Brimhall Turns Detective, Judy Delton (Carolrhoda Books, 1983).

Footprints Under the Window, Hardy Boys, Franklin Dixon (Grosset & Dunlap, 1965).

Footprints and Shadows, Anne Wescott Dodd (Simon & Schuster Books for Young Readers, 1992).

Mark Trail's Book of Animals (North American Mammals), Ed Dodd (Scholastic Book Services, 1968, c1955).

Animal Tracks, Arthur Dorros (Scholastic, 1991).

Barnyard Tracks, Dee Dee Duffy (Bell Books, 1992).

On the Tracks of Dinosaurs, James O. Farlow (Franklin Watts, 1991).

How to Invite Wildlife Into Your Backyard, David Alan Herzog (Greatlakes Living Press, 1977).

The Case of the Fantastic Footprints: A McGurk Mystery, E.W. (Edmund Wallace) Hildick (Macmillan, 1994).

The Mystery of the Giant Footprints, Fernando Krahn (Dutton, 1977).

Nature's Footprints in the African Grasslands, Q.L. (Querida Lee) Pearce and W.J. Pearce (Silver Press, 1990).

Nature's Footprints in the Barnyard, Q.L. (Querida Lee) Pearce and W.J. Pearce (Silver Press, 1990).

Nature's Footprints in the Desert, Q.L. (Querida Lee) Pearce and W.J. Pearce (Silver Press, 1990).

Nature's Footprints in the Forest, Q.L. (Querida Lee) Pearce and W.J. Pearce (Silver Press, 1990).

Let's Go Dinosaur Tracking!, Miriam Schlein (Harper Collins, 1991).

The Ghost Town Monster, Robert Wise (EMC Corp., 1974).

INTRODUCTORY ACTIVITIES

DAY ONE

Objective: The students will look at footprints in sand and determine how the person walked across the sand.

Curriculum subject: Science

Teacher: Many people look at footprints or tracks. Bird watchers look at bird tracks to learn what birds have been in the area. The police look at tracks to learn who was at the crime scene. Paleontologists look at fossilized dinosaur tracks to learn how dinosaurs walked. Can you think of anyone else who looks at tracks?

Imagine a snowy day. Three sets of animal tracks run across the fresh snow. What can you learn by looking at the tracks?

Today we'll look at tracks. We'll see if we can tell what the person who made the tracks was doing.

Reading Tracks
Materials

◆ a long box no more than 2" tall

◆ plastic trash bags

◆ sand

◆ watering can

◆ stiff hand-held brush

◆ newspaper

Procedure

1. Lay the box on newspaper in front of the class. Cut open the trash bags. Line the box with the plastic.

2. Fill the box with a thin layer of sand. Using the watering can, dampen the sand with water. The sand must be wet enough to hold the shape of a footprint, yet not so wet that it is soggy. Smooth the sand. (You might prefer to use a sandbox if one is available.)

3. Ask all the students to put their heads down and cover their eyes. Help a student with very small feet walk across the sand. Brush off the student's shoes with the brush.

4. Show the footprints to the rest of the class. Who do they think made the footprints? Why do they think so? What was the person who made the tracks doing? (The student was walking.) How can you tell?

5. Repeat the activity, asking a student to hop across the sand. Other students might drag one foot, or come up with other ways to make tracks.

6. Why might it be important to look at footprints and know what the person or animal was doing?

DAY TWO

Story Lesson

Follow the *Presenting the Story Lesson* instructions in the Introduction. Each story lesson follows the same procedure; however, say the following in step 4:

"The title of the story we're reading today is *Reading Tracks*. What do you think the story is about? What do you already know about reading tracks?"

EXTENSION ACTIVITIES

1. The students will visit the zoo, petting zoo, farm, or other animal facility. They will make a catalogue of animal tracks.

◆ Before the field trip, contact the zoo. Ask for a guide who can help the students look for animal tracks.

◆ Teacher:

Today we'll visit the zoo. Everyone will take a drawing pad. As you go through the zoo, look for animal tracks. Draw a picture of the track and the animal who made the track. Be sure to label you picture.

◆ When you return to class, review the drawings. What does a deer track look like? Why is it different from the elephant or monkey track? What can you learn about the animal by looking at its tracks?

2. The students will listen to a story about dinosaur tracks. They will predict what scientists millions of years in the future might learn about people of our time when they find our tracks.

◆ Teacher:

In 1938, Roland Bird found fossilized dinosaur tracks in Texas. The tracks told a story about the dinosaur who left them. Paleontologists study these fossils. What could a paleontologist learn about dinosaurs when he or she looks at their tracks?

Today we'll listen to the story *Let's Go Dinosaur Tracking!* by Miriam Schlein. We'll learn how to study dinosaur tracks.

3. The students will make clay prints of their hands.

◆ Teacher:

Today you'll make a clay fossil of your hand print. Unlike the dinosaurs, we can leave a message in our fossil. You'll press a cookie cutter shape next to your hand print. The shape will tell people what you enjoy. If you like to read about space travel, you might choose the rocket cookie cutter. If you like dogs, you might choose the dog cutter. Look at the cookie cutter shapes. Think about the message you'd like to send to people who find your hand print millions of years from now.

Make Your Own Hand Print Fossil
Materials

◆ clay
◆ cookie cutters of various shapes

Procedure

◆ Roll out a piece of clay large enough for a student's hand and a cookie cutter shape.
◆ The student presses his or her hand into the clay. Next to the hand print, the student presses in the cookie cutter shape. Cut all the way through the clay.
◆ After the clay dries, the students share the hand prints and their messages with the class.

4. Display two sets of pictures: one set of animal tracks and a matching set of animal pictures. Ask the students to match the animal to its tracks. Discuss why the students think the animal would make a given track pattern.

5. You can find other activities in *Keepers of the Animals: Native American Stories and Wildlife Activities for Children*, pages 197–200.

READING TRACKS

After it rains, look for bird tracks. Look in places where there is mud. Did you know that you can tell what kind of bird walked in the mud?

Most bird tracks look alike in many ways. Birds have three front toes and one back toe. The way a bird walks makes its tracks special.

Sparrows are hopping birds. They put both feet together. When they hop, they land on both feet. What do you think sparrow tracks look like?

Starlings are walking birds. They walk like people. They put one foot in front of the other. What do you think starling tracks look like?

Some birds, like robins, hop and walk. What do you think robin tracks look like?

Look at the picture of bird tracks. Were you right?

Look for pictures of other animal tracks. As you learn more, you will know what tracks frogs, turtles, ducks and even dinosaurs make.

Bird Tracks

Sparrow

Starling

Robin

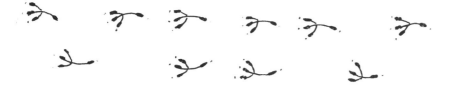

QUESTIONS FOR READING TRACKS

1. Where is a good place to look for bird tracks?

   _____

   _____

2. How are most bird footprints <u>alike</u>?

   _____

   _____

3. What makes bird tracks special?

   _____

   _____

4. Name the three birds in the story.

   _____

   _____

5. Which bird tracks did you read about <u>first</u>?

   _____

   _____

6. Which bird tracks did you read about <u>last</u>?

   _____

   _____

7. People found dinosaur tracks in rocks. After reading this story, what is one thing you might learn about a dinosaur by looking at its tracks?

   _____

   _____

8. The story tells us to look for bird tracks after it rains. Why would a dry day be a bad time to look for tracks?

   _____

   _____

9. What might a robin's tracks look like just before it begins to fly? Next, draw a picture of what these tracks might look like.

_____

_____

10. Some people look for animal tracks as a hobby. A hobby is something you like to do when you are not working. Why do you think looking at animal tracks is fun for these people?

_____

_____

11. Write a title for the story. Use as few words as possible.

_____

_____

12. Look at the picture of bird tracks. How are the tracks of a sparrow like the tracks of a starling? How are the tracks different?

_____

_____

13. In your own words, tell about the tracks made by robins.

_____

_____

14. Imagine that a sparrow hurt one of its legs. Tell what its tracks might look like. Next, draw a picture of the tracks you might see.

_____

_____

15. The story says, "Every bird makes its own special tracks." Is this a fact, or someone's opinion? How do you know?

_____

_____

16.

_____

_____

Name _____ Date _____

© 1997 by The Center for Applied Research in Education

IN THE DEEP SEA

ABOUT THE STORY

This story tells about animals in the deep sea that people have never seen before. It describes some of the strange animals found by oceanographers in the deep sea.

PREVIEW WORDS

oceanographers   gulper eel   blink

angler fish

THROUGHOUT THE WEEK—While the students work, or enter and leave the class, play the cassette *What's in the Sea?: Songs About Marine Life and Ocean Ecology* by Lois Skiera-Zucek (Long Branch, NJ: Kimbo, 1990).

BOOKS TO READ

A Thousand Yards of Sea: A Collection of Sea Stories and Poems, compiled by Laura Cecil (Greenwillow Books, 1993).

Underseas Frontiers: An Introduction to Oceanography, C.B. Colby (Coward, McCann & Geoghegan, 1977).

The Magic School Bus on the Ocean Floor, Joanna Cole (Scholastic, 1992).

Window on the Deep: The Adventures of Underwater Explorer Sylvia Earle, Andrea Conley (Franklin Watts, 1991).

Ocean Life, David Cook (Crown Publishers, 1983).

The Ocean World of Jacques Cousteau, a twenty-volume set (Danbury Press, 1973).

Jacques Cousteau: Man of the Oceans, Carol Greene (Childrens Press, 1990).

A Fish of the World, Terry Jones (Peter Bedrick Books, 1994).

The Beachcomber's Book, Bernice Kohn Hunt (The Viking Press, 1970).

Sea Songs, Myra Cohn Livingston (Holiday House, 1986).

I Am the Ocean, Suzanna Marshak (Arcade Publishers, 1991).

Mysteries and Marvels of Ocean Life, Rick Morris (Usborne, 1983).

The Underwater Alphabet Book, Jerry Pallotta (Charlesbridge Publishing, 1991).

Life in the Dark, Joyce Pope (Steck-Vaughn, 1992).

The World's Oceans, Cass R. Sandak (Franklin Watts, 1987).

I Can Be an Oceanographer, Paul P. Sipiera (Childrens Press, 1987).

Make Your Own Paper Ocean, Sally and Stewart Walton (Smithmark Publishers, 1994).

Jacques Cousteau: Free Flight Undersea, Paul Westman (Dillon Press, 1980).

VIDEOS

Mr. Know-It-Owl Presents: Under the Sea from the Concord Children's Video Encyclopedia. Apollo Educational Video, Concord Video, 1987. Length: 35 minutes.

Deep Sea Dive, National Geographic Kids Video. Burbank, CA: Columbia Tristar Home Video, 1994. Length: 30 minutes.

Fish, Shellfish and Other Underwater Life, Penguin Home Video, 1988. Length: 30 minutes.

Exploring Colors and Shapes of the Deep Blue Sea, Video Treasures, 1994.

CDS, RECORDS, AND CASSETTES

Walt Disney Presents the Story of 20,000 Leagues Under the Sea (cassette and book set) Jules Vernes (Buena Vista Distribution Co., 1982).

What's in the Sea?: Songs About Marine Life and Ocean Ecology (cassette: lyrics enclosed), music and lyrics by Lois Skiera-Zucek (Kimbo, 1990).

INTRODUCTORY ACTIVITIES

DAY ONE

Objective: The students will watch a film about deep sea animals.

Curriculum subject: Science

Watch the film *Deep Sea Dive.*

Before showing the video, tell the students they will answer these questions after the film.

1. Which sea animal did you like the most? Why?

2. Which sea animal was the strangest?

3. Name three sea animals from the movie.

DAY TWO

Story Lesson

Follow the *Presenting the Story Lesson* instructions in the Introduction. Each story lesson follows the same procedure; however, say the following in step 4:

"The title of the story we're reading today is *In the Deep Sea.* What do you think the story is about? What do you already know about the deep sea?"

EXTENSION ACTIVITIES

1. Read the story *The Magic School Bus on the Ocean Floor* by Joanna Cole. Ask the students to look for any animal that lives in the ocean. Tell them that they will choose an animal to draw after hearing the story (Extension Activity 2).

2. In this activity, the students make posters of deep sea animals.

Deep Sea Animal Posters
Materials

◆ one poster board for every two students

◆ art sponges

◆ blue and green poster paint

◆ sand, sea shells, other deep sea decoration

◆ glue

◆ construction paper

◆ drawing paper

Procedure

◆ Cut each poster board in half; each student takes one piece.

◆ Dip a sponge into green poster paint. Widely dot the poster with the sponge. Dip another sponge into blue poster paint. Dot the sponge over the remaining white of the poster. Overlapping the colors and leaving small amounts of the white showing adds to the effect.

◆ If the animal you draw lives on the floor of the ocean, glue sand along the bottom of the poster. Glue shells and construction paper plants along the sea floor.

◆ While the paint dries, choose a deep sea animal to draw. On drawing paper, draw and color a large picture of your animal. If your animal travels in schools, make several of the same animal.

◆ Cut out the animal drawing.

◆ Glue scattered pieces of tightly wadded paper balls about ¼″ round on the back of the animal. Make sure none of the paper balls shows from the front of the drawing.

◆ Using glue only on the paper balls, glue the animal to the painted poster board. The animal will appear to be floating off the board.

◆ Using reference books, write a brief description of the animal. Be sure to tell the name of the animal, what the animal eats, where it lives, and what is unique about the animal.

For example:

Angler Fish

The angler fish is a mean-looking fish. It lives in the deep ocean where there is very little light. An angler fish has many long, sharp teeth. A string that looks like a fishing line hangs from its nose. The end of the string lights up. Other fish come close to the angler fish to see what the light is. That's when the angler fish eats them for lunch.

◆ Glue the description to the poster.

◆ Display the posters around the room.

3. The students will make large models of deep sea submersibles. This activity takes several days to complete.

◆ For the teacher:

Several weeks before the lesson, collect large boxes. The boxes must be large enough for one to two students to sit in. Collect one box for every two to four students in your class. Lay the box on one side. The students will enter the box from the open end. On the three closed sides of the box, trace a dinner plate to make a circle—one circle on each side. Carefully cut out the circles with a utility knife. These are the portholes.

Also, cut one circle large enough for the students to reach through on the side opposite the open end—about one foot from the floor of the submersible. Like the robotic arm of submersibles, the students reach through the hole to collect specimens.

Before the lesson begins, ask the students to browse through books with pictures of deep sea submersibles.

If you have a large class, you might want to enlist the help of adult volunteers during this project.

Submersible Model
Materials

For each group of two to four students:

◆ one large box lying on its side so that the students can crawl in the open end. Three circular portholes are on each of the remaining sides, with an armhole on the end.
◆ blue plastic wrap
◆ construction paper
◆ drawing paper
◆ blue wrapping paper
◆ sea shells, coral, starfish
◆ tape
◆ glue stick

Procedure

◆ Draw and color deep sea animals onto drawing paper. Cut out the drawings.
◆ While the students draw, the teacher stretches and tapes a sheet of blue plastic wrap tightly over each porthole.
◆ With a glue stick, the students glue their deep sea animals to the outside of the plastic wrap.
◆ The students color the inside of the box to make the controls of the submersible.
◆ Set sea shells, coral, and starfish on the classroom floor in front of the arm hole. A student can then reach through the arm hole to collect specimens, like the robotic arm of a submersible.

◆ The students tour each submersible. The overhead light will shine through the blue plastic wrap and into the submersible, giving the look of light filtering through water.

IN THE DEEP SEA

People have seen all of the Earth. We have seen all the animals. We have walked on every spot of Earth. Is this true?

No, it is not true. No one has seen most of the animals in the sea. No one has walked on the deep sea floor.

Many people are looking in space to find new life. People called oceanographers look for new life right here on Earth. They look in the sea.

There is no light deep in the sea. The sun cannot reach deep under water. Nine out of ten animals in the deep sea shine. Some blink their lights on and off, like the angler fish with its shining string.

The gulper eel looks as if it could live only on Mars. Most of its body is a large, open mouth with many sharp teeth.

Someday oceanographers will live in the deep sea. Then they will look for more wonderful animals. Would you like to join them?

QUESTIONS FOR IN THE DEEP SEA

1. Have people seen all the animals on Earth?

   _____

   _____

2. Who looks in the sea for new life?

   _____

   _____

3. How many deep sea animals shine?

   _____

   _____

4. What does the gulper eel look like?

   _____

   _____

5. Name the first animal described in the story.

   _____

   _____

6. What will oceanographers do after they live in the deep sea?

   _____

   _____

7. Why is the deep sea eel called the gulper eel?

   _____

   _____

8. Do oceanographers think it is good to look for life in the deep sea? Why do you think so?

   _____

   _____

9. Will oceanographers always look for new animals? Why do you think so?

_____

_____

10. Why would someone want to be an oceanographer?

_____

_____

11. Write a title for the story. Use as few words as you can.

_____

_____

12. How are oceanographers and astronauts alike? How are they not alike?

_____

_____

13. Tell about the two animals in the story. Use as few words as you can.

_____

_____

14. How will people feel about the sea when oceanographers find new animals? Why do you think so?

_____

_____

15. The story said, "Someday oceanographers will live in the deep sea." Is this a fact? Why do you think so?

_____

_____

16.

_____

_____

Name _____   Date _____

"LITTLE PETER" THE CLOWN

ABOUT THE STORY

The story tells about the first clown to paint his face and wear baggy clothes. Little Peter, or Pierrot, originated in France. He was a sad character who covered his sad face with white paint. Most adults know Little Peter from the opera *Pagliacci,* made famous by Enrico Caruso.

Note: Pierrot is the diminutive form of the name Pierre. It means Little Peter. It is pronounced pē′ ẽr- ō or pye-rō′.

PREVIEW WORDS

Little Peter	Pierrot	clown
France	laugh	

BOOKS TO READ

Here Come the Clowns, Gale Brennan (Childrens Press, 1980).

The Laugh Book: A New Treasury of Humor for Children, compiled by Joanna Cole and Stephanie Calmenson (Doubleday, 1986).

The Best Trick of All, Nora Dale (Raintree Publishers, 1989).

Jingle, the Christmas Clown, Tomie de Paola (Putnam's, 1992).

Clowning Around, Cathryn Falwell (Orchard Books, 1991).

Creative Clowning, Bruce Fife, Tony Blanco, et. al. (Java Publishing Company, 1988).

A Day in the Life of a Circus Clown, Carol Gaskin (Troll Associates, 1988).

The Great Balloon Game Book and More Balloon Activities, Arnold E. Grummer (G. Markin, 1987).

The Carnival With Mr. and Mrs. Bumba, Pearl Augusta Harwood (Lerner Publications, 1971).

Face Painting: From Cowboys to Clowns, Pirates to Princesses, 40 Amazingly Original Designs for the Perfect Children's Party, Lynsy Pinsent (Chartwell Books, 1993).

The Book of Clowns, Felix Sutton (Grosset & Dunlap, 1953, c1974).

Clowning Around: Jokes About the Circus, Rick and Ann Walton (Lerner Publications, 1989).

Clown Games, Harriet Ziefert (Viking, 1993).

VIDEO

Jim Henson Play-Along Video: Hey, You're As Funny As Fozzie Bear: A Comedy Show Starring Fozzie Bear and You, Henson Associates, Inc. (Lorimar Home Video, 1988). Length: 30 minutes.

INTRODUCTORY ACTIVITIES

DAY ONE

Objective: The students will watch a clown act. They will listen to a clown tell about his or her job and the history of clowns.

Curriculum subject: Language Arts

Invite a clown to your class. Many towns and cities have clown schools. Some student clowns are willing to come practice their act for your students. Ask the clown to tell a little about the history of clowns.

Before the clown comes, discuss which questions the students should ask. Write the questions on a chart. Try to include who, what, when, where, and why questions.

After the clown finishes his or her act, conduct a question-and-answer session.

DAY TWO

Objective: The students will make a picture of a clown, using geometric shapes.

Curriculum subject: Art

Three-Dimensional Clown Pictures
Materials

- ◆ construction paper shapes of various sizes of circles, ovals, triangles, and squares
- ◆ colored poster board, cut in half
- ◆ construction paper
- ◆ colorful confetti
- ◆ pencils and crayons
- ◆ yarn, old buttons, pompoms, jingle bells, other decorations
- ◆ scissors
- ◆ glue stick
- ◆ white glue, slightly thinned with water in a Styrofoam dish or small aluminum pie tin
- ◆ paintbrushes

Procedure

1. The students work in groups to share materials and ideas. Each group needs a set of materials. Each student works on half a poster board.

2. Using pencils, the students trace the shapes onto the poster board to make clowns. Next, they draw around the shapes to fill in the clowns. Example:

Step A

Step B

3. Outline the final clown drawing with black crayon. Now it is time to decorate the clown.

4. Quickly paint inside the lines of the clown suit with thinned glue. Do not paint outside the suit lines. Make sure all the area is covered with glue. Pour confetti over the glue.

5. Let the glue dry.

6. Brush off any excess confetti.

7. Cut white paper to fit over the clown's head. Use a glue stick to glue it over the head. (Glue stick will not pucker the paper.) Using crayons, give it a clown face.

8. Using yarn or pompoms, glue on the clown's hair.

9. Glue buttons down the front of the clown suit. Add jingle bells or any other decorations you might like.

10. Make construction paper shoes. Glue them onto the clown with glue stick.

11. To make a stand-up ruffle collar, cut a piece of construction paper 1½″ wide and 6″ long, or the size to fit your clown's neck. Fold the paper like a fan. Glue one end of the fan along the clown's left shoulder. Wrap the paper around the clown's neck and glue the other end along his right shoulder.

12. Write the name of the clown at the top of the poster board. Display the clowns in the room.

DAY THREE

Story Lesson

Follow the *Presenting the Story Lesson* instructions in the Introduction. Each story lesson follows the same procedure; however, say the following in step 4:

"The title of the story we're reading today is *"Little Peter" the Clown.* What do you think the story is about? What do you already know about clowns?"

EXTENSION ACTIVITIES

1. Read the book *A Day in the Life of a Circus Clown* by Carol Gaskin. Would the students like to become clowns? Why?

2. Watch the video *Jim Henson Play-Along Video: Hey, You're As Funny As Fozzie Bear: A Comedy Show Starring Fozzie Bear and You.* The students interact with Fozzie and Kermit to put on a comedy show.

◆ How is Fozzie Bear like a clown? How is he different from a clown?

◆ How is Fozzie's act like a clown's act?

3. Read from the book *Clowning Around!: Jokes About the Circus* by Rick and Ann Walton.

◆ For homework, send the students on a joke hunt. They can get their jokes from anyone they know. They must bring the joke written on paper to the class for Extension Activity 4.

4. Hold a Clown Day on Friday. Decorate the room with balloons and banners.

◆ Center all curriculum subjects around clowns. For example, *Balloon Science: A Science Book Bursting With More Than 50 Balloon Experiments and Activities* by Etta Kaner (Reading, Massachusetts: Addison-Wesley, 1990) is full of science projects using balloons.

◆ Ask the students to wear clownlike clothes to class. They are to use their imaginations. They can wear hats, bandannas, and so forth.

◆ Ask volunteers to help paint the students' faces. Check first, however, for any allergies the students might have to face paint. For face painting ideas, see *Face Painting* by Pinsent, Lynsy. (Pierrot face is on pages 41–43.)

◆ The students will share their jokes from the joke hunt while dressed as clowns. Read every joke before the students tell them. Be sure the jokes are appropriate.

"LITTLE PETER" THE CLOWN

Who was the first clown? The first clown worked for kings. His job was to make the king laugh. He did not look like the clowns we see today. He did not wear big clothes or paint his face.

The first clown to paint his face was from France. They called their clown Little Peter, or Pierrot.

Little Peter painted his face white. Even his clothes were white. His big clothes, pointed hat, and large buttons made him look like today's clowns.

Little Peter was a smart clown. He was also very sad. He painted his face white so no one could see his sad face.

The next time you see a clown, look at the way he or she dresses. Are the clown's clothes big? Does the clown paint his or her face? If the clown does, he or she is following in the steps of the sad clown, Little Peter.

QUESTIONS FOR "LITTLE PETER" THE CLOWN

1. For whom did the first clowns work?

   _____

   _____

2. Where was Little Peter from?

   _____

   _____

3. How did Little Peter feel?

   _____

   _____

4. What color were Little Peter's face and clothes?

   _____

   _____

5. Which clowns did the story tell about first?

   _____

   _____

6. Who was the first clown to paint his face?

   _____

   _____

7. What one word best tells about Little Peter?

   _____

   _____

8. Was Little Peter a good clown? Why do you think so?

   _____

   _____

9. Will clowns always dress in big clothes? Why do you think so?

_____

_____

10. Why did Little Peter want to paint his sad face?

_____

_____

11. Write a name for the story. Use only a few words.

_____

_____

12. How was Little Peter like today's clowns? How was he not like today's clowns?

_____

_____

13. In a few words, tell what Little Peter looked like.

_____

_____

14. How did Little Peter change the way clowns look?

_____

_____

15. The story said, "Little Peter painted his face white." Is this a fact? Why do you think so?

_____

_____

16.

_____

_____

Name _____   Date _____

MARY READ: LADY PIRATE

ABOUT THE STORY

This story tells about the life of Mary Read. Mary Read was one of the few lady pirates in the early 1700's.

PREVIEW WORDS

pirate	Mary Read	Anne Bonny
countries	enemy's	disappeared
Navy		

THROUGHOUT THE WEEK—Read the story *It Was a Dark and Stormy Night* by Janet and Allan Ahlberg.

*During Extension Activity 3, the students will dress as pirates. Prepare them early by telling them that they should wear jeans, T-shirts, and bandannas on that day.

BOOKS TO READ

> **Note:** Some pirate books are graphic in their description of pirate brutality. Look over each book and judge whether its content is appropriate for the age of your students.

Skeleton Crew, Allan Ahlberg (Greenwillow Books, 1992).

It Was a Dark and Stormy Night, Janet and Allan Ahlberg (Viking, 1993).

Peter Pan, J.M. (James Matthew) Barrie (Henry Holt, 1987).

Wiggy and Boa, Anna Fienberg (Houghton Mifflin, 1990).

Pirates: Robbers of the High Seas, Gail Gibbons (Little, Brown, 1993).

The Golden Book of Buccaneers, John Gilbert (Golden Press, 1975).

Songs of the Sea, Paul Glass and Louis C. Singer (Grossett & Dunlap, 1966).

Jason and the Lizard Pirates, Gery Greer (HarperCollins Publishers, 1992).

The Mystery of the Pirate Ghost, Geoffrey Hayes (Random House, 1985).

Lo-Jack and the Pirates, William H. Hooks (Bantam Books, 1991).

Secret in the Pirate's Cave, The Bobbsey Twins, Laura Lee Hope (Pocket Books, 1980).

The Pirates of Bedford Street, Rachel Isadora (Greenwillow Books, 1988).

The Forgetful Pirate, Leonard Kessler (Garrard Publishing, 1974).

Secret Spaces, Imaginary Places: Creating Your Own Worlds for Play, Elin McCoy (Macmillan, 1986).

Pirates, Karen McWilliams (Franklin Watts, A First Book, 1989).

The Horrendous Hullabaloo, Margaret Mahy (Viking, 1992).

Pirates Past Noon, Mary Pope Osborne (Random House, 1994).

Fact or Fiction: Pirates, Stewart Ross (Copper Beech Books, 1995).

The Not-So-Jolly Roger, Jon Scieszka (Viking, 1991).

Sheep on a Ship, Nancy Shaw (Houghton Mifflin, 1989).

Pirates, Hazel Songhurst (Derrydale Books, 1994).

Pirates, Brenda Thompson and Rosemary Giesen (Lerner Publications, 1977).

VIDEO

Treasure Island, Walt Disney's Studio Film Collection, 1950. Burbank California: Buena Vista Home Video. Length: 96 minutes.

INTRODUCTORY ACTIVITIES

DAY ONE

Objective: The students will watch the Walt Disney film *Treasure Island.* They will discuss the depiction of pirates in the story.

Curriculum subject: Language Arts

Teacher: This week we'll learn about pirates. Many writers tell stories about pirates. Why do you think pirates are such a popular subject?

Watch the film *Treasure Island.* It's based on a book called *Treasure Island* by Robert Louis Stevenson. Stevenson wrote the book in 1883 to entertain his twelve-year-old stepson. After the film we'll talk about the pirates.

After the film is over, discuss the pirate characters. Why do you think Robert Louis Stevenson wrote a book around the subject of pirates? Do you think his stepson enjoyed the story about pirates? Why do you think so? Why is the story, *Treasure Island,* popular more than 100 years after it was written? Do you think *Treasure Island* will be a popular story 100 years from today? Why do you think so?

DAY TWO

Story Lesson

Follow the *Presenting the Story Lesson* instructions in the Introduction. Each story lesson follows the same procedure; however, say the following in step 4:

"The title of the story we're reading today is *Mary Read: Lady Pirate.* What do you think the story is about? What do you already know about pirates?"

EXTENSION ACTIVITIES

1. The students will write a description of a pirate.

Read the story *Sheep on a Ship* by Nancy Shaw before beginning the lesson.

◆ Teacher:

Let's imagine seeing a pirate. As you picture this pirate in your mind's eye, try to remember the details. When we're finished, you'll write a description of your pirate. (Read the following exercise to your students.)

Close your eyes and lay your head down. Everyone must stay very quiet. Imagine a bright, sunny day. You're on a tall pirate ship. Look up and see the black flag flapping in the breeze. The wind is gently tossing the waves and they rock the ship slowly under your feet. If you listen carefully, you can hear the creaking and moaning of the wooden planks of the ship.

At the front of the ship, a pirate is at the wheel. Imagine him or her clearly as if you're really there. What is the pirate wearing? What colors are the clothes? Is the pirate tall or small? Does he or she have a peg leg? Look at his or her face. What is the expression on the pirate's face? What is the pirate thinking about? How does he or she feel?

Continue to watch the pirate as the ship rocks gently over the waves. Take in what you see and remember every detail about your pirate.

Now quietly sit up. Without talking, write a description of your pirate. Tell me exactly what you saw. Include any details you can remember. If you can't spell a word, quietly raise your hand and I will help you.

◆ After the students finish their descriptions, ask them to give their descriptions to their neighbors. Each neighbor will read the description, then draw a picture of the pirate he or she read about. The neighbor will share his or her picture with the author of the description. Did the picture look like the pirate the author imagined? Was the description clear enough for the reader to correctly see the pirate the author described? Read the most successful descriptions to the class. Why was each a good description?

2. The students will learn and sing sea chanteys. One source for sea chanteys is *Songs of the Sea,* compiled by Paul Glass and Louis C. Singer. The book includes music for voice and piano, with guitar chords.

◆ Other sea chanteys include "Blow the Man Down," "Haul Away, Joe," and "Sacramento."
  *Remind the students to dress as pirates for Extension Activity 3.

3. The students will pretend to be pirates and work on subject areas using the pirate theme.

◆ Prior to this activity, ask a fellow teacher or volunteer to make a treasure map. First, the teacher will hide a box filled with chocolate foil-covered coins. Then the teacher will draw a map to show where he or she hid the box. Fray the edges of the map to make it look old. Roll the map into an empty tennis ball can, and decorate the outside of the can with construction paper.

◆ Before the students come to class, decorate the room like a pirate ship. Follow these suggestions and use your imagination:

  ◆ Hang the Jolly Roger.

  ◆ Set barrels around the room.

  ◆ Replace individual desks with long cafeteria tables.

  ◆ Make a ship's wheel and mount it in the front of the class.

  ◆ Place a toy parrot on a shelf.

  ◆ Hang lanterns around the classroom.

◆ As the students come to class, they will complete their costumes. An excellent source of pirate costumes and prop designs is *Pirates* (a *Make and Play* book) by Hazel Songhurst. This book also describes art projects on the pirate theme.

◆ Subject activities:

Math

Before beginning the day's lesson, ask story problems involving pirates based on the lesson's objective. For example, for a subtraction lesson:

Mary Read found 10 gold pieces in a treasure chest. She gave Anne Bonny 3 of the gold pieces. How many gold pieces are left?

Social Studies

Map reading: Using the treasure map made earlier, the students track down the hidden treasure.

Music

The students sing sea chanteys.

◆ Continue in this manner for _every_ subject of the day.

MARY READ: LADY PIRATE

We think of pirates as men. On dark ships, men with peg legs are ready to fight.

Not all pirates were men. Some pirates were women. One of these lady pirates was Mary Read.

Mary ran away from home when she was 14. She ran away to sail the sea. One time she joined the army. Soon she went back to the sea she loved.

Mary Read became a pirate. She stole ships. She used a gun and knife. Next, she worked for countries at war. They asked Mary to steal their enemy's ships.

One day Mary met Anne Bonny. The two women worked together. They dressed like men and were as mean as any pirate.

In 1720, the Navy caught Mary and Anne. Mary Read died in prison from a fever. Anne Bonny disappeared. No one ever saw Anne again.

QUESTIONS FOR MARY READ: LADY PIRATE

1. Were all pirates men?

   _____

   _____

2. Name the two lady pirates in the story.

   _____

   _____

3. When did the Navy catch Mary Read?

   _____

   _____

4. How did Mary Read die?

   _____

   _____

5. What did Mary Read do before she was a pirate?

   _____

   _____

6. What happened to Mary after the Navy caught her?

   _____

   _____

7. What one word best tells about Mary Read?

   _____

   _____

8. Was Mary Read a friendly person? Why do you think she was or she wasn't?

   _____

   _____

9. Do you think Anne Bonny was a pirate after she disappeared? Why do you think so?

_____

_____

10. Why was Mary Read put in prison?

_____

_____

11. Write a title for the story. Use as few words as you can.

_____

_____

12. How was Mary Read like other pirates? How was she not like other pirates?

_____

_____

13. Tell about Mary Read's life in your own words.

_____

_____

14. How did Mary Read make people on other ships feel? Why do you think so?

_____

_____

15. The story said, "(Mary Read and Anne Bonny) were as mean as any pirate." Is this a fact or an opinion? Why do you think so?

_____

_____

16.

_____

_____

Name _____ Date _____

JOHN ROCK

ABOUT THE STORY

This story tells about John Rock. John Rock was the first African-American lawyer recognized by the Supreme Court (1865).

PREVIEW WORDS

John Rock	Civil War	slaves
medical school	dentist	recognized
law	lawyer	Supreme Court
throughout	fellow human beings	

THROUGHOUT THE WEEK—If possible, conduct these lessons during Black History Month (February). February is also the month (February 1, 1865) in which the Supreme Court recognized John Rock. Decorate the room with pictures of African-Americans and African-American art. Play music by important black American artists such as Louis Armstrong, Marian Anderson, and Duke Ellington as the students work and when they enter and leave the classroom.

Read the book *Little Louis and the Jazz Band: The Story of Louis "Satchmo" Armstrong,* by Angela Shelf Medearis, to the class. (New York: Lodestar Books, 1994.)

BOOKS TO READ

Extraordinary Black Americans From Colonial to Contemporary Times, Susan Altman (Childrens Press, 1988).

Martin Luther King, Jr.: The Story of a Dream, a play by June Behrens (Childrens Press, 1979).

Addy's Craft Book (1864): A Look at Crafts From the Past With Projects You Can Make Today, Rebecca Sample Bernstein (Pleasant Company Publications, 1994).

Thurgood Marshall and Equal Rights, Seamus Cavan (Millbrook Press, 1993).

Mary McLeod Bethune: Champion for Education, Carol Greene (Childrens Press, 1993).

The Picture Life of Jesse Jackson, Warren J. Halliburton (Franklin Watts, 1984).

One More River to Cross, The Stories of Twelve Black Americans, by Jim Haskins (Scholastic, 1992).

Best Friends (Includes poet Langston Hughes), selected by Lee Bennett Hopkins (Harper & Row, 1986).

Poems for Spring (Includes poet Langston Hughes), selected by Robert Hull (Steck-Vaughn Library, 1992).

The Value of Responsibility: The Story of Ralph Bunche, Ann Donegan Johnson (Value Communications, 1978).

The Value of Courage: The Story of Jackie Robinson, Spencer Johnson (Value Communications, 1977).

Our Martin Luther King Book, Pat McKissack (Childrens Press, 1986).

Little Louis and the Jazz Band: The Story of Louis "Satchmo" Armstrong, Angela Shelf Medearis (Lodestar Books, 1994).

Duke Ellington: King of Jazz, Elizabeth Rider Montgomery (Garrard Publishing, 1972).

Rosa Parks, My Story, Rosa Parks (Dial Books, 1992).

Jesse Owens, Rick Rennert (Chelsea House Publishers, 1992).

Langston Hughes: American Poet, Alice Walker (Crowell, 1974).

Kids Explore America's African-American Heritage, Westridge Young Writers Workshop (John Muir Publications, 1993).

Black Scientists, Lisa Yount (Facts on File, 1991).

*This book is an adult book; however, it exposes students to the contributions of black Americans to science.

CDS, RECORDS, AND CASSETTES

A Picture Book of Martin Luther King, Jr. (cassette and book set), David Adler (Holiday House, 1989).

Disney Songs the Satchmo Way (CD), (Walt Disney, 1987).

Louis Armstrong and Duke Ellington: An Historic Recording Event (CD), (Roulette Records, 1985).

All Star Road Band (CD), Duke Ellington (Teresa Gramophone Co., 1983).

Carl Lewis: The Second Jesse Owens (cassette and book set), Bert Rosenthal (Childrens Press, 1984).

INTRODUCTORY ACTIVITIES

DAY ONE

Objective: The students will listen to and discuss a biography of Martin Luther King, Jr.

Curriculum subject: Language Arts or History

Teacher: Throughout the history of the United States, black Americans made enormous contributions in every area of our society. One such American was Martin Luther King, Jr.

Today we'll listen to a story about Martin Luther King, Jr.'s life. We call a story about a person's life a biography. We'll read many biographies as we spend the week learning about the achievements of black Americans.

Play the cassette and book set *A Picture Book of Martin Luther King, Jr.,* by David A. Adler. After listening to the story, display this question chart which you have prepared in advance. Discuss the questions, encouraging the students to answer in complete sentences.

1. Who was the story about?

   Where was he or she born?

   When was he or she born?

2. What important contribution did the person make?

3. When did the person make this contribution?

4. Where did the person make this contribution?

5. Why are the person and his or her work important?

DAY TWO

Story Lesson

Follow the *Presenting the Story Lesson* instructions in the Introduction. Each story lesson follows the same procedure; however, say the following in step 4:

"The title of the story we're reading today is *John Rock*. What do you think the story is about?"

EXTENSION ACTIVITIES

1. The students will make a Black Americans' Hall of Fame.

Black Americans' Hall of Fame
Materials

◆ poster boards (one for each black American in the Hall of Fame)

◆ poster paints

◆ glue, scissors

◆ drawing paper

◆ magazine photographs of black Americans highlighted in the Hall of Fame

◆ clay

Procedure

◆ Break the students into groups. Assign each group a black American to be featured in the Hall of Fame. Each group can make more than one display. Make sure that no one repeats a subject.

Suggestions:

Matthew Henson: Explorer

Martin Luther King, Jr.: Civil Rights Activist

Jesse Owens: Track-and-Field Athlete

Jesse Jackson: Minister, Civil Rights Leader

Rosa Parks: Civil Rights Activist

Jackie Robinson: Baseball Player

Frederick McKinley Jones: Inventor

Guion Stewart Bluford, Jr.: Pilot, Astronaut

Mary McLeod Bethune: Educator

Louis Armstrong: Musician, singer, composer

Duke Ellington: Band leader, musician, composer

Thurgood Marshall: U.S. Supreme Court Justice

Percy Lavon Julian: Chemist

Ralph Bunche: Statesman, diplomat

Langston Hughes: Poet

Daniel "Chappie" James, Jr.: Pilot, four-star general

Charles Richard Drew: Scientist, educator, surgeon

*For more names, refer to *Extraordinary Black Americans From Colonial to Contemporary Times,* by Susan Altman.

◆ Display the question chart from Day One. Change question 1 to "Who is this poster about?" The students will make a poster of their subject. The poster will answer the questions on the chart. Encourage the students to be creative. They can make a collage or a picture biography of their subject. For example, if the Langston Hughes group chooses to feature his poem "April Rain Song," they might make three-dimensional umbrellas stand out from their poster.

◆ The students make a small clay statue of their subject to set in front of the poster.

2. The students will celebrate Black History Month, and open their Black Americans' Hall of Fame to the school.

◆ Prepare for an exhibition of the Black Americans' Hall of Fame in the school cafeteria. During the day, students from other classes can walk through the displays.

◆ Mount a large chart of the following quote at the front of the exhibit:

Black History Month

> It is not interested so much in Negro History as it is in history influenced by the Negro; for what the world needs is not a history of selected races or nations but the history of the world void of national bias, race hate, and religious prejudice ...The aim has been to emphasize important facts in the belief that facts properly set forth will speak for themselves.[1]

> Dr. Carter G. Woodson
> "Father of Black History"
> October 1927

3. Your students can prepare and serve African-American food and drink to the visitors to the Hall of Fame. Recipes for *Fresh Mint Tea, Bread Pudding, Emancipation Proclamation Snackin' Cake,* and others are in *Kids Explore America's African-American Heritage,* by the Westridge Young Writers Workshop, pp. 63–78.

4. Ask members of the black community to come to the class to talk about the accomplishments of blacks in America. End with a question-and-answer session.

---

[1]"Annual Report of the Director." *Journal of Negro History,* October 1927, p. 573.

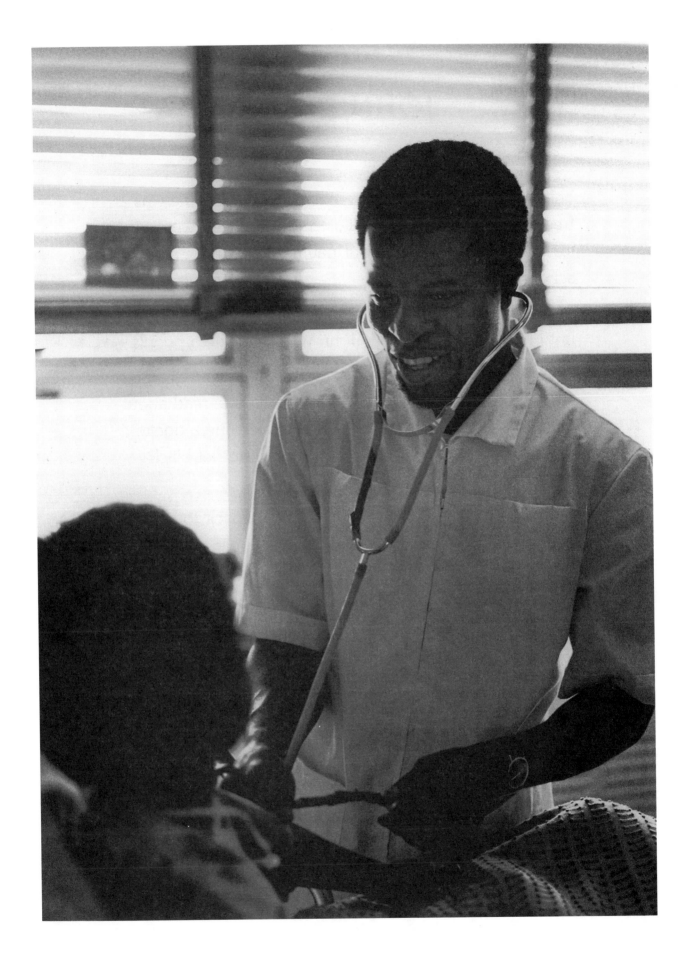

JOHN ROCK

John Rock was an American black man born before the Civil War. He lived in the North, so he was a free man. People with black skin in the South were slaves. They worked without pay, and could not go to school.

John Rock was born in 1825. He stayed in school until he was 18 years old. John wanted to help people. At the age of 19, he became a teacher.

John Rock never stopped learning. He read about medicine. He tried to go to school to become a doctor. The school did not let him in. They did not let black people go to medical school.

John did not give up. He taught himself to be a dentist. He worked very hard to help people. John worked so hard he became sick. Still, he did not give up.

When John felt better, he studied law. In 1865, John Rock became the first black lawyer recognized by the Supreme Court.

Throughout his life, John Rock helped his fellow human beings. He died in 1866.

QUESTIONS FOR JOHN ROCK

1. In what year was John Rock born?

   _____

   _____

2. How old was John Rock when he became a teacher?

   _____

   _____

3. What kept John Rock from going to medical school?

   _____

   _____

4. In what year was John Rock recognized as a lawyer by the Supreme Court?

   _____

   _____

5. What was John Rock's first job?

   _____

   _____

6. What did John Rock become after he was told he could not go to medical school?

   _____

   _____

7. What one word do you think best describes John Rock?

   _____

   _____

8. Do you think that staying in school until the age of 18 helped John Rock become such a great man? Why do you think so?

   _____

   _____

9. John Rock understood that he needed to learn as much as he could to make his life important. He worked hard and never gave up.
What do you want to do when you finish school? What will you need to do to reach your goal?

_____

_____

10. Why do you think that John Rock kept working to make his dreams come true? Why do you think he did not give up?

_____

_____

11. Write a title that best describes this story. Use as few words as possible.

_____

_____

12. John Rock wanted to be a doctor. He became a dentist instead. How is a doctor like a dentist? How are they different?

_____

_____

13. In your own words, tell why John Rock never became a doctor.

_____

_____

14. After reading about John Rock, have your ideas about your future changed? How have they changed?

_____

_____

15. The story said, "Throughout his life, John Rock helped his fellow human beings." Is this a fact or an opinion? Why do you think so?

_____

_____

16.

_____

_____

Name _____ Date _____

BRER RABBIT AND ANANSI THE SPIDER

ABOUT THE STORY

This story tells about animal trickster stories from Africa. Brer Rabbit and Anansi the Spider are greedy and selfish creatures who trick their friends to get what they want.

PREVIEW WORDS

Brer Rabbit

Anansi the Spider

Africa

African

THROUGHOUT THE WEEK—Set up displays of African folk art. Decorate the room with African art. Play African music as the students work.

During the week, read stories from *African-American Folktales for Young Readers*, collected and edited by Richard and Judy Dockrey Young, to the class. Be sure to read the introductions at the beginning of each chapter. These introductions give historical backgrounds to the story styles and characters.

Young, Richard Dockrey and Judy Dockrey Young, *African-American Folktales for Young Readers*. Little Rock: August House Publishers, 1993.

You can also read *Jump Again! More Adventure's of Brer Rabbit* by Joel Chandler Harris, adapted by Van Dyke Parks (New York: Harcourt Brace Jovanovich, 1987). This book received the 1987 Redbook Children's Picturebook Award and the New York Times Best Illustrated Children's Book Award.

BOOKS TO READ

Afro-American Folktales: Stories From Black Traditions in the New World, edited and selected by Roger D. Abrahams (Pantheon Books, 1985).

Stencil It!, Sandra Buckingham (Camden House, 1993).

The People Could Fly: American Black Folktales, told by Virginia Hamilton (Alfred A. Knopf, 1987).

Brer Rabbit, Barbara Hayes (Rourke Enterprises, 1984).

All Stuck Up, Linda Hayward (Random House, 1990).

Apples on a Stick: The Folklore of Black Children, collected and edited by Barbara Michels and Bettye White (Coward-McCann & Geoghegan, Inc., 1983).

Jump! The Adventures of Brer Rabbit, adapted by Van Dyke Parks (Harcourt Brace Jovanovich, 1986).

Jump Again! More Adventures of Brer Rabbit, adapted by Van Dyke Parks (Harcourt Brace Jovanovich, 1987).

Jump on Over! The Adventures of Brer Rabbit and His Family, adapted by Van Dyke Parks (Harcourt Brace Jovanovich, 1989).

Mufaro's Beautiful Daughters: An African Tale, John Steptoe (Lothrop, Lee & Shepard Books, 1987). A Caldecott Honor Book.

The Kids' Multicultural Art Book: Art and Craft Experiences From Around the World, Alexandra M. Terzian (Williamson Publishing, 1993).

Kids Explore America's African-American Heritage, Westridge Young Writers Workshop (John Muir Publications, 1992).

African-American Folktales for Young Readers, collected and edited by Richard and Judy Dockrey Young (August House Publishers, Inc., 1993).

Classic American Folk Tales, retold by Steven Zorn (Courage Books, 1992).

VIDEOS

Diana Colson's African Singalongs: A Music Video of 19 Original Songs for Children Ages 4 to 12, Hank Swain Productions, 1989. Length: 35 minutes.

Anansi, Brian Gleeson (Rabbit Ears Production, Inc., 1992.) Told by Denzel Washington. Music by UB40. From the Rabbit Ears' *Children's Classics From Around the World* series. Length: 26 minutes.

Brer Rabbit and Boss Lion, Brad Kessler (Rabbit Ears Productions, Inc., 1992). Told by Danny Glover. Music by Dr. John. From the Rabbit Ears' *American Heroes and Legends* series. Length: 30 minutes.

Anansi and the Moss-Covered Rock, Eric A. Kimmel (Live Oak Media, 1990). Length: 11 minutes.

Anansi Goes Fishing, Eric A. Kimmel (Live Oak Media, 1992). Length 12 minutes.

INTRODUCTORY ACTIVITIES

DAY ONE

Objective: The students will listen to and watch Brer Rabbit and Anansi stories.
Curriculum subject: Reading or Language Arts
Teacher: Today we'll see the videos *Brer Rabbit and Boss Lion* and *Anansi.* Brer Rabbit and Anansi the spider are characters created in Africa many years ago. As you watch the stories, look for ways that Brer Rabbit and Anansi are alike.

Show the following videos, which are also available in book and cassette packages: *Brer Rabbit and Boss Lion* and *Anansi.*
Teacher: How are Brer Rabbit and Anansi alike? How are they different?

DAY TWO

Story Lesson
Follow the *Presenting the Story Lesson* instructions in the Introduction. Each story lesson follows the same procedure; however, say the following in step 4:

"The title of the story we're reading today is *Brer Rabbit and Anansi the Spider.* What do you think the story is about? What do you already know about Brer Rabbit and Anansi the Spider?"

EXTENSION ACTIVITIES

1. The students will prepare and perform shadow puppet plays based on stories about Brer Rabbit or Anansi the Spider.

◆ See the books to read list for stories about Brer Rabbit or Anansi the Spider.

◆ Break the students into groups of five to six people. The groups will look for a Brer Rabbit or Anansi the Spider story they would like to perform.

◆ After choosing a story, the students will make shadow puppets of the characters in the story.

◆ Shadow Puppets:

Using construction paper of any color, cut out shapes of the characters. (The stencil patterns on page 63 are good examples of outlines of Brer Rabbit and Anansi the Spider.) Tape the top of a long dowel, tongue depressor or straw to the back of the construction paper figure.

◆ The Stage:

Stretch a white sheet or white bulletin board paper across the front of the class. Raise the sheet off the floor approximately three feet, or to a height where students can sit comfortably below the screen. Shine a bright light on the back of the sheet. The students work between the sheet and the light. The audience sees the shadows on the front side of the sheet. *Be sure the students and the sheet are far away from the hot lamp bulb.*

◆ The Play:

The students sit below and behind the sheet. The students hold the lower end of the puppet's dowel. When the students raise the puppets between the light and the sheet, the puppets cast a shadow onto the sheet. By moving the puppets, the students act out their story.

Note: The students can cut out construction paper props, and tape them to the back of the sheet. For example, if Brer Rabbit goes to a well, cut the shape of the well out of construction paper. Tape the well to the back of the sheet.

2. The students will write a Brer Rabbit or Anansi the Spider story.

◆ Write the following story-starter on chart paper.

◆ Break the students into groups. The students will write the ending of the story, or write a Brer Rabbit or Anansi the Spider story of their own. After they finish the stories, the students will share them with the class. (Adapted from "Goobers Gone, Rabbit Gone" (*Afro-American Folktales: Stories From Black Traditions in the New World,* edited and selected by Roger D. Abrahams, pp. 200–201).

Brer Rabbit and the Goobers

One day Brer Rabbit saw Brer Bear.

He saw Brer Bear going to the goober fields. Goobers are peanuts. Brer Rabbit likes goobers. He likes goobers a lot.

Brer Rabbit saw Brer Bear digging. Brer Bear dug up many goobers. Soon Brer Bear's wagon was full of goobers.

"Those goobers look good," said Brer Rabbit. Brer Rabbit is very lazy. He will not dig for goobers.

"I will trick Brer Bear," said Brer Rabbit. "Soon I will have his goobers."

◆ If the students do not have the writing skills needed for this activity, break the class into groups. The students draw pictures of the ending of the story. Move from group to group, writing the ending for the students as they dictate it to you.

3. The students will make painted cloth patches in Brer Rabbit and Anansi the Spider motifs. The patches will be sewn into a quilt.

◆ Your local craft store carries materials to make stencils; however, Sandra Buckingham in her book *Stencil It!* describes an inexpensive way to make stencils from freezer paper.

Brer Rabbit and Anansi Stencil Quilt
Materials

◆ freezer paper or store-bought stencil kits

◆ copies of Brer Rabbit and Anansi the Spider patterns or designs made by the students

◆ carbon or tracing paper

◆ stencil spray adhesive

◆ scissors

◆ protective mouth and nose masks

◆ cotton fabric cut into 12″ squares, as many as needed for the desired size of the quilt.

◆ sponges, paint rollers, paint brushes, rolled-up rags, or any creative applicator to paint the stencil design

◆ mud paint

Mud Paint
(From African Tribes in Mali)

*For more information about African mud paint ("Korhogo Mud Cloth") and other African art techniques, see *The Kids' Multicultural Art Book: Art and Craft Experiences from Around the World,* p. 116, by Alexandra M. Terzian. Terzian suggests using mud in the cleaning process; I prefer to use dry dirt. Both techniques are effective.

◆ Put one cup dry dirt into a sieve.

◆ Hold the sieve over a bowl. Work the dirt through the sieve. Throw away the pebbles and other debris left in the sieve.

◆ Continue to resift the dirt until there is no more debris left in the sieve after sifting.

◆ Add water to the dirt until it is the consistency of latex house paint.

◆ Slowly add tempera paint to the mud until it reaches the desired color.

◆ The mud paint can be stored for later use. It is thinned with water.

Procedure

(Prepare mud paint before making the stencil.)

◆ Using carbon paper, transfer the rabbit and spider designs onto freezer paper or store-bought stencil material.

◆ Carefully cut out the design from the inside. Avoid jagged edges.

◆ Wearing a protective mask, lightly spray the stencil with stencil spray adhesive. Use the spray outside or with plenty of ventilation.

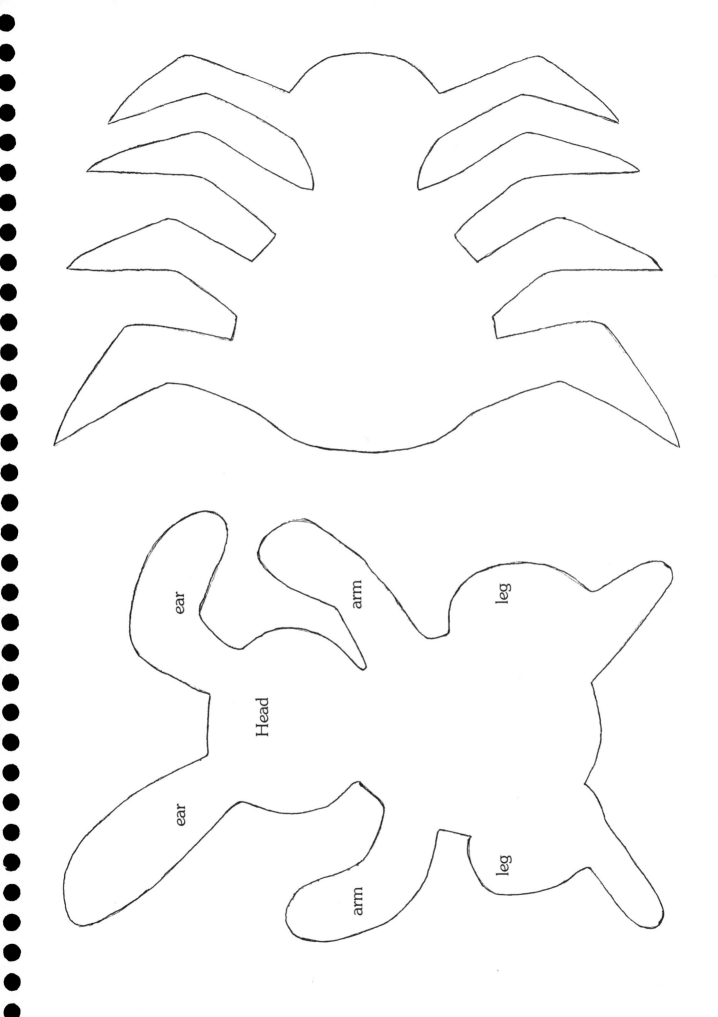

ear

arm

leg

Head

ear

arm

leg

◆ Position stencil in the center of the fabric square. Leave at least a ¾″ edge around the stencil for the seam.

◆ Using sponges, paint rollers, brushes, or rolled-up rags, paint the motif onto the fabric.

◆ Let the paint set before removing the stencil.

◆ Repeat the procedure until all squares are painted.

◆ After the fabric squares dry, sew them together to make a quilt top. Sew long strips 4″ wide around the edges of the quilt top. Display the quilt top as is or ask a volunteer to sew on quilt batting and backing. The students quilt the blanket by tying knots in the corners of each square. Donate the quilt to a local charity.

Quilt Knot

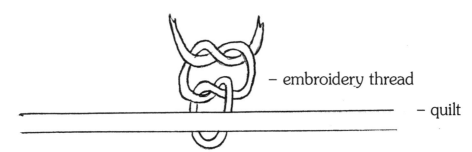

– embroidery thread

– quilt

BRER RABBIT AND ANANSI THE SPIDER

Brer Rabbit likes to play tricks. He plays tricks on his friends. You can read about Brer Rabbit in very old stories from Africa.

There are many African stories about small animals. These animals want all the food. They do not like to share. How do these small animals get what they want? They trick their friends.

Anansi the Spider also likes to play tricks. Anansi likes to eat. He likes to eat everything he can. The spider tries to trick his friends to get a lot of food. One day his trick did not work. Anansi lost all the hair on his head.

Brer Rabbit and Anansi stories are funny. They teach something, too. They tell you to be good to your friends.

QUESTIONS FOR BRER RABBIT AND ANANSI THE SPIDER

1. Where do the Brer Rabbit stories come from?

   _____

   _____

2. How do Brer Rabbit and Anansi get what they want?

   _____

   _____

3. What does Anansi the Spider like to do?

   _____

   _____

4. What do Brer Rabbit and Anansi stories teach you?

   _____

   _____

5. What does Brer Rabbit do before he gets what he wants?

   _____

   _____

6. What does Anansi get after he tricks his friends?

   _____

   _____

7. What one word tells about Brer Rabbit?

   _____

   _____

8. Do you think people like Brer Rabbit and Anansi stories? Why do you think so?

   _____

   _____

9. Do you think people will tell Brer Rabbit and Anansi stories for a long time? Why do you think so?

_____

_____

10. Why did Brer Rabbit and Anansi use tricks to get what they wanted?

_____

_____

11. Write a title for this story. Use only a few words.

_____

_____

12. How are Brer Rabbit and Anansi alike? How are they not alike?

_____

_____

13. Tell how Anansi the Spider gets what he wants.

_____

_____

14. Anansi the Spider is very small. He tricks his friends to get what he wants. How would Anansi get what he wanted if he was a big lion?

_____

_____

15. The story says, "Brer Rabbit and Anansi stories are funny." Is this a fact or what someone thinks? Why do you think so?

_____

_____

16.

_____

_____

Name _____   Date _____

THE CALDECOTT MEDAL

ABOUT THE STORY

This story tells about the life of Randolph Caldecott. The Caldecott Medal, a prize for the best picture book of the year, is named after Randolph Caldecott.

PREVIEW WORDS

Randolph Caldecott   Caldecott Medal

Old Christmas

BOOKS TO READ

Art Through Children's Literature: Creative Art Lessons for Caldecott Books, Debi Engle-baugh (Teacher Ideas Press, Libraries Unlimited, Inc., 1994).

Speak!: Children's Book Illustrators Brag About Their Dogs, edited by Michael J. Rosen (Harcourt Brace & Jovanovich, 1993).

Caldecott Medal Winners

Grandfather's Journey, Allen Say (illustrator)/Walter Lorraine (editor) (Houghton Mifflin, 1993).

Mirette on the High Wire, Emily Arnold McCully (Putnam's, 1992).

The Polar Express, Chris Van Allsburg (Houghton Mifflin, 1985).

Tuesday, David Wiesner (Clarion Books, 1991).

Black and White, David Macaulay (Houghton Mifflin, 1990).

Lon Po Po: A Red Riding Hood Story From China, Ed Young (Philomel Books, 1989).

Song and Dance Man, Stephen Gammell (illustrator)/Karen Ackerman (author) (Knopf, 1988).

Owl Moon, John Schoenherr (illustrator)/Jane Yolen (author) (Philomel Books, 1987).

*See your librarian for a complete list of Caldecott Medal books.

VIDEOS

It Could Always Be Worse by Margot Zemach, and *Sam, Bangs, and Moonshine* (Length: 14 minutes) by Evaline Ness. American School Publishers, Random House Video: Caldecott Video Collection.

CDS, RECORDS, AND CASSETTES

The Polar Express (cassette), by Chris Van Allsburg. Read by William Hurt. (Listening Library, Inc., Houghton Mifflin, 1989).

INTRODUCTORY ACTIVITIES

DAY ONE

Objective: The students will listen to three Caldecott Medal books. They will discuss why the books received the medal.

Curriculum subject: Reading or Language Arts

Before reading one or more of the following books to the class, tell the students that the artists won a prize called the Caldecott Medal. As you read the story, they will look for reasons why the illustrations won the award. Read *Mirette on the High Wire* and/or *The Polar Express*.

Discuss the quality of the illustrations. The students will give reasons why they think the illustrations won the Caldecott Medal. Write the list on the board.

DAY TWO

Story Lesson

Follow the *Presenting the Story Lesson* instructions in the Introduction. Each story lesson follows the same procedure; however, say the following in step 4:

"The title of the story we're reading today is *The Caldecott Medal*. What do you think the story is about? What do you already know about the Caldecott Medal?"

EXTENSION ACTIVITIES

1. Read the story *Tuesday* by David Wiesner to the class. After the story, ask them why they think the book won the Caldecott Medal.

2. This activity directly follows Extension Activity one.

◆ Before beginning this art project, blow out the whites and yolks of several eggs (one for every student plus extras in case one breaks). Blow out the eggs by punching small holes in each end of an egg with a pin. Cover one hole with your mouth and blow the yolks and whites out the other hole.

◆ Dye half the eggs light brown and the others light green.

Flying Frogs
Materials

◆ dyed egg shells

◆ green, brown, and black permanent markers

◆ wiggly eye buttons

◆ two pieces of green construction paper per student

◆ brown and green construction paper

◆ white glue and glue sticks

◆ white thread, needle

◆ paper clips

Procedure

◆ Give each student an egg shell. Brown eggs make brown frogs. Green eggs make green frogs. These are the frogs' bodies.

◆ Using the frog leg patterns, the students cut out two front legs and two back legs from construction paper that matches their frog bodies.

◆ Using the lily pad pattern, the students cut out two green construction paper lily pads.

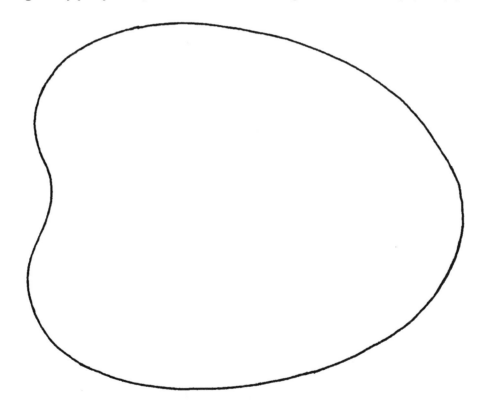

◆ Using the glue stick, the students glue the two lily pads together to make one sturdy lily pad. Draw green veins on the lily pad. Let dry.

◆ Glue two wiggly eye buttons on either side of the small end of the egg. Glue on front and back legs (as shown in the example.) Let dry.

◆ Using the green or brown markers, draw the spots on the frog's back. Look at the pictures in *Tuesday* for an example.

◆ Using the black marker, draw a wide, goofy smile on the frog's face.

◆ Glue the frog to the center of the lily pad using white glue. Let dry.

◆ The teacher will thread the needle with the white thread. Tie a knot in the end of the thread. Draw the needle from the bottom and in the corner of the lily pad. Pull the thread up to the top of the pad, and let the thread slide out of the eye of the needle. Repeat on three sides of the pad, making sure that each thread is the same length. Hold all three threads over the head of the frog and tie them together. Dot each knot with a touch of white glue. Let dry.

◆ Open a paper clip so that it looks like an ornament hanger. Hook one end of the clip onto the threads. Hook the other end to the ceiling or lamp fixtures. The frog will appear to be flying on a lily pad. Vary the length of threads for each frog so that they fly at different heights from the floor. Example:

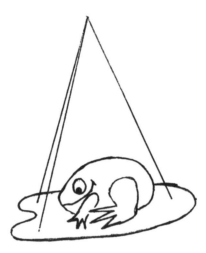

3. The students will make book covers for Caldecott Medal books in your school or local library. The students will write critiques of the books they cover.

Caldecott Book Covers
Materials

◆ bulletin board paper of various colors

◆ crayons, markers

◆ tape

◆ notebook paper

◆ glue stick

◆ clear tape

Procedure

◆ The students choose a Caldecott book.

◆ Open the book and trace its shape onto colored bulletin board paper. Draw an extra 3″ at each end of the book.

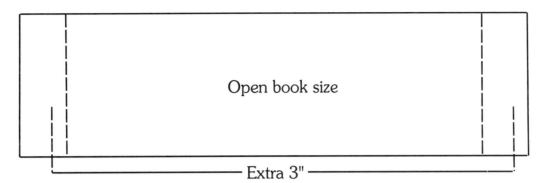

Open book size

— Extra 3" —

- ◆ The students design and color a front cover only.
- ◆ Cut notebook paper to fit the back cover of the book. The students will write a critique of the book. Example:

    I liked the story *Tuesday* because the pictures were beautiful. They made you feel like you were really seeing frogs fly on lily pads. The story was funny, too. The man eating a midnight snack made me laugh. I think everyone should read *Tuesday* by David Wiesner.

    Kate Jones

    Rusk School, 2A

- ◆ Glue the critique to the back cover with a glue stick.
- ◆ Laminate the book covers.
- ◆ Wrap the 3″ ends of the book cover around the corners of the book. Using clear tape, tape the 3″ ends to the front and back of the book cover at the top and bottom, leaving space to insert the book.

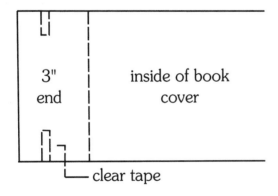

3"
end

inside of book
cover

— clear tape

- ◆ Set up a display of Caldecott Medal books in the library. Donate the covers to the library.

4. Read the story *Where the Wild Things Are* by Maurice Sendak (Harper & Row, 1963). Discuss why the story won the Caldecott Medal.

Wild Cookies

◆ Make *Wild Cookies* before class.

   ◆ 1 cup softened unsalted margarine

   ◆ 3 tablespoons chocolate sprinkles

   ◆ ½ cup chopped nuts

   ◆ 1 cup sugar

   ◆ 2 tablespoons milk

   ◆ 1 teaspoon vanilla

   ◆ 2½ cups flour

plus

   ◆ ¼ cup chopped nuts

   ◆ 1 cup coconut flakes

   ◆ chocolate chips

◆ Cream together margarine and sugar. Stir in vanilla and milk. Add flour, chocolate sprinkles, and ½ cup chopped nuts. Roll dough into two 8" logs. Roll the logs over ¼ cup chopped nuts and the coconut flakes. Cover in waxed paper and refrigerate until chilled. Cut into ¼" cookie slices. Lay out onto ungreased cookie sheet. Place two chocolate chips on the front of each cookie as eyes. Bake at 375° for about 12 minutes or until done. Serve the cookies on the day the students hear the story *Where the Wild Things Are*.

5. The students will make paper bag "Wild Things."

Wild Things
Materials

◆ large paper bags

◆ paper scraps

◆ fake fur

◆ glue

◆ construction paper scraps

◆ crayons

◆ clear tape

Procedure

◆ Stuff a large paper bag with paper scraps. Tape the bag closed.

◆ Cut out legs and arms to look like those of "Wild Things." Glue the arms to the side of the bag. Glue the legs to the bottom of the bag so they dangle off the table. The "Wild Thing" will sit on the edge of a table or bookcase with its legs dangling off.

◆ Glue a piece of fake fur to the top of the "Wild Thing." Draw on a face and decorate the "Wild Thing" with construction paper scraps.

6. See the book *Art Through Children's Literature: Creative Art Lessons for Caldecott Books* by Debi Englebaugh for more art projects.

THE CALDECOTT MEDAL

Randolph Caldecott was born in 1846. Randolph walked in the woods when he was a little boy. He drew pictures of the animals. Randolph wanted to be an artist.

"Randolph should learn about money," his father said. "He needs a real job."

Randolph tried to make his father happy. When he grew up, he worked in a bank. Randolph was very sad. At night Randolph went to art school. He loved to draw pictures.

In 1875, Randolph Caldecott drew pictures for the book *Old Christmas*. Everyone liked his pictures. More people wanted his drawings in their books. Randolph drew many pictures for picture books.

In 1886, Randolph Caldecott died. He was only 40 years old. He was an artist for only ten years.

In 1939, people began to give prizes to the best picture book of the year. They called the prize the Caldecott Medal. Now we will always remember the joy and beauty Caldecott gave the children of the world.

QUESTIONS FOR THE CALDECOTT MEDAL

1. When was Randolph Caldecott born?

    _____

    _____

2. Where did Randolph work when he grew up?

    _____

    _____

3. What book did Randolph Caldecott draw pictures for in 1875?

    _____

    _____

4. What is the name of the prize given to the best picture book of the year?

    _____

    _____

5. Where did Randolph Caldecott work before he drew the pictures for Old Christmas?

    _____

    _____

6. Which came first, the Caldecott Medal or Randolph Caldecott's death?

    _____

    _____

7. What one word best tells about Randolph Caldecott?

    _____

    _____

8. Why was Randolph Caldecott sad when he worked for a bank?

    _____

    _____

9. Look at *several* picture books printed this year. Which one do you think will win the Caldecott Medal? Ask your librarian to tell you if you were right.

_____

_____

10. Why was the prize for the best picture book named after Randolph Caldecott?

_____

_____

11. Write a title for this story. Use as few words as you can.

_____

_____

12. Look at a picture by Randolph Caldecott. Now look at pictures by Chris Van Allsburg. How are the pictures alike? How are they different?

_____

_____

13. In your own words, tell how Randolph Caldecott became a picture book artist.

_____

_____

14. How did Randolph Caldecott's father affect his life?

_____

_____

15. The story said, "He (Randolph Caldecott) was an artist for only ten years." Is this a fact or someone's opinion? How can you prove your answer?

_____

_____

16.

_____

_____

Name _____ Date _____

THE COLOR WHEEL

ABOUT THE STORY

The story tells about the colors of the color wheel. The author explains how artists mix the colors red, blue and yellow to make any color they want.

PREVIEW WORDS

color wheel	painting	colors
rainbow	painters	mix
few	yellow	blue
red		

THROUGHOUT THE WEEK—Display brightly colored prints around the room. Include several watercolor paintings in your display.

BOOKS TO READ

The Science of Color: Investigating the Color Yellow, Barbara J. Behm (Gareth Stevens Publishing, 1993).

Also in the series: *Investigating the Color Red, Investigating the Color Green,* and *Investigating the Color Blue.*

The Art of Color Mixing, Walter Brooks (A Grumbacher Library Book, 1966).

The Mixed-Up Chameleon, Eric Carle (Crowell, 1984).

Harlequin and the Gift of Many Colors, Remy Charlip (Parents' Magazine Press, 1973).

Danger Colors, edited by Jennifer Coldrey and Karen Goldie-Morrison (Putnam, 1986).

Let's Explore Science: Color and Light, David Evans and Claudette Williams (Dorling Kindersley, 1993).

Nature's Colors: Dyes From Plants, Ida Grae (Macmillan, 1974).

Luka's Quilt, Georgia Guback (Greenwillow Books, 1994).

Colors, Gallimard Jeunesse and Pascale de Bourgoing (Scholastic, 1991).

Color Dance, Ann Jonas (Greenwillow Books, 1989).

Look at Rainbow Colors, Rena K. Kirkpatrick (Raintree Editions, 1978).

Hailstones and Halibut Bones: Adventures in Color, Mary O'Neil (Doubleday, [1989] c1961).

Coat of Many Colors, Dolly Parton (HarperCollins, 1994).

First Arts and Crafts: Painting, Sue Stocks (Thomson Learning, 1994).

A Color Sampler, Kathleen Westray (Tichnor & Fields, 1993).

I See Colors, Rozanne Lanczak Williams (Creative Teaching Press, 1994).

Colors, Philip Yenawine (Museum of Modern Art: Delacorte Press, 1991).

VIDEOS

All About Colors, Little Schoolhouse, Vol. 6 (Hi-Tops, 1987).

Easy Watercolor Techniques: Art Lessons for Children, vol. 1, Donna Hugh (Coyote Creek Productions, 1991). Length: 50 minutes.

More Fun With Watercolors: Art Lessons for Children, vol. 3, Donna Hugh (Coyote Creek Productions, 1992. Distributed by Clearvue/eav, 1-800-253-2788.) Length: 53 minutes.

CDS, RECORDS, AND CASSETTES

Mr. Al Sings Colors and Shapes (cassette), Mr. Al (Melody House, 1989).

Paintbox Penguins: A Book About Colors (cassette and book set), Marcia Leonard (Troll Associates, 1992).

INTRODUCTORY ACTIVITIES

DAY ONE

Objective: The students will make a color wheel. They will mix colors in various mediums.
Curriculum subject: Art or Science

Read the book *Colors* by Gallimard Jeunesse and Pascale de Bourgoing.

Teacher: In the story *Colors,* we saw that the basic colors are red, blue, and yellow. We mixed these colors to make orange, purple, and green. These are the colors of the color wheel. Artists use the color wheel to help them make new colors.
(Copy and hand out the color wheel illustrated in this section.)
This is a color wheel. Take out your crayons and color the space marked "red" with your red crayon. Continue coloring each space with the named color until the whole wheel is colored.

While the students color, take out clear cups filled with egg dye and six hard-boiled eggs. You need three cups of yellow dye, three cups of blue dye, and three cups of red dye.

Teacher: Look at these cups of egg dye. Can you find these colors on your color wheel? Notice that we don't have all the colors from the color wheel. What colors are missing? (Answer: The missing colors are purple, green, and orange.)
We can make a purple dye with these colors. How might I make the color purple? (Answer: You pour a red dye into a blue cup.) Watch while I pour the red dye into the blue cup. Look at your color wheel. What color is between the blue and red? (Answer: Purple is between the blue and the red.) This tells us that blue and red make purple.

Continue in this fashion until you have all six colors of the color wheel. Dye the eggs in each color.

You can continue this lesson by mixing red gelatin with blue gelatin. What color does it make? Will the gelatin taste like grape? Why, or why not? Ask volunteers to taste the gelatin to see if it tastes like grape.

COLOR WHEEL

Red

Purple

Orange

Blue

Yellow

Green

DAY TWO

Story Lesson

Follow the *Presenting the Story Lesson* instructions in the Introduction. Each story lesson follows the same procedure; however, say the following in step 4:

"The title of the story we're reading today is *The Color Wheel.* What do you think the story is about? What do you already know about the color wheel?"

EXTENSION ACTIVITIES

1. Show the video *Easy Watercolor Techniques: Art Lessons for Children,* vol. 1, with Donna Hugh. The video features four lessons. Each lesson takes two days to complete. The techniques include experimenting with mixing colors.

2. The students will look at objects through colored water.

Materials

◆ three clear, wide-bottom plastic glasses

◆ red, blue, and yellow food color

◆ red, blue, and yellow paper

◆ water

Procedure

◆ Fill each glass with only ¼″ of water.

◆ Add liquid food coloring to each glass. Make one glass red, one blue, and one yellow. Do not make the color dark.

◆ Hold the red glass inches above red paper.

◆ Look down through the water. What color do you see?

◆ Repeat the activity holding the red glass over the blue paper, then the yellow paper. What colors do you see now?

◆ The students continue the activity, moving each glass over the colored paper.

◆ The colors were not mixed or blended together. Why does the color of the water seem to change when you look through it to the colored paper?

3. Many common plants make beautiful dyes. Ida Grae's *Nature's Colors: Dyes From Plants* is filled with recipes for dyes. Many of her dyes require no chemicals. For example, her Dock Blossom dye calls for only dock blossoms and tap water.

◆ You must have a heating element to make these dyes. Use caution with heating elements around children. They will marvel, however, at the beautiful dyes they can make from everything from pansies to purple cabbage to cactus. Which recipe you use depends on the plants available in your region.

◆ Tie dye T-shirts in the dyes.

◆ Not all plants make the color you would expect. Why do the green leaves of a black walnut tree make a tan dye?

4. Read *Hailstones and Halibut Bones* by Mary O'Neil to the class. The students will write color poems of their own.

◆ Give each student half of a poster board. The students make a collage of color by gluing pictures and small objects to the poster. All the objects on the poster must be of the same color. They can glue on buttons, yarn, paper, small plastic toys, and magazine pictures. Use paint to fill in empty places.

◆ The students write a poem about the color they used in their poster. Mount the poem next to the poster.

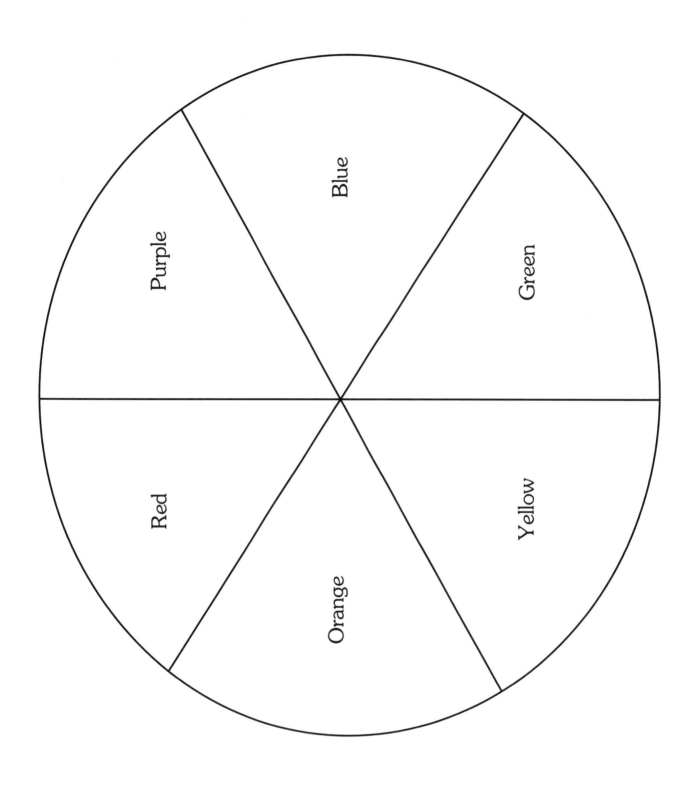

THE COLOR WHEEL

Painting is fun. You can paint a rainbow if you have many colors. You can make any color you want if you know how.

Painters make their own paint colors. They get just a few colors. Then they mix the paint to make the color they need.

If you need paint, you can just get red, blue, and yellow. Painters use color wheels to help them make colors.

Look at the color wheel. It tells you to mix red and blue to make purple. If you mix yellow and blue, you get green. What color do you make if you mix yellow and red?

With the colors red, blue, and yellow you can make any color you want. Someday your teacher will say, "You may have only three paint colors." What colors will you ask for?

QUESTIONS FOR THE COLOR WHEEL

1. How do painters make the colors they need?

   _____

   _____

2. What three colors do you need to make any color you want?

   _____

   _____

3. Name the six colors on the color wheel.

   _____

   _____

4. What color will you get if you mix red and blue?

   _____

   _____

5. What is the first color the story teaches you to make?

   _____

   _____

6. What is the second color the story teaches you to make?

   _____

   _____

7. Why is the picture in the story called a color wheel?

   _____

   _____

8. Look at the color wheel. What two colors do you mix together to make orange?

   _____

   _____

9. Name one way you might use the color wheel to help you in the future.

_____

_____

10. Why might a painter want to mix her or his own colors?

_____

_____

11. Write a title for this story. Use as few words as possible.

_____

_____

12. Would you like to buy the color paint you need, or mix paint to make your own colors? Why do you feel this way?

_____

_____

13. In your own words, tell how you use the colors red, blue, and yellow to make three new colors.

_____

_____

14. After reading this story, will you change the way you use paints? Why do you think so?

_____

_____

15. The story tells you to mix red and blue paint to make purple. Is this a fact? How can you prove your answer?

_____

_____

16.

_____

_____

Name _____   Date _____

TO FLY OVER THE OCEAN

ABOUT THE STORY

This story tells about Charles Lindbergh's flight from New York to Paris. The author describes the hardships Lindbergh endured on his historic flight.

PREVIEW WORDS

Charles Lindbergh	mirrors
May 20, 1927	Washington, D.C.
parties	special
The Spirit of St. Louis	

THROUGHOUT THE WEEK—Display model airplanes around the room. Ask students to bring their model airplanes to class.

BOOKS TO READ

At the Controls: Women in Aviation, Carole S. Briggs (Lerner Publications, 1991).

Flight: The Journey of Charles Lindbergh, Robert Burleigh (Philomel Books, 1991).

Anne Morrow Lindbergh: Pilot and Poet, Roxane Chadwick (Lerner Publications, 1987).

Fabulous Paper Airplanes, E. (Elmer) Richard Churchill (Sterling Publishing, 1992).

The Story of the Spirit of St. Louis, R. Conrad Stein (Childrens Press, 1984).

The Elephant's Airplane and Other Machines, Anne-Marie Dalmais (Western, 1984).

Airplane Ride, Douglas Florian (Crowell, 1984).

The Flight of the Lone Eagle: Charles Lindbergh Flies Nonstop From New York to Paris, John T. Foster (Franklin Watts, 1974).

Flying Free: America's First Black Aviators, Phillip S. Hart (Lerner Publications, 1992).

Amelia Earhart: Courage in the Sky, Mona Kerby (Viking, 1990).

Up in the Air, Poetry by Myra Cohn Livingston (Holiday House, 1989).

We're Taking an Airplane Trip, Dinah L. Moche (Golden Press, 1982).

The Funcraft Book of Flying Models, Derek Beck (Scholastic, 1976).

The Glorious Flight: Across the Channel With Louis Blériot, July 25, 1909, Alice and Martin Provensen (Viking, 1983). Caldecott Award.

Flying Paper Airplane Models, Frank Xavier Ross (Lothrop, Lee & Shepard, 1975).

Famous Aviators of World War II, James B. Sweeney (Franklin Watts, 1987).

The First Flight Across the United States: The Story of Calbraith Perry Rogers and His Airplane, the Vin Fiz, Richard L. Taylor (Franklin Watts, 1993)

The First Solo Flight Around the World: The Story of Wiley Post and His Airplane, the Winnie Mae, Richard L. Taylor (Franklin Watts, 1993).

The Wright Brothers: Conquering the Sky, Becky Welch (Fawcett Columbine, 1992).

VIDEO

There Goes an Airplane, Dave Hood, presenter (Kid Vision, 1994). Length: 35 minutes.

INTRODUCTORY ACTIVITIES

DAY ONE

Objective: The students will listen to a story about Charles Lindbergh.

Curriculum subject: Language Arts or Reading

Teacher: Has anyone flown in an airplane? How big was the plane? How fast did it fly? Has anyone flown over an ocean?

When people first began to fly, airplanes were very slow and small. People said pilots were brave because flying was dangerous.

Today I'm going to read a story about a man named Charles Lindbergh. We will learn about the first flight from New York to Paris. (Using a large map, show where New York and Paris are.) Read the book *Flight: The Journey of Charles Lindbergh* to the class.

Teacher: Why is Charles Lindbergh's flight important? Why do people think he was a brave man? How is Charles Lindbergh like Neil Armstrong, the first man to walk on the moon?

DAY TWO

Story Lesson

Follow the *Presenting the Story Lesson* instructions in the Introduction. Each story lesson follows the same procedure; however, say the following in step 4:

"The title of the story we're reading today is *To Fly Over the Ocean.* What do you think the story is about?" If the students' answers include Charles Lindbergh, ask, "What do you already know about Charles Lindbergh?"

EXTENSION ACTIVITIES

1. Arrange for a field trip to an air museum, air show, or airport. If this is not possible, invite a pilot to visit the class. Ask him or her to discuss the importance of Charles Lindbergh's flight. Why does he or she enjoy flying? What did she or he need to do to become a pilot? What kinds of jobs might a pilot have?

2. Show the video *There Goes an Airplane* presented by Dave Hood. Dave Hood shows the students what it is like to be a pilot. The video also discusses the various uses of airplanes with a sense of humor.

3. Read the Caldecott Medal book *The Glorious Flight: Across the Channel With Louis Blériot, July 25, 1909* by Alice and Martin Provensen. Compare the lighter-than-air craft to Blériot's airplane. How are they alike? How are they different?

4. The students will make a model of a lighter-than-air craft.

Lighter-than-Air Craft Model
Materials

- medium-size balloons of the standard shape
- strawberry baskets from a grocer
- newspaper
- salt
- colorful ribbons
- masking tape
- paintbrushes
- blank newsprint
- flour
- water
- acrylic paints
- paper clips
- glue

Procedure

- Tear 1″ strips of newspaper. Soak them overnight.
- Make the papier mâché paste.

  Mix together ½ cup flour and one tablespoon of salt.

  Add 1 cup warm water and mix. The final paste should be thick like white paste. Add water to thin the paste, or flour to thicken it.
- Blow up a balloon. Open a paper clip to a 90° angle. Tape one hook to the balloon with masking tape. The other hook points straight up.
- Tie a string around the knot of the balloon. Hang the balloon above your work area. This will allow you to work without holding the balloon. Cover your work area with newspaper to keep it clean.
- Dip a newspaper strip into the paste. Run the strip between two of your fingers to push off any excess paste. Lay the strip on the balloon. Cover the taped end of the paper clip with the papier mâché, but leave the other hook exposed. Continue in this way until the balloon is completely covered. Repeat a second layer with blank newsprint. Make sure none of the printed newspaper shows.
- Let the balloon hang overnight to dry.
- Take down the balloon and cut off the string. Tie the string to the exposed hook of the paper clip. Hang the balloon over your work area.
- Using bright colors, paint the balloon with acrylic paint. Encourage the students to use their imaginations. Have they seen hot-air balloons? What were the designs like? Try making a design of your own. To make a chevron design or other straight-line designs, use the masking tape to mask off the straight lines. Let dry.
- Cut two long lengths of ribbon. Cross them at their centers at the top of the balloon. The length of the ribbon depends on the size of your balloon. One ribbon end ties to the basket, reaches to the top of the balloon, then drapes back down to the opposite corner of the basket. Glue them in place with a drop of white glue. Let dry.
- Tie each end of a ribbon to a corner of the strawberry basket. For added color, lace ribbons through the mesh of the baskets.
- Hang the balloons on varying lengths of string from the ceiling or light fixtures.

TO FLY OVER THE OCEAN

In 1927, planes did not fly far. The planes were small. They did not go fast.

Planes could not fly over the ocean. Charles Lindbergh wanted to be the first person to fly over the ocean.

On May 20, 1927, Lindbergh began to fly over the ocean. He had a very small plane. Lindbergh called his plane The Spirit of St. Louis.

Lindbergh could not see out the window. To see out, he looked in mirrors. He had one mirror to see behind him.

After 33 hours, he landed on the other side of the ocean. There were many parties. People were happy he flew over the ocean.

You can see his plane today. It is in a special place in Washington, D.C.

"Charles A. Lindbergh ... landed at Le Bourget Airport, Paris, at 5:24 this afternoon, thus becoming the first person to fly from New York to Paris nonstop."—Lowell Thomas, May 21, 1927

QUESTIONS FOR TO FLY OVER THE OCEAN

1. What did Charles Lindbergh do?

   _____

   _____

2. What did he call his plane?

   _____

   _____

3. On what day did Lindbergh begin to fly over the ocean?

   _____

   _____

4. How did Lindbergh see out of his plane?

   _____

   _____

5. What did people do after Lindbergh flew over the ocean?

   _____

   _____

6. How many planes flew over the ocean before May 20, 1927?

   _____

   _____

7. The story said, "People were happy Lindbergh flew over the ocean." Why do you think they were happy?

   _____

   _____

8. Reread the fourth paragraph. Do you think it was easy for Lindbergh to fly over the ocean? Why do you think so?

   _____

   _____

9. Will people always enjoy reading about the flight of Charles Lindbergh? Why do you think so?

_____

_____

10. Why did Charles Lindbergh want to fly over the ocean?
Would you like to do something no one has done before? Why do you feel this way?

_____

_____

11. Write a title for the story. Use as few words as possible.

_____

_____

12. Look at a picture of The Spirit of Saint Louis. Look at a picture of a jet plane. How are the two planes alike? How are they different?

_____

_____

13. In your own words, tell about Charles Lindbergh's flight over the ocean.

_____

_____

14. Charles Lindbergh was the first person to fly across the ocean. How did his flight change the way people traveled around the world?

_____

_____

15. The story said, "People were happy he (Lindbergh) flew over the ocean." Is this a fact or someone's opinion? Why do you think so?

_____

_____

16.

_____

_____

Name _____   Date _____

SUPER-FAST TRAINS

ABOUT THE STORY

The story tells about the high-speed trains of Japan and France. The author compares the speed of the trains to that of steam engines. Magnetic trains in airtight tubes are the super-fast trains of the future.

PREVIEW WORDS

Japan	France	Bullet Train
magnets	tubes	steam

THROUGHOUT THE WEEK—Set up model trains in the classroom. Decorate the room with pictures of trains.

BOOKS TO READ

The Ghost Train, Allan Ahlberg (Greenwillow Books, 1992).

What About?: Trains, Ron and Joyce Cave (Gloucester Press, 1982).

Rail Travel, Alan Cooper (Thompson Learning, 1993).

Terror Train!, Gilbert B. Cross (Atheneum, 1987).

On the Railway, Young Engineer Malcolm Dixon (The Bookwright Press, 1984).

Mac and Marie and the Train Toss Surprise, Elizabeth Fitzgerald Howard (Four Winds Press, 1993).

Finding Papa, Laura Leonard (Atheneum, 1991).

The Owl Who Became the Moon, Jonathan London (Dutton Children's Books, 1993).

Advanced Model Railroads: A Practical Manual for Designing and Constructing Your Dream Layout, Dave Lowery (Courage Books, 1993).

Black and White, David Macaulay (Houghton Mifflin, 1990). A Caldecott Book.

All Aboard ABC, Doug Magee and Robert Newman (Dutton, 1990).

The Sunday Outing, Gloria Jean Pickney (Dial Books for Young Readers, 1994).

Technology in Action: Train Technology, Michael Pollard (Bookwright Press, 1990).

Trains, Angela Royston (Aladdin Books, 1992).

The Young Engineer Book of Supertrains, Jonathan Rutland (Usborne, 1978).

Railroad Toad, Susan Schade and Jon Buller (Random House, 1993).

Train Song, Diane Siebert (HarperCollins, 1989, c1981).

Trains, Philip Steele (Crestwood House, 1991).

Getting Started With Model Trains, John Townsley (Sterling Publishing, 1991).

City Trains: Moving Through American Cities by Rail, Roger B. Yepsen (Macmillan, 1993).

VIDEOS

The Polar Express, Chris Van Alsburg (American School Publisher, A Macmillan/McGraw-Hill Company, 1988). A Caldecott Video Collection. Length: 11.33 minutes.

Awesome Trains, Simitar Entertainment, Inc., 1994. Length: 30 minutes.

Kids Love Trains, Atlas Video, 1994. Length: 30 minutes.

There Goes a Train, Engineer Dave (Kid Vision, 1994). Length: 35 minutes.

CDS, RECORDS, AND CASSETTES

The Polar Express (cassette), Chris Van Allsberg (Listening Library, 1989). Narrated by William Hurt. A Caldecott Medal Book.

The Christmas Train (cassette and book), Ivan Gantschev (Little, Brown, 1984).

Choo Choo (cassette and book set), Virginia Lee Burton (Houghton Mifflin, 1989).

INTRODUCTORY ACTIVITIES

DAY ONE

Objective: The students will watch the video *There Goes a Train* with Engineer Dave. They will discuss the various trains shown in the movie.

Curriculum subject: Language Arts

Show the video *There Goes a Train,* with Engineer Dave. This is part of a series that includes *There Goes an Airplane,* which the students saw with the previous story *To Fly Over the Ocean.*

Before watching the video, ask the students if they have ridden on a train. Where did they go? What kind of train did they ride on? Did they eat or sleep on the train? What was the experience like?

After the video, discuss the types of trains that Engineer Dave showed them. What did they learn about trains that they did not already know?

DAY TWO

Story Lesson

Follow the *Presenting the Story Lesson* instructions in the Introduction. Each story lesson follows the same procedure; however, say the following in step 4:

"The title of the story we're reading today is *Super-Fast Trains.* What do you think the story is about? What do you already know about trains?"

EXTENSION ACTIVITIES

1. Ask a local train representative to speak to the class. The person might be involved in freight trains, in-city mass transit trains, AMTRAK, or antique trains.

◆ Before the speaker arrives, discuss the questions the students might ask. Include who, what, when, where, and why questions. Write the questions on a chart. These questions might include:

Do trains affect our lives in ways we do not know? Can trains compete with airplanes? If so, how can they compete?

What is the future of long-distance passenger trains? What can we expect in the future of trains? Is a career in trains something the students should consider, and why?

How can airtight tubes and magnetic trains help trains to go much faster in the future?

◆ The representative should talk about how trains affect the lives of the students. End with a question-and-answer session.

2. During Science, read the book *On the Railway* by Malcolm Dixon. Conduct some of the experiments in the book. Emphasize the text and experiments in "Make a Hovertrain" and "Mag-Lev Trains" on pp. 22 and 23.

3. Read the story *Mac and Marie and the Train Toss Surprise* by Elizabeth Fitzgerald Howard.

◆ Ask the students to tell about their experiences with trains. Maybe they know someone who works on a train like the children in the story, whose uncle did. Perhaps they went on a trip that they really enjoyed on a train. Has anyone ridden on an antique train? If not, do they hear a train engine and whistle late at night while they are in their beds? How did the sound make them feel? Where do they think the train was going?

◆ Teacher:

     Write a story about your train. Use words like "rumbling," "rocking," or "clickity-clack." These words touch off the listeners' imagination and make them feel that they're hearing and feeling the motion of the train. It might help to close your eyes, and imagine the sound and feel of your train.

◆ Help the students write their stories. If someone has a good descriptive word, write the word on the board so that everyone can share it. Why is the word a good word to describe the sound or feelings of a train?

◆ Share the stories with the class. While you read the stories, ask the students to put down their heads and close their eyes. Have them picture the train in their imaginations as they listen to the story.

4. The teacher cuts out pictures of trains from magazines before the lesson. Cut out one train for each student. Cut along the outline of the train so that none of the background is included.

◆ The students close their eyes as they listen to the cassette *The Polar Express* by Chris Van Allsburg. Where is the Polar Express taking them? Would they like to ride on a magic train that took them anywhere they would like to go?

◆ Hand out the train pictures. Each train is the student's magic train. The trains can take the students anywhere they want to go. Is the magic train taking them to a person they would like to visit? Is the magic train taking them to outer space? Maybe their magic train is taking them back or forward into time? Perhaps someone always wanted to see the Statue of Liberty? The magic train can even take them to imaginary places.

◆ On drawing paper, the students draw a picture of where they would like their magic train to take them. They can glue on construction paper trees, and other things to add interest. Encourage them to use their imaginations. The students draw empty tracks in the scene.

◆ Finally, the students use a glue stick to glue their train picture into the scene.

◆ The students will write poems about their magic trains.

SUPER-FAST TRAINS

When we think of trains, we think of slow trains rolling across the West. That picture of trains is changing, and it's changing fast!

In Japan and France, high-speed trains are racing across the land. They are so fast that people use trains, not planes.

New tracks help the trains move very fast. Turning tracks do not lie flat on the ground. They rise up on the outside, like race tracks for cars. The trains can turn without slowing down.

The Bullet Train of Japan runs up to 130 miles per hour. It runs on electric wires that are over the train.

France's trains can move people faster than an airplane. Their trains move up to 254 miles per hour. The fastest steam train can go only 126 miles per hour.

Someday trains will run in big tubes. Magnets will lift them off the ground. These speeders will move at over 745 miles per hour.

QUESTIONS FOR SUPER-FAST TRAINS

1. What is the name of Japan's fast train?

   _____

   _____

2. How fast does the Bullet Train run?

   _____

   _____

3. How fast does France's train move?

   _____

   _____

4. How fast can the fastest steam train go?

   _____

   _____

5. Which train does the story tell about first?

   _____

   _____

6. What is the second train the story tells about?

   _____

   _____

7. What one word best tells about the Bullet Train?

   _____

   _____

8. Do people want to ride on very fast trains? Why do you think so?

   _____

   _____

9. Will people make trains that go faster in the future? Why do you think so?

_____

_____

10. Why do Japan and France make such fast trains?

_____

_____

11. Write a name for the story. Use only a few words.

_____

_____

12. How is the Bullet Train of Japan like steam trains? How are they not alike?

_____

_____

13. In your own words, tell about the tracks used by super-fast trains.

_____

_____

14. How will a train that goes 745 miles in one hour change the way people go from place to place?

_____

_____

15. The story said, "The Bullet Train of Japan runs up to 130 miles per hour." Is this a fact or an opinion? How can you show you are right?

_____

_____

16.

_____

_____

Name _____   Date _____

THOMAS EDISON'S NEWSPAPER

ABOUT THE STORY

The story tells about a newspaper printed by Thomas Edison at the age of 15. Edison printed and sold his newspaper on a train.

PREVIEW WORDS

Thomas Edison	newspaper	light bulb
train	printing press	
the War Between the States		

THROUGHOUT THE WEEK—Collect permission slips from the parents. You need permission to use the students' names in a class newspaper. Many districts require parent permission to use a student's name when circulating any flier or newspaper.

Ask the school principal or assistant principal if he or she could give an interview. Also, ask the principal if he or she could take a picture when the students make a *Day at Our School* photojournalism book (see Extension Activity 4, page 105).

Read chapters from *Germy Blew "The Bugle"* by Rebecca C. Jones to the class every day. The story tells about Jeremy Bluett who starts a school paper. (New York: Arcade Publishing, 1990.)

BOOKS TO READ

The Berenstain Bears and the School Scandal Sheet, Stan Berenstain (Random House, 1994).

The Secrets of Santa, Anne Civardi (Simon & Schuster, 1991).

What's It Like to Be a Newspaper Reporter, Janet Palazzo-Craig (Troll Associates, 1990).

Running a School Newspaper, Vivian Dubrovin (Franklin Watts, 1985).

James Weldon Johnson, Ophelia Settle Egypt (Crowell, 1974).

American Women of Achievement: Nellie Bly, Elizabeth Ehrlich (Chelsea House Publishers, 1989).

Morrie Turner, Creator of "Wee Pals," Mary Kentra Ericsson (Childrens Press, 1986).

I Can Be a Reporter, Christine Maloney Fitz-Gerald (Childrens Press, 1986).

Deadline!: From News to Newspaper, Gail Gibbons (Crowell, 1987).

Journalism, Ray Eldon Hiebert (Boy Scouts of America, 1976).

What's Inside?: Great Inventions, edited by Hilary Hockman (Dorling Kindersley, 1993).

Hot Off the Press!: A Day at the Daily News, Margaret Miller (Crown Publishers, 1985).

The Value of Creativity: The Story of Thomas Edison, Ann Donegan Johnson (Value Communications, 1981).

The Value of Fairness: The Story of Nellie Bly, Ann Donegan Johnson (Value Communications, 1977).

Germy Blew "The Bugle," Rebecca C. Jones (Arcade Publishing, 1990).

Careers for Wordsmiths, interviews by Andrew Kaplan (Millbrook Press, 1991).

One Spooky Night and Other Scary Stories, Mauri Kunnas with Tarja Kunnas (Crown, 1986, c1985).

The Furry News: How to Make a Newspaper, Loreen Leedy (Holiday House, 1990).

Tell Me About Yourself: How to Interview Anyone, From Your Friends to Famous People, D.L. Mabery (Lerner Publications, 1985).

Karen's Newspaper, Ann M. Martin (Scholastic, 1993).

Mark Twain? What Kind of Name Is That?: A Story of Samuel Langhorne Clemens, Robert M. Quackenbush (Prentice-Hall, 1984).

Jace the Ace, Joanne Rocklin (Collier Macmillan, 1990).

Stephanie's Big Story, Susan Saunders (Scholastic, 1989).

Mysteriously Yours, Maggie Marmelstein, Marjorie Weinman Sharmat (HarperCollins Publishing, 1982).

The News Media, Ruth Wolverton (Franklin Watts, 1981).

Weekly Reader: 60 Years of News for Kids, 1928–1988, introduction by Hugh Downs, prepared by the staff of the *Weekly Reader* (*World Almanac,* 1988).

VIDEO

The Great Muppet Caper, Jim Henson Video, distributed by Buena Vista Home Video, 1993. Length: 98 minutes.

CDS, RECORDS, AND CASSETTES

Meet the Author Series: The Man Who Invented Snoopy (cassette and filmstrip set with booklet) (Random House, 1982).

INTRODUCTORY ACTIVITIES

DAY ONE

Objective: The students will visit a newspaper office, or speak to a reporter in class.
Curriculum subject: Language Arts or Social Studies

If possible, take the students on a field trip to a local newspaper office. Ask to speak to a reporter, editor, photographer, cartoonist, sports writer, or printer.

Before leaving the classroom, review the five questions beginning with who, what, when, where, and why. When a reporter gets information for a story, he or she must answer these questions. Why are these questions important to a reporter?

Look for the answers to these questions as the students visit the newspaper office:

◆ *Who* decides which stories are printed?

◆ *What* do you use to print the stories onto paper?

◆ *When* do you print your newspaper?

◆ *Where* do you find your stories?

◆ *Why* did you become involved in the newspaper?

If you cannot visit a newspaper office, ask a reporter to visit your class. Ask the same questions, and end with a question-and-answer session.

DAY TWO

Objective: The students will learn about a printing press, and why it was important to the development of newspapers.

Curriculum subject: History, Art

If possible, have antique letter blocks from a printing press available for the students to look at.

Teacher: Yesterday we went to a newspaper office. We saw how reporters write news stories. The editor read the stories and suggested changes. Finally, the printer made many copies of the newspaper.

Think about the printing machine. What would happen if there wasn't a printing machine of any kind? How would they make copies of the newspaper? (Answer: They would have to make copies of the newspaper by hand.)

One of the most important inventions in history was the printing press. A man named Johannes Gutenberg invented the printing press about 550 years ago.

(Show the students several stamps.)

Look at these stamps. When I put the stamp in ink and press it on paper, I make a copy of the picture on the stamp. This stamp has words on it. Look at the words carefully. What is strange about the words? (Answer: The letters are backward.) Were the letters backward when I stamped them on a piece of paper?

First, Gutenberg made many little stamps with backward letters on them. Each stamp had only one letter. He put one stamp at a time on what looked like a big cookie sheet. When he put all the stamps together, he could make words and sentences.

Next, he brushed ink over all the letters. He laid a piece of paper over the letters.

Finally, Gutenberg lowered a heavy block onto the paper. The block pressed the paper tightly against the letters. When he raised the press and took out the paper, the words were printed on the paper like the words on a newspaper.

(Show the students the picture of a printing press in the book *What's Inside?: Great Inventions,* edited by Hilary Hockman, pp. 16–17. Read the text to the students.)

Why do you think they called this invention a printing press? Why was the printing press an important invention?

(Follow the instructions on p. 17 of *What's Inside?: Great Inventions* to make stamp designs on potato halves.)

DAY THREE

Story Lesson

Follow the *Presenting the Story Lesson* instructions in the Introduction. Each story lesson follows the same procedure; however, say the following in step 4:

"The title of the story we're reading today is *Thomas Edison's Newspaper.* What do you think the story is about? What do you already know about newspapers?"

EXTENSION ACTIVITIES

1. Read the book *The Furry News: How to Make a Newspaper* by Loreen Leedy to the class. The book is a delightful story about animals making their own newspaper. It clearly explains the jobs of the people who work at a newspaper.

◆ The end of the book tells how to set up a newspaper. Read the section "Making Your Own Newspaper for Your Family, Neighborhood, or School." Follow the directions, and make a school or class newspaper.

2. The students will make a list of important issues facing your school. They will choose one of the issues to investigate. On a piece of chart paper, write the who, what, when, where, and why questions that the class must answer.

◆ Next, make a list of people to interview. A school board member, the principal, or other administrator might visit the class to answer the students' questions. If no one can come to the class, try scheduling a telephone interview. If the students do not have the skills to take notes, the teacher should take notes for them.

◆ After the interview, review what you learned. What were the answers to the questions? Write a story about the issue you investigated. Include the story in your newspaper.

3. Watch the filmstrip *Meet the Author Series: The Man Who Invented Snoopy*. After the filmstrip, the students will make comic strips of their own.

◆ Hand out several copies of the funny pages. Read the comics to the students. Ask: "Which comics do you think are funny? Why do you think so?"

◆ Give each student a paper with four rectangles on it. (See the black-line master (page 106) in this section.) The students will make a four-part comic strip. They can give their characters words, or let the pictures speak for themselves. The students can do this activity in groups.

◆ Include the comic strips in your newspaper.

4. Before class, look at the book *A Day in the Life of America* (New York: Collins Publishers, 1986). The book is a collection of photographs taken by several photojournalists in one day. Some of the photographs are not suitable for the students; however, you can see the concept clearly in the book. I would not make the book available to the students.

◆ Teacher:

There is a type of reporter we call a photojournalist. A photojournalist takes pictures of a subject. The picture tells the story as well, if not better, than a story made of words.

Tomorrow we'll be photojournalists. Starting early in the morning and before school, we'll take pictures. We'll take a picture every 30 minutes. Everyone will have a turn taking a picture. Even our principal will take a picture.

We'll look for something happening that tells about a day at our school. For example, we'll take a picture of students eating breakfast or getting their class picture taken. Don't warn the people that you're taking the pictures. We want the pictures to show them as the really are and not posed.

◆ Bring an inexpensive camera loaded with film for 24 photographs to class. Make a list of students in the order they will take a picture. Each student will take one picture, then pass the camera on to the next student. Let each student take one picture every 30 minutes. The teacher and the student might be the only people who know the content of the picture.

◆ The teacher begins by taking pictures when the first person, perhaps the custodian, comes to school. The teacher finishes with a photograph of the last person leaving. The pictures should reflect a day at your school—such as the raising of the flag, students running in P.E., and other regular activities.

◆ Develop the film to large-size prints. Number the backs of the prints in the order in which they were taken. The students will mount the photographs in an album. Put the pictures in chronological order, with the morning picture on the first page and the evening picture on the last page. Do not write words with the pictures. The photographs will speak for themselves. Put the title *A Day at (your school's name)* on the front of the album.

◆ Discuss the story the photographs tell about the school. How is the album like a story written in words? How is it different? Which way do you like telling a story best, with pictures or words?

5. Distribute the class newspaper to the other classes. Present the *Day at Your School* book to the principal.

THOMAS EDISON'S NEWSPAPER

Do you know the name Thomas Edison? Edison made the first light bulb. Did you know Edison made his own newspaper? He made his newspaper when he was only 15 years old.

Edison was a newspaper boy during the War Between the States. He sold the paper to people riding on a train. The people wanted to know about the war. By the time the newspaper got to the train, the news was old. Edison wanted to get news to the people faster.

First, Edison got an old printing press. He put it on the train. Edison got off the train when it stopped. Then he talked to people who knew about the war.

Next, Edison printed his own newspaper on the train. He wrote about the war. Edison also wrote about the men who worked on the train.

People liked Edison's newspaper. At first he made 100 papers. Soon he was making 300 newspapers.

Today we think about Thomas Edison and his light bulb. Maybe we should also think of him as the boy with his own newspaper.

QUESTIONS FOR THOMAS EDISON'S NEWSPAPER

1. Who made the first light bulb?

   _____

   _____

2. How old was Thomas Edison when he made his newspaper?

   _____

   _____

3. Where did Edison sell his newspapers?

   _____

   _____

4. Where did Edison print his newspaper?

   _____

   _____

5. What was the <u>first</u> thing Edison did to make his newspaper?

   _____

   _____

6. What was the <u>next</u> thing Edison did to make his newspaper?

   _____

   _____

7. What one word best tells about Thomas Edison?

   _____

   _____

8. Why did people like Edison's newspaper?

   _____

   _____

9. Will people always want a newspaper like Edison's on a train? Why do you think so?

_____

_____

10. Why did Edison want to get the news to the people fast?

_____

_____

11. Write a name for the story. Use only a few words.

_____

_____

12. How are Edison's newspaper and today's newspaper alike? How are they not alike?

_____

_____

13. Tell how Edison made his newspaper. Use as few words as you can.

_____

_____

14. Did Edison's paper help the people on the train? Why do you think so?

_____

_____

15. The story said, "People liked Edison's newspaper." Is this a fact? How do you know?

_____

_____

16.

_____

_____

Name _____   Date _____

SEQUOYAH AND THE CHEROKEE ALPHABET

ABOUT THE STORY

This story tells how Sequoyah created the Cherokee alphabet. The author discusses how the alphabet changed the lives of the Cherokee people.

PREVIEW WORDS

Sequoyah   Cherokee   alphabet

English   Cherokee Phoenix

THROUGHOUT THE WEEK—Decorate the classroom with Native American designs. Include blankets, pottery, and baskets.

Play Native American music as the students enter and leave the classroom, and as they work. For example:

Talking Spirits: Native American Music From the Hopi, Zuni and San Juan Pueblos. Music
    of the World, 1992.

Read a story each day from *Native American Stories* told by Joseph Bruchac. (Colorado: Fulcrum Publishing, 1991.)

BOOKS TO READ

Only the Names Remain, Alex W. Bealer (Little, Brown, 1972).

Powwow, June Behrens (Childrens Press, 1983).

Native American Crafts Workshop, Bonnie Bernstein and Leigh Blair (Pitman Learnings, Inc.,
    1982).

Flying With the Eagle, Racing the Great Bear: Stories From Native North America, Joseph
    Bruchac (BridgeWater Books, 1993).

Native American Stories, Joseph Bruchac (Fulcrum Publishing, 1991).

*Keepers of Life: Discovering Plants Through Native American Stories and Earth Activities
    for Children,* Michael J. Caduto and Joseph Bruchac (Fulcrum Publishing, 1994).

The Cherokee Indians, Nicole Claro (Chelsea House Publishers, 1992).

Indian Crafts, Janet and Alex D'Amato (Lion Press, 1968).

Indian Two Feet Rides Alone, Margaret Friskey (Childrens Press, 1980).

Easy to Make North American Indian Crafts, Frieda Gates (Harvey House, Publishers, 1981).

Wilma Mankiller: Chief of the Cherokee Nation, Bruce Glassman (A Blackbirch Press Book,
    1992).

The Girl Who Loved Wild Horses, Paul Goble (Bradbury Press, 1978). Caldecott Medal Book.

The Trail on Which They Wept: The Story of a Cherokee Girl, Dorothy and Thomas Hoobler
    and Carey-Greenberg Associates (Silver Burdett Press, a division of Simon & Schuster,
    1992).

Something for the Medicine Man, Flora Mae Hood (Melmont, 1962).

The Complete Book of Indian Crafts and Lore, W. Ben Hunt (Golden Press, 1954).

The Art of American Indian Cooking, Yeffe Kimball and Jean Anderson (Doubleday, 1965).

Native Harvests: Botanicals and Recipes of the American Indian, Barrie Kavasch (Random House, 1979).

Mandie and the Cherokee Legend, Lois Gladys Leppard (Bethany House Publishers, 1983).

The Cherokee, a New True Book, Emilie U. Lepthien (Childrens Press, 1985).

The Cherokee, Barbara A. McCall (Rourke Publications, 1989).

The Cherokee, Theda Perdue (Chelsea House, 1988).

North American Indians, a Civilization Project Book, Susan Purdy and Cass R. Sandak (Franklin Watts, 1982).

The Story of the Trail of Tears, R. Conrad Stein (Childrens Press, 1985).

The Kids' Multicultural Art Book: Art and Craft Experiences From Around the World, Alexandra M. Terzian (Williamson Publishing, 1993).

American Indian Clothes and How to Make Them, Alex Whitney (McKay, 1979).

VIDEO

The Girl Who Loved Wild Horses, Paul Goble, 1988. American School Publishers, Random House Video: Caldecott Video Collection.

CDS, RECORDS, AND CASSETTES

Myth, Music and Dance of the American Indian (cassette and book set), Ruth De Cesare, Ph.D., ed. (Alfred Publishing Co. Inc., 1988).

Dream Catcher (CD), Tokeya Inajin (Kevin Locke) (Earth Beat!, 1992). "The songs in this collection are from three magnificent Indian nations, the *Lakota, Dakota* and *Meskwaki.*"

Talking Spirits: Native American Music From the Hopi, Zuni and San Juan Pueblos (cassette), Music of the World, 1992.

INTRODUCTORY ACTIVITIES

DAY ONE

Objective: The students will watch the video of the Caldecott book *The Girl Who Loved Wild Horses.* The students will make a list of Native American tribes.

Curriculum subject: Language Arts or Social Studies

Show the video *The Girl Who Loved Wild Horses* by Paul Goble (1988). If the video is not available, read the book to the class.

Teacher: Before Columbus came to America, there were many Native American tribes. In North America, which now includes the United States, Mexico and Canada, there were over 250 tribes. Each tribe had its own language and culture.

How these tribes lived depended on where they settled. Tribes living in the cold, icy climate of what we call Alaska hunted marine animals for food. Indians living in the plains hunted buffalo.

Ask the students to call out names of tribes. Write the tribe names on the board. Examples: Pawnee, Omaha, Cheyenne, Arapaho, Blackfoot, Crow, Comanche, Pueblo, Eskimo, Apache, Hopi, Iroquois, Navajo, Osage, Sioux.

DAY TWO

Story Lesson

Follow the *Presenting the Story Lesson* instructions in the Introduction. Each story lesson follows the same procedure; however, say the following in step 4:

"The title of the story we're reading today is *Sequoyah and the Cherokee Alphabet.* What do you think the story is about? What do you already know about the Cherokee people?"

EXTENSION ACTIVITIES

1. Break the class into groups of three to four students. Assign each group one of the following tribes: Pueblo, Navajo, Pawnee, Cherokee, Apache, Maya, Aztec. Give each group a large cardboard square. Each group will make a model of a village of their tribe. Did they live in hogans or log cabins? Did they have totem poles? Did they hunt buffalo or plant crops? All these questions should be answered by the model. Include details (e.g., Navajo sand paintings and pictographs on stretched skins). Use whatever materials are available, Allow the students to use their imaginations.

◆ If needed, here is a simple clay the students can make themselves.

Clay

◆ Mix together well: 1½ cup flour, ½ cup salt, and ½ tablespoon alum.

◆ Divide the flour and salt mixture into fourths (½ cup each) and put into separate bowls.

◆ Combine ⅛ cup water and 1 teaspoon vegetable oil. Dye the liquid with food coloring.

◆ Mix the dyed water and oil into one of the bowls of dry ingredients. Add more water to a dry clay. Add more flour to a sticky clay.

◆ Repeat steps 3 and 4 for each bowl of dry ingredients, using a different color for each bowl.

2. The students will spend the day making Native American costumes, food, and crafts. For designs of paper bag costumes see *The Kids' Multicultural Art Book: Art and Craft Experiences from Around the World* by Alexandra M. Terzian.

◆ Consult books listed in the *Books to Read* section for a variety of Native American crafts and activities.

3. If possible, arrange for a Native American to visit the class to discuss Native American culture and language.

Cherokee Nation Communications

P.O. Box 948 * Tahlequah, OK * 74465-0948

Cherokee Alaphabet

D a	**R** e	**T** i	**Ꮊ** o	**O** u	**i** v
Ꮪ ga **Ꮝ** ka	**Ᏺ** ge	**Ᏻ** gi	**A** go	**J** gu	**E** gv
Ꮗ ha	**Ꮄ** he	**Ꮅ** hi	**F** ho	**Γ** hu	**Ꮎ** hv
W la	**Ꮆ** le	**Ꮇ** li	**G** lo	**M** lu	**Ꮸ** lv
Ꮉ ma	**Ꮉ** me	**H** mi	**Ꮊ** mo	**Ꮍ** mu	
Ꮎ na **Ꮏ** hna **G** nah	**Ꮑ** ne	**ꭿ** ni	**Z** no	**Ꮔ** nu	**O** nv
Ꮖ qua	**Ꮗ** que	**Ꮙ** qui	**Ꮖ** quo	**Ꮗ** quu	**Ɛ** quv
Ꮜ sa **Ꮝ** s	**Ꮞ** se	**Ꮟ** si	**Ꮠ** so	**Ꮡ** su	**R** sv
Ꮣ da **Ꮤ** ta	**Ꮥ** de **Ꮦ** te	**Ꮧ** di **Ꭲ** ti	**V** do	**S** du	**Ꮫ** dv
Ꮪ dla **Ꮮ** tla	**L** tle	**C** tli	**Ꮰ** tlo	**Ꮱ** tlu	**P** tlv
Ꮳ tsa	**Ꮴ** tse	**Ꮵ** tsi	**K** tso	**Ꮷ** tsu	**Ꮿ** tsv
Ꮹ wa	**Ꮺ** we	**Ꮻ** wi	**Ꮼ** wo	**Ꮽ** wu	**6** wv
Ꮿ ya	**ß** ye	**Ꭹ** yi	**Ꮒ** yo	**G** yu	**B** yv

Sounds Represented by Vowels

a, as a in father, or short as a in rival

e, as a in hate, or short as e in met

i, as i in pique, or short as i in pit

o, as o in note, approaching aw in law

u, as oo in fool, or short as u in pull

v, as in u but, nasalized

Consonant Sounds

g nearly as in English, but approaching to k. d nearly as in English but approaching to t; h k l m n q s t w y as in English. Syllables beginning with g except **Ꮪ** (ga) have sometimes the power of k. **A** (go), **S** (du), **Ꮫ** (dv) are sometimes sounded to, tu, tv and syllables written with tl except **Ꮮ** (tla) sometimes vary to dl.

Reprinted by permission of Cherokee Nation Communications, Tahlequah, Oklahoma.

SEQUOYAH AND THE CHEROKEE ALPHABET

For many years, the Cherokee could not write. They did not know about letters. The Cherokee could not write to their friends. They could not read stories. If a Cherokee child wanted to hear a story, someone had to tell it.

One day a Cherokee man named Sequoyah saw white people writing. He called this writing "talking leaves." Sequoyah wanted to make a Cherokee alphabet.

Sequoyah had to make up his letters. The English letters did not work for Cherokee. Sequoyah worked for almost 10 years. He made 86 Cherokee letters. Each letter stood for a part of a word. Sequoyah was the first person to make a new alphabet by himself.

The new Cherokee letters were easy to learn. Most Cherokees learned to read and write in only a few days.

For the first time, the Cherokee had a newspaper. They called it the Cherokee Phoenix. Cherokee children could now read a story without finding someone to tell it.

QUESTIONS FOR SEQUOYAH AND THE CHEROKEE ALPHABET

1. Name the man who made the Cherokee alphabet.

   _____

   _____

2. How many years did Sequoyah work on his letters?

   _____

   _____

3. How long did it take most Cherokees to learn to read and write?

   _____

   _____

4. What was the name of the Cherokee newspaper?

   _____

   _____

5. How did the Cherokee children hear a story before Sequoyah made his alphabet?

   _____

   _____

6. What could the Cherokee people do after Sequoyah made his alphabet?

   _____

   _____

7. What one word best tells about Sequoyah?

   _____

   _____

8. Was Cherokee life better after Sequoyah made his alphabet? Why do you think so?

   _____

   _____

9. Will the Cherokee always use Sequoyah's alphabet? Why do you think so?

_____

_____

10. Why did Sequoyah make a Cherokee alphabet?

_____

_____

11. Write a name for the story. Use as few words as you can.

_____

_____

12. How are Sequoyah's Cherokee letters and English letters alike? How are they not alike?

_____

_____

13. Tell how Sequoyah made his alphabet. Use as few words as you can.

_____

_____

14. How did Sequoyah's alphabet change the lives of his people?

_____

_____

15. The story said, "Sequoyah was the first person to make a new alphabet by himself." Is this a fact? How do you know?

_____

_____

16.

_____

_____

Name _____   Date _____

PIÑATAS

ABOUT THE STORY

The story tells the history of piñatas. The author explains how the three-point star piñata represents the Three Wise Men and the gifts they took to the baby Jesus.

PREVIEW WORDS

piñata	Spain	Mexico
Christmas	Three Wise Men	Jesus

THROUGHOUT THE WEEK—Decorate the class with bright colors and Mexican folk art. Display a Mexican flag. As the students work or leave and enter the room, play traditional Mexican music, such as:

Ronstadt, Linda. *Canciones de Me Padre* (CD). New York: Elektra/Asylum, 1987.

Read a story a day from *The Boy Who Could Do Anything and Other Mexican Folk Tales* by Anita Brenner. (Hamden, Conn.: Linnet Books, 1992.)

BOOKS TO READ

Pablo Remembers: The Fiesta of the Days of the Dead, George Ancona (Lothrop, Lee & Shepard Books, 1993).

The Piñata Maker = El Piñatero, George Ancona (Harcourt Brace & Jovanovich, 1994). Texas Bluebonnet Award Nominee.

Baja Cars, T.J. Anderson (Crestwood House, 1988).

Mexico, Donna Bailey and Anna Sproule (Steck-Vaughn Library, 1990).

Fiesta!: Cinco de Mayo, June Behrens (Childrens Press, 1978).

The Boy Who Could Do Anything and Other Mexican Folk Tales, Anita Brenner (Linnet Books, 1992).

Piñatas, Virginia Brock (Abingdon Press, 1966).

Count Your Way Through Mexico, James Haskins (Carolrhoda Books, 1989).

Cooking the Mexican Way, Rosa Coronado (Lerner Publications, 1982).

Las Navidades: Popular Christmas Songs from Latin America, selected by Lulu Delacre (Scholastic, 1990).

The Legend of the Poinsettia, Tomie De Paola (Putnam, 1993).

Latin American and Caribbean Crafts, Judith Hoffman Corwin (Franklin Watts, 1991).

The Nelson A. Rockefeller Collection of Mexican Folk Art: A Gift to the Mexican Museum, Mexican Museum with text by Carlos Espejel (Chronicle Books, 1986).

Frida Kahlo: Mysterious Painter, Nancy Frazier (Blackbirch Press, 1992).

Mexico, the People, Bobbie Kalman (Crabtree Publishing Co., 1993).

The Christmas Piñata, Jack Kent (Parents' Magazine Press, 1975).

The Days of the Dead, Kathryn Lasky (Hyperion Books for Children, 1994).

Fiesta Time in Mexico, Rebecca B. Marcus (Garrard, 1974).

Soccer Sam, Jean Marzollo (Random House, 1987).

Fiesta!: Mexico's Great Celebrations, Elizabeth Silverthorne (Millbrook Press, 1992).

Hernando Cortes, R. Conrad Stein (Childrens Press, 1991).

Fiesta of Folk Songs from Spain and Latin America, Henrietta Yurchenco (Putnam, 1967).

CDS, RECORDS, AND CASSETTES

Piñata!: Bilingual Songs for Children, Sarah Barchas (High Heaven Music, 1991.

Canciones de Mi Padre (CD), Linda Ronstadt (Elektra/Asylum, 1987).

First Folk Dances, vol. 2: Good Neighbors, Latin American Dances (record), Ruth S. White (Tom Thumb, 1988).

INTRODUCTORY ACTIVITIES

DAY ONE

Objective: The students will listen to the story *The Piñata Maker = El Piñatero* by George Ancona.

Curriculum subject: Language Arts or Art

Bring several piñatas to class and a bag of candy. Hold up one piñata for the students to see.

Teacher: What do you call this toy? It's a piñata. Does anyone know how to play with a piñata? First, the piñata is hung by a rope overhead. It may be tied to the ceiling, or a tree. You cover your eyes with a blindfold. Then you hold a long stick in your hand. Someone helps you turn in a circle three times. Next, you have three chances to swing at the piñata with the stick. Everyone gets a turn. Finally, the piñata breaks open. Candy that is inside the piñata falls out. Everyone runs to pick up the candy. Look closely at our piñata. What is it made of? What makes the fluffy look on the outside of the piñata? Now look at the top of our piñata. Do you see that hole? The candy goes into this hole to fill the piñata. Let's fill our piñata with this bag of candy. (Open the bag of candy and fill the piñata.)

This week we'll learn about fiestas. People in Mexico call their big parties fiestas. We'll learn about piñatas, learn Mexican dances, and even have our own fiesta on Friday.

Today we'll begin by reading a story about a man who makes piñatas. Look closely at the pictures. How are his piñatas different from ours? What other toys does he make for the children's fiesta?

Read the story *The Piñata Maker = El Piñatero* by George Ancona. Discuss the questions after reading the story.

DAY TWO

Story Lesson

Follow the *Presenting the Story Lesson* instructions in the Introduction. Each story lesson follows the same procedure; however, say the following in step 4:

"The title of the story we're reading today is *Piñatas*. What do you think the story is about? What do you already know about piñatas?"

EXTENSION ACTIVITIES

1. The students will make piñatas. These are piñatas that are close to the design of traditional piñatas. Traditional piñatas were made around clay pots like those the piñata maker made in the story. The students will make a pot out of papier-mâché. Before beginning the activity, show the students the piñata in the class. It is not made from a clay pot. How is it different from the piñata maker's piñata?

Piñatas
Materials

- round balloons
- string
- newspaper
- papier-mâché paste
- rope
- several colors of tissue and crepe paper
- white glue
- construction paper scraps
- scissors
- straight-edge

Procedure

- Make papier-mâché. Display this chart as you make the papier-mâché.

Papier-mâché

1. Soak sheets of newspaper overnight.
2. Mix 2 tablespoons of flour with 2 to 3 tablespoons of cold water.
3. Mix together until the paste is smooth.
4. Ask your teacher to quickly pour in a little boiling water.
5. Stir until the paste is thick and shiny.

◆ Blow up a round balloon.

◆ If possible, hang the balloon on a string by its knot over a covered work area.

◆ Dip the newspaper completely into the papier-mâché paste. Slide the newspaper strip through your fingers to remove excess paste.

◆ Cover the balloon with papier-mâché. Leave the knot end exposed so that an opening is in the top. This will make the pot. The opening must be about 2″ wide so that the candy can pour into it.

◆ Let the balloon dry over night.

◆ DO NOT POP THE BALLOON. Use your imagination to make a design for the piñata. Look at the many piñata books in the *Books to Read* section for ideas. You can make a star piñata, a super-hero, an animal, an alien spaceship, or a bug. Be sure to encourage the students to use their imaginations.

◆ Make the paper covering for the balloon by cutting long, 3″ wide strips from crepe or tissue paper. Fold the strips in half. Cut 1″ into the folded side. Make sure your cuts are straight and evenly distributed along the strips.

(glue side)

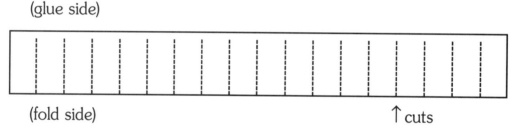

(fold side)   ↑ cuts

◆ Run a bead of white glue along the glue side of the strip.

◆ Wrap the strips around the piñata in rows, starting at the bottom of the piñata.

◆ When the piñata is finished and dry, pop the balloon. Throw away all the balloon pieces for the safety of the students.

2. The students will make colorful Mexican vests.

◆ Because this activity can be used at any age level, you will need to measure the students for the size of the vest patterns. If needed, you can make small, medium, and large patterns. Measure the students from shoulder to shoulder. Then measure the students from the lower neck to the waist.

◆ Collect many colors of bright bulletin board paper. Multiply the shoulder-to-shoulder measurement by two. Cut a piece of bulletin board paper to that width and the length from neck to waist.

◆ Fold the paper in half, matching the edges of the shorter sides. Cut the lower corners along a curved line.

fold →

← length from neck to waist

← cut on curved line

◆ Open the paper and lay it flat. Fold the left side to the center line. Fold the right side to the center line.

◆ Follow the drawing below to cut the arm and neck holes.

↓cut out neck and arm holes

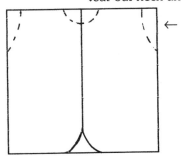

◆ Use clear packing tape to tape the shoulders closed.

◆ The students draw colorful designs and stripes on their vests. The students can look at pictures of traditional Mexican clothing and art for inspiration.

3. The students will learn Latin American folk dances. While listening to the record *First Folk Dances, vol. 2: Good Neighbors, Latin American Dance* by Ruth S. White, the students will learn Latin American folk dances. The students can perform the dances wearing blue jeans, a white shirt, and their paper vests.

4. The students make Mexican food.

Guacamole
Ingredients

◆ ripe avocados

◆ mild bottled salsa

◆ one lemon

◆ baked tortilla chips

Procedure

◆ The teacher will cut the avocados in half and remove the pit. (You can save the pit to grow an avocado plant during Science.)

◆ The students use spoons to scoop out the meat of the avocado. Put the meat in a bowl and discard the skin.

◆ Mash the avocado with a fork.

◆ Mix in mild salsa to taste.

◆ The teacher will cut the lemon in half, and squeeze the lemon over the guacamole. This prevents the avocado from turning brown.

◆ Pour the guacamole into colorful bowls.

◆ Serve with baked tortilla chips.

5. Ask a member of the Hispanic community to visit the class. Discuss what a Mexican fiesta is, and its history. What other games do they play at a fiesta? What food do they serve at a fiesta?

6. On Friday, hold a fiesta. The students can dance. They can break their piñatas. If possible, buy mild tamales wrapped in corn husks at the grocery stores. Warm them in a microwave, and serve them with the guacamole and tortilla chips for lunch.

◆ Remember that Mexican food can be too spicy for young children. Always taste the salsa and tamales before serving them to make sure they are very mild.

PIÑATAS

Have you been to a party and played with a piñata? Some piñatas are paper bulls filled with candy. Children hit the bull with sticks. The bull breaks and the children run for the falling candy.

The paper bull was a piñata. Piñatas are very old toys.

In Spain, children played with piñatas at Christmas. The Christmas piñata looked like a star. The star had three points. They said each point was one of the Three Wise Men who visited Jesus. The candies in each point were like the gifts the Three Wise Men took to Jesus.

When people from Spain came to Mexico they brought piñatas. The people of Mexico liked the toys. They made them for their children.

The children of Mexico have played with piñatas for many years. Today you can find piñata animals, people, and stars.

You can play with a piñata, too. First, cover your eyes and hold a stick. Next, turn around three times. Last, hit the piñata three times. When it breaks, everyone shares the candy that falls from Mexico's piñata.

QUESTIONS FOR PIÑATAS

1. What did the piñata of Spain look like?

   _____

   _____

2. What was inside the points of the star piñata?

   _____

   _____

3. Where did the people of Spain take their piñatas?

   _____

   _____

4. For whom did the people of Mexico make their piñatas?

   _____

   _____

5. What is the first thing you do when you play with a piñata?

   _____

   _____

6. What is the last thing you do when you play with a piñata?

   _____

   _____

7. Why did the people of Spain play with their piñatas at Christmas?

   _____

   _____

8. Are piñatas hard to break? Why do you think so?

   _____

   _____

9. Will children always like playing with piñatas? Why do you think so?

_____

_____

10. Why do children play with piñatas?

_____

_____

11. Write a title for the story. Use as few words as possible.

_____

_____

12. How are the animal and people piñatas of today like Spain's star piñata? How are they not alike?

_____

_____

13. In your own words, tell how to play with a piñata.

_____

_____

14. How would a party change if someone brought a piñata?

_____

_____

15. The story says, "When people from Spain came to Mexico they brought piñatas." Is this a fact? How can you prove your answer?

_____

_____

16.

_____

_____

Name _____   Date _____

READING LEVEL 1
BIBLIOGRAPHY

"Animal Tracks," *The Audubon Nature Encyclopedia* (1973), 1, 68–74.

Brooks, Walter. *The Art of Color Mixing.* New York: A Grumbacher Library Book, 1966.

Colflesh, Linda. *Making Friends: Training Your Dog Positively.* New York: Howell Book House, 1990.

Conley, Andrea. *Window on the Deep: The Adventures of Underwater Explorer Sylvia Earle.* New York: Franklin Watts, 1991.

Guthridge, Sue. *Tom Edison: Boy Inventor.* Indianapolis, Indiana: The Bobbs-Merrill Company, Inc., 1959.

Johnson, Ann Donegan. *The Value of Creativity: The Story of Thomas Edison.* La Jolla, CA: Value Communications, Inc., 1981.

Kalman, Bobbie, and Tammy Everts. *Frogs and Toads.* New York: Crabtree Publishing Company, 1994.

Lepthien, Emilie U. *The Cherokee.* A New True Book. pp. 18–21. Chicago: Childrens Press, 1985.

"Lindbergh, Charles Augustus," *Pictorial Encyclopedia: People Who Made America,* p. 753. Skokie, IL: United States History Society, Inc., 1973.

Morgan, Alfred. *A Pet Book for Boys and Girls.* New York: Charles Scribner's Sons, 1949.

Perdue, Theda. *Indians of North America: The Cherokee,* pp. 43–45. New York: Chelsea House Publishers, 1989.

Peterson, Linda Kauffman and Marilyn Leathers Solt. *Newbery and Caldecott Medal and Honor Books: An Annotated Bibliography,* pp. 22–23. Boston, MA: G.K. Hall & Co., 1982.

Pollard, Michael. *Technology in Action: Train Technology,* pp. 32–33 and 41. New York: The Bookwright Press, 1990.

"Rock, John," *Pictorial Encyclopedia: People Who Made America,* p. 1146. Skokie, IL: United States History Society, Inc., 1973.

Ross, Stewart. *Fact or Fiction: Pirates,* pp. 18–19. Brookfield, Conn.: Copper Beech Books, 1995.

Rutland, Jonathan. *The Young Engineer Book of Supertrains,* p. 29. Ontario, Canada: Usborne Publishing Ltd., 1978.

Sutton, Felix. *The Book of Clowns,* p. 2. New York: Grosset & Dunlap, 1974.

Westridge Young Writers Workshop. *Kids Explore America's Hispanic Heritage,* pp. 50–51. Sante Fe, NM: John Muir Publications, 1992.

Young, Richard and Judy Dockrey Young, eds. *African-American Folktales for Young Readers,* p. 75. Little Rock: August House Publishers, Inc., 1993.

READING LEVEL 2

FAST-FOOD COMPUTERS

ABOUT THE STORY

People who frequent fast-food restaurants look for low prices and fast service. With this in mind, major fast-food chains are considering replacing workers behind the counters with computers. This story looks at the overall impact of such a move.

PREVIEW WORDS

fast-food restaurants   computers   fries

order

BOOKS TO READ

Grace Hopper: Navy Admiral and Computer Pioneer, Charlene W. Billings (Enslow Publishers, 1989).

How It Works: Computers, Ian Graham (Gloucester Press, 1992).

A Computer Went A-Courting: A Love Song For Valentine's Day, Carol Greene (Childrens Press, 1983).

Dr. An Wang: Computer Pioneer, Jim Hargrove (Childrens Press, 1993).

The Ghost in the Computer, Laura Lee Hope (Wanderer Books, 1984).

Careers for Computer Buffs, interviews by Andrew Kaplan (Millbrook Press, 1991).

Computer Graphics: How It Works, What It Does, Larry Kettelkamp (Morrow Junior Books, 1989).

The Age of Computers: The Story of Computers, Ian Litterick and Chris Smithers (Bookwright Press, 1984).

Kids' Computer Capers: Investigations for Beginners, Sandra Markle (Lothrop, Lee & Shepard Books, 1983).

Skeeter and the Computer, Frank Modell (Greenwillow, 1988).

Miss Pickerell and the War of the Computers, Dora Pantell (Franklin Watts, 1984).

VIDEOS

Computers for Kids, M-USA Video, 1990. Length: 40 minutes.

Rumpelstiltskin, Rabbit Ears Productions, 1991 (Electronic music by Tangerine Dream). Length: 30 minutes.

CDS, RECORDS, AND CASSETTES

Citizen of Time (CD: Electronic music), David Arkenstone (Narada Productions, Inc., 1990).

INTRODUCTORY ACTIVITIES

DAY ONE

Objective: The students will use role playing to order food at a fast-food restaurant, giving orders to people behind the counter. Afterward, they will discuss the experience.

Curriculum subject: Language Arts

Before reading the story, the students act out a fast-food restaurant scene.

Materials

◆ trays from the cafeteria

◆ food from a local fast-food restaurant, or ask local fast- food restaurants for donated empty hamburger boxes, and other containers.

◆ a long, cafeteria-style table for the counter

◆ fast-food restaurant props made by the students during art class. Examples: price signs, cash registers, paper bags with restaurant logo.

◆ play money (can also be made during art class)

Procedure

Before beginning, use the tables, trays, and so forth to make a make-believe counter at a fast-food restaurant.

◆ Choose three students to act as restaurant cashiers.

◆ Choose one student to act as manager.

◆ The other students walk through, giving orders and returning to their desks with their meals.

◆ After lunch, discuss what it was like to talk to people while giving the food orders. Did they like talking to people? Would the students rather order with computers? Why do they feel this way?

DAY TWO

Objective: The students will act out using computers instead of dealing with people in fast-food restaurants and discuss the experience. Afterward, they will make comparisons between Day One and Day Two.

Curriculum subject: Language Arts

Repeat yesterday's activity; however, replace the cashiers with computers. (Simply turn the cash registers toward the customers to make computers.) Keep the manager behind the counter to supervise the distribution of food.

Discuss what it felt like to order through computers. Did they like dealing with the computer or the people? Would they like the fast-food restaurants to change to computers? Why, or why not?

DAY THREE

Story Lesson

Follow the *Presenting the Story Lesson* instructions in the Introduction. Each story lesson follows the same procedure; however, say the following in step 4:

"The title of the story we're reading today is *Fast-Food Computers*. What do you think the story is about? What do you already know about fast-food restaurants? What do you know about computers?"

EXTENSION ACTIVITIES

1. Ask parents and grandparents to talk to the class. Discuss how computers and technology have changed their lives. How did they play and work before computers? Do they talk to fewer people and deal with more computers? Do they like the changes or do they miss the personal contact?

Conduct a discussion that expands on what the students learned. These changes happened during their parents' or grandparents' lifetimes. What changes might occur in the students' lives by the time they are grandparents?

2. Imagine the world in twenty-five years. Talk about how computers will change our lives in home, work, school, entertainment, medicine, and other areas. Discuss what our homes, schools, and communities will look like. What role would the students like to play in making this future a reality?

Next, break the class into small groups. Give each group a sheet of white bulletin board paper. These students will work together to create, draw, and color murals that depict what the students expect their community will look like in twenty-five years. Display the murals around the room for a panoramic view of the future.

3. Ask a computer design engineer, a college professor in a related field, or anyone dealing in the future of computers to visit the class. Ask him or her to bring examples and pictures of the latest computer advances. Ask the speaker to discuss the following topics:

◆ What new computer products will consumers find in the near future?

◆ How will jobs change in the future? (Which jobs will disappear? What skills should the students develop for employment?)

◆ How will work, school, and play change over the next twenty-five years?

FAST-FOOD COMPUTERS

At every fast-food restaurant there are many people who help you. They take your order, and make sure you get what you want. Some day you might give your order to a computer.

First, the computer will show you a list of food and drinks. You touch the word or picture that tells what you want. The computer can even ask, "Would you like any fries with your order?"

In the kitchen, the cooks also have a computer. Their computer tells them what you ordered.

The people who own fast-food restaurants hope the computers will help them sell more food. The computers will also save time, and will not make mistakes.

QUESTIONS FOR FAST-FOOD COMPUTERS

1. In the future, what might take your order at fast-food restaurants?

   _____

   _____

2. How will you tell the computer what you want?

   _____

   _____

3. How will the cooks know what you ordered?

   _____

   _____

4. Name two ways these computers will help people who own fast-food restaurants.

   _____

   _____

5. What is the first thing the computer will do when you want to give an order?

   _____

   _____

6. What will the computer do next?

   _____

   _____

7. What is a good name for these computers? The name must tell what the computer is used for.

   _____

   _____

8. The story tells us that owners of fast-food restaurants hope computers will help them sell more food. How might the use of a computer do this?

   _____

   _____

9. Computers are taking the place of people in many jobs. Yet people who do not have an education or are working to get their education need these jobs. What might happen to the people who need to work?

_____

_____

10. Would you like to go to a fast-food restaurant where you give your orders to people or to computers? Why do you feel this way?

_____

_____

11. Write a title for this story. Use as few words as possible.

_____

_____

12. Compare a restaurant where people take orders to a restaurant using computers. How do they look and sound alike? How do they look and sound different?

_____

_____

13. Explain why fast-food restaurant owners want to use computers. Tell about the good things the owners hope computers will do for them.

_____

_____

14. What effect might the use of computers have on people who eat at fast-food restaurants? Do you believe they will enjoy eating at these restaurants? Why do you think so?

_____

_____

15. Fast-food restaurant owners say computers will help them sell more food. Is this a fact or an opinion? Why do you think so?

_____

_____

16.

_____

_____

Name _____   Date _____

HOW MUCH DO YOU WEIGH?

ABOUT THE STORY

This story explores gravity and how it affects our weight. The students learn how to calculate their weight according to which planet in the solar system they visit.

> **Note:** This story coordinates with multiplication and division lessons. If you prefer, read the story out of sequence to match it with appropriate Math lessons.

PREVIEW WORDS

weigh	craters	surface gravity
Mercury	Venus	Mars
Jupiter	Saturn	Uranus
Neptune	Pluto	

BOOKS TO READ

Gravity Is a Mystery, Franklyn M. Branley (Crowell, 1986).

Weight and Weightlessness, Franklyn M. Branley (Crowell, 1971).

What the Moon Is Like, Franklyn M. Branley (Crowell, 1986).

Why Doesn't the Earth Fall Up?: And Other Not Such Dumb Questions About Motion, Vicki Cobb (Lodestar Books, 1988).

Famous Firsts in Space, Edward F. Dolan (Dutton, 1989).

Gravity at Work and Play, Sune Engelbrektson (Holt, Rinehart & Winston, 1963).

Make It Balance, David Evans (Dorling Kindersley, 1992).

Astronauts, Carol Greene (Childrens Press, 1984).

Science in a Nanosecond, James A. Haught (Prometheus Books, 1990).

The Forces With You!, Tom Johnston (Gareth Stevens, 1988).

Space Science, Projects for Young Scientists, David W. McKay (Franklin Watts, 1986).

The Astronauts, Dinah L. Moche (Random House, 1978).

C.O.L.A.R.: A Tale of Outer Space, Alfred Slote (J.B. Lippincott, 1981).

Science for Kids: 39 Easy Astronomy Experiments, Robert W. Wood (Tab Books, 1991).

VIDEO

The Absent-Minded Professor, Disney Home Video, 1984. Length: 96 minutes.

CDS, RECORDS, AND CASSETTES

Adventures in the Solar System: Planetron and Me (book and cassette set), Geoffrey T. Williams and Dennis F. Regan (Price Stern Sloan, 1986).

INTRODUCTORY ACTIVITIES

DAY ONE

Objective: The students will review the concept of gravity. They will discuss how to measure
gravity with a bathroom scale.

Curriculum subject: Science

Gravity and the Bathroom Scale
Materials

◆ diagram of the inner workings of a simple spring scale

◆ bathroom scale

◆ large spring

◆ one coin (penny)

Procedure

◆ Teacher: Gravity pulls things down toward the center of the earth. (Drop a penny on
the floor.) Why did the penny fall?

   Students: Gravity made the penny fall. (The students must answer in complete sentences.)

   Teacher: What does gravity do?

   Students: Gravity pulls things down toward the center of the earth.

◆ (Show the students a large spring. Set the spring on a flat surface. Set a book on the spring.)

   Teacher: The book pushes down and squeezes the spring. Gravity pulls the book down
toward Earth. As gravity pulls down the book, the book squeezes the spring.

◆ (Display a scale and a diagram showing the inside of a simple scale.)

   Teacher: A scale is a set of springs under a plate. When you stand on the plate, you
squeeze the springs. The more you weigh, the tighter you squeeze the springs.

◆ (Ask two students to volunteer to stand on the scale. Weigh each student individually. Write
their weight on the board.)

   Teacher: The scale measures how hard a person's weight presses down on the springs.
This depends on how hard gravity pulls on the body. The scale turns this information into numbers on the dial. This number tells in pounds how much the
person weighs. Student 1 weighs more than Student 2 because his or her body
weight squeezed the springs more tightly.

Why does the scale say Student 1 weighs _____ pounds? Why does the scale say Student
2 weighs _____ pounds?

DAY TWO

Objective: The students will observe the effects of lower gravity on astronauts on the moon.
Curriculum subject: Science

Show a movie about the Apollo missions to the moon. The movie must show astronauts walking on the moon. Before the film begins, ask the students to watch for signs that grav-

ity on the moon is different from that on Earth. Tell them they will discuss their observations after the film is over.

After the movie, discuss what the students observed as they watched the astronauts walk on the moon. Is gravity on the moon stronger or weaker than on Earth? Why do they think so?

DAY THREE

Story Lesson

Follow the *Presenting the Story Lesson* instructions in the Introduction. Each story lesson follows the same procedure; however, say the following in step 4:

"The title of the story we're reading today is *How Much Do You Weigh?* What do you think this story is about? What do you already know about weighing yourself?"

EXTENSION ACTIVITIES

1. Invite a speaker to discuss gravity and space. Such a speaker might be a professor in a related field, a planetarium volunteer or a retired high school science teacher.

   Topics for discussion should include problems found in space travel due to gravity differences. What are some of the careers in the areas of space and the study of the solar system? What does a person need to do to prepare for such a career? What does the speaker find exciting about his or her field?

2. Review the various gravity strengths on the planets of our solar system. Discuss how buildings, clothing, and vehicles must change to adapt to stronger or weaker gravity.

   The students will draw a picture of what a community on their favorite planet (except Earth) would look like. What inventions would they create to live in the weak gravity of Pluto? What inventions would they create to live in the strong gravity of Jupiter?

   Next, write stories telling about the inventions. How would cars and trucks work? How would children walk to school? What would it be like shopping for eggs? Share the stories with the class.

HOW MUCH DO YOU WEIGH?

How much do you weigh? It's an easy question to answer. Just climb on a scale and read the number. The scale tells you how much you weigh on Earth.

How much do you weigh on the moon? Imagine flying to the moon with your scale. Setting your scale down among the craters and rocks, you weigh yourself. Do you weigh more on the moon or less?

The surface gravity on the moon is only .16 of Earth's. That means a 90-pound boy weighs only 14.4 pounds on the moon. To learn your moon weight, multiply your Earth weight by .16.

How much would you weigh on the sun? That same 90-pound boy weighs 2,511 pounds on the sun. The surface gravity on the sun is 27.9 times stronger than Earth's. If you multiply your Earth weight by 27.9, you'll know your sun weight.

How can you learn how much you weigh on the other planets in our solar system? You multiply your Earth weight by the surface gravity of each planet.

OUR SOLAR SYSTEM	90-POUND BOY	SURFACE GRAVITY
Earth	90 pounds	1
Moon	14.4 pounds	.16
Sun	2,511.0 pounds	27.9
Mercury	34.2 pounds	.38
Venus	81.9 pounds	.91
Mars	34.2 pounds	.38
Jupiter	237.6 pounds	2.64
Saturn	101.7 pounds	1.13
Uranus	105.3 pounds	1.17
Neptune	107.1 pounds	1.19
Pluto	7.2 pounds	.08

QUESTIONS FOR HOW MUCH DO YOU WEIGH?

1. What is the surface gravity of the moon?

   _____

   _____

2. How much would a 90-pound boy weigh on the moon?

   _____

   _____

3. What is the surface gravity of the sun?

   _____

   _____

4. How much would a 90-pound boy weigh on the sun?

   _____

   _____

5. To learn how much you weigh, what do you do after you climb on the scale?

   _____

   _____

6. Which does the author tell about first, the moon's gravity or the sun's?

   _____

   _____

7. On which <u>planet</u> would you weigh the least? On which <u>planet</u> would you weigh the most?

   _____

   _____

8. Does the author think you will go to the moon to weigh yourself? Why do you think so?

   _____

   _____

9. When men walked on the moon, they could jump high. They didn't weigh as much on the moon as they did on Earth. What would happen if the same men tried to jump on the sun?

_____

_____

10. Why are astronauts interested in gravity?

_____

_____

11. Write a title for the story. Use as few words as possible.

_____

_____

12. How many more pounds does the 90-pound boy weigh on Saturn than on Earth?

_____

_____

13. In your own words, tell about gravity on the sun and the moon.

_____

_____

14. How would life on Earth change if the gravity suddenly became very weak?

_____

_____

15. The story says, "That means a 90-pound boy weighs only 14.4 pounds on the moon." Is this a fact or an opinion? How can you prove your answer?

_____

_____

16.

_____

_____

Name _____ Date _____

STORIES IN THE STARS

ABOUT THE STORY

Ancient civilizations told stories about pictures they saw in the patterns of the stars. This story tells about a few of the patterns these people saw.

PREVIEW WORDS

dot-to-dot	Big Dipper	Seven Sisters
Bull	Hunter	Swan
Dragon		

BOOKS TO READ

Mythology and the Universe, Library of the Universe, Isaac Asimov (Gareth Stevens, 1990).

The Legend of the Milky Way, Jeanne M. Lee (Holt, Rinehart and Winston, 1982).

The Heavenly Zoo: Legends and Tales of the Stars, Alison Lurie (Farrar, Straus & Giroux, 1980).

The Drinking Gourd, F. N. Monjo (Harper & Row, 1970).

Star Tales: North American Indian Stories About the Stars, Gretchen Wills Mayo (Walker, 1987).

A Young Astronomer's Guide to the Night Sky, Michael R. Porcellino (Tab Books, 1991).

The Shining Stars: Greek Legends of the Zodiac, Ghislaine Vautier (Cambridge University Press, 1981).

They Dance in the Sky: Native American Star Myths, Jean Guard Monroe and Ray A. Williamson (Houghton Mifflin, 1987).

VIDEOS

Follow the Drinking Gourd: A Story of the Underground Railroad, Rabbit Ears Productions, 1992. Length: 30 minutes.

Jack Horkheimer: Star Hustler, PBS stations around the country broadcast "Star Hustler." You may record episodes of "Star Hustler" for classroom use.[1]

IN-CLASS PLANETARIUM

Star Theater (for ages 8 and up). Star Theater is a small projector that displays stars, planets, constellations and their names on ceilings and walls. Star Theater includes a 50-minute audiocassette, telling myths and legends of the night sky, and an activities guide. Star Theater is available through *Signals: A Catalog for Fans and Friends of Public Television.*

---

[1]Information from *Reflector: The Astronomical League Newsletter,* vol. 47, no. 3, May, 1995, p. 11.

INTRODUCTORY ACTIVITIES

DAY ONE

Objective: The students will explore the concept of constellations, their designs and myths.
Curriculum subject: Science

Read *Mythology and the Universe* by Isaac Asimov to the class. Discuss why the ancient people told myths about the constellations. Why do we still use these constellations to find our way around the night sky?

Teacher: (Display a picture of a bull.) Ancient people named a constellation Taurus. They saw Taurus as a giant bull. What story might go with this constellation? Write your own story about Taurus the Bull. Tell how and why the bull is in the night sky. This is your myth, so use your imagination.

DAY TWO

Objective: The students will learn the designs and names of constellations.
Curriculum subject: Science

Materials

◆ black construction paper
◆ sharp pencils
◆ overhead projector

Procedure

◆ Break the class into small groups.
◆ Each group chooses one constellation. Suggested constellations include:

Orion, the Giant Hunter

Canis Major, the Great Dog

Gemini, the Twins

Scorpio, the Scorpion

Pleiades, the Seven Sisters

◆ Using reference books as guides, the students draw dots on the black construction paper. Each dot represents a star in their constellation.
◆ Where the students made the dots, poke holes in the construction paper with a sharp pencil.
◆ The students will write a short description of their constellation's myth.
◆ Set the black construction paper on the overhead projector. The students share the myth about their constellation as the constellation shines on the screen.

DAY THREE

Story Lesson

Follow the *Presenting the Story Lesson* instructions in the Introduction. Each story lesson follows the same procedure; however, say the following in step 4:

"The title of the story we're reading today is *Stories in the Stars*. What do you think this story is about? What do you already know about star stories?"

EXTENSION ACTIVITIES

1. Teacher: Today we'll watch a video called, *Follow the Drinking Gourd.* The Drinking Gourd was a common name for the Big Dipper among slaves of the American South. Listen to the story; it told slaves how to escape slavery by going north.

   (Show the video. If you cannot find the video, read the book *The Drinking Gourd* by F. N. Monjo.)

   Teacher: In what other ways might people use the constellations to find their way at night? Imagine you're a camper lost at night. How could the constellations help you find your way home?

2. Organize the students to draw a large mural of the night sky. Following a star map, students paint the stars using fluorescent paint on deep blue or black bulletin board paper. The students label the constellations and important stars. Display the mural on a prominent wall.

Atmosphere of Betelgeuse · Alpha Orionis
Hubble Space Telescope · Faint Object Camera

Size of Star
Size of Earth's Orbit
Size of Jupiter's Orbit

STORIES IN THE STARS

Long ago, people looked at the stars and saw pictures of animals, people, and things. They even gave these big dot-to-dot star pictures names. At night, they told stories about the pictures in the sky.

The Big Dipper is easy to find. It looks like a large pot. Sailors use the Big Dipper to find their way at night. The two end stars point north.

The Seven Sisters is a small group of stars. A story tells us that these stars were seven beautiful sisters. The gods turned the sisters into stars and set them in the sky.

The Bull is a large group of stars. The eye of the Bull is a red star. It makes the Bull look mad.

The stories about the stars are very old. Read more about the Hunter, the Swan, or the Dragon. People use these stories today to help find their way in the stars.

QUESTIONS FOR STORIES IN THE STARS

1. Long ago, what did people see in the stars?

   _____

   _____

2. What star picture do sailors use to find their way at night?

   _____

   _____

3. What makes the Bull look mad?

   _____

   _____

4. According to a story, who turned the Seven Sisters into stars and put them in the sky?

   _____

   _____

5. What did the gods do before they set the Seven Sisters in the sky?

   _____

   _____

6. What can sailors do after they find the Big Dipper?

   _____

   _____

7. Sailors use the Big Dipper to find their way at night. If you are lost in the desert, could you use the Big Dipper to guide you? Why do you think this way?

   _____

   _____

8. Read the story about the Seven Sisters. How do you think the gods felt about the sisters?

   _____

   _____

9. People saw pictures in the stars a long time ago. We still use these pictures today. We use the pictures in the stars to help us find our way. Do you think people will use these pictures in the future? If so, how might they use them?

_____

_____

10. Why do you think people made up stories about the stars?

_____

_____

11. Write a title for the story. Use as few words as possible.

_____

_____

12. How are the Seven Sisters and the Big Dipper star pictures (constellations) alike? How are they different?

_____

_____

13. Briefly describe in your own words how a sailor would use the Big Dipper to guide a ship at night.

_____

_____

14. If sailors used only the Big Dipper to guide their ships at night, what would happen on a cloudy night?

_____

_____

15. The story says, "The Big Dipper is easy to find." Is this a fact or an opinion? How can you prove your answer?

_____

_____

16.

_____

_____

Name _____ Date _____

SET A WORLD'S RECORD

ABOUT THE STORY

The students learn about Noureddine Morceli who set a world's record in running in 1994. The story teaches students how to time themselves while running around a track.

PREVIEW WORDS

world's record	Noureddine Morceli	simple
healthy	multiply	seconds
football field	minutes	equals
illness	exercise	watch

BOOKS TO READ

Tiger Runs, Derek Hall (Sierra Club, Knopf, 1984).

The Adventures of Albert, the Running Bear, Barbara Isenberg (Clarion Books, 1982).

Albert the Running Bear's Exercise Book, Barbara Isenberg (Clarion Books, 1984).

Albert the Running Bear Gets the Jitters, Barbara Isenberg (Clarion Books, 1987).

Julie Brown, R. Rozanne Knudson (Viking Kestrel, 1988).

Running Is for Me, Fred Neff (Lerner, 1980).

Running a Race, Steve Parker (Franklin Watts, 1991).

My Mom Is a Runner, Mary Gallagher Reimold (Abingdon Press, 1987).

Track Athletics, Robert Sandelson (Crestwood House, 1991).

CDS, RECORDS, AND CASSETTES

Carl Lewis: The Second Jesse Owens (book and cassette set), Bert Rosenthal (Childrens Press, 1994).

INTRODUCTORY ACTIVITIES

DAY ONE

Objective: The students will discuss people who run. They will design construction paper running suits for bulletin board characters.

Curriculum subject: Art

Teacher: Have you seen people running for fun? Where did you see them? What were they wearing? We will read and talk about running this week. Today you are going to design a running suit for a construction paper person. Try to make the person look like you. You can use yarn, paper, or cotton balls to make the hair. Use your imagination to make the most creative running suit you can. You can decorate the tennis shoes, too.

Materials

◆ one copy of Runner Pattern for each student. (See the following pages for the pattern.)

◆ various colors of construction paper scraps

◆ scissors

◆ glue

◆ yarn, glitter, crayons, paints, buttons (anything the students might use to decorate their runners' suits)

Procedure

◆ Pass out the materials and let the students share as much as possible. Move from group to group, talking about track events they have seen. Do they know people who run for exercise or in races? Why do they like to run?

◆ When the students finish their characters, display them on a bulletin board entitled *See How They Run!*

◆ Encourage those who finish early to read a book about athletes from the display table.

DAY TWO

Objective: The students will learn about track and field sports from high school, college, or professional athletes. Included safety tips and proper equipment.
Curriculum subject: Physical Education or Language Arts

Invite local high school, college, or professional athletes to speak to the class. Topics should include equipment, techniques, and safety, such as stretching before running. Ask the athletes to tell about their role models, and why they admire these athletes. How has the discipline they learned in athletics affected other aspects of their lives? End the lesson with a question-and-answer session.

DAY THREE

Story Lesson
Follow the *Presenting the Story Lesson* instructions in the Introduction. Each story lesson follows the same procedure; however, say the following in step 4:
"The title of the story we're reading today is *Set a World's Record*. What do you think this story is about? What is a world's record?"

Note: Ask the students to wear comfortable clothes and shoes they can run in for tomorrow's lesson (Extension Activity 1).

Runner Pattern

Shoe
(cut two)

Arm
(cut two)

Leg
(cut two)

Head
(cut one)

Shorts
(cut one)

T-Shirt
(cut one)

EXTENSION ACTIVITIES

1. During this activity, the students will practice increasing running speed.

Materials

◆ notebook paper
◆ pencils
◆ stopwatches (one per two to three students)

Procedure

◆ Give each student one piece of notebook paper. Mark the page in the following manner:

(Student's Name) _____

Date	Time

◆ Take the students to a track.

◆ Break the students into groups of two or three.

◆ Give each group a stopwatch.

◆ Follow the instructions in yesterday's story, and the safety and stretching exercises discussed by the speaker on Day Two. The students time each person in their group as they run around the track.

◆ Multiply the time it took each student to run around the track once by four. Enter the number under the column marked Time.

◆ Ask the students to practice running around the track one time every day.

◆ Repeat this activity once a week for one month. Compare the time on the first day to that of the last day. Are the students running faster? Why do they think so?

◆ If a student is physically unable to run due to a handicap or illness, ask that student to time the others. Try to find an activity the student can participate in if possible. For example, a child in a wheelchair can time his or her own speed to a reasonable distance.

2. The students will choose an academic area in need of improvement, such as learning the multiplication tables. They will use the techniques for increasing running speed to improve the chosen academic area.

◆ Teacher:

Everyone in this room could do better in a school subject. Maybe you don't know your multiplication tables. Perhaps you need to improve your spelling grade. How can you use the information about learning to run faster to help you improve in this area? What subject would you like to improve in? (The students, particularly the learning disabled, improve their self-concept if they see that *everyone* has something they need to work on).

◆ Break the students into groups of two or three working on the same subject. Ask them to make a chart like the one they made yesterday. This time make the chart appropriate to what they want to learn. For example, if the student wants to do better in spelling, she or he might have a column marked "Grade" instead of "Time." Be sure the student writes a title for the chart that tells what subject he or she is working on.

◆ Allow the students fifteen minutes a day to practice. For example, if they are working on multiplication tables, the students will coach one another in their group.

◆ Once a week for a month, let the students test one another and mark their charts. Have they improved? Why do they think so? This is a good activity to continue throughout the year.

SET A WORLD'S RECORD

In 1994, Noureddine Morceli set a world's record in running. Can you run as fast as Morceli?

If you would like to know, give yourself a simple test. First, you must be healthy. Don't run if you have an illness that gets worse if you exercise.

Next, go to a track. Many schools have tracks that go around a football field. Take a watch that counts seconds with you. Ask a friend to time you.

Run around the track one time. Write down how many minutes and seconds it took you to run, then multiply that number by four. One mile equals four trips around the track.

How fast do you think you can run? Morceli ran one mile in 3 minutes and 44.39 seconds.

If you did not run as fast as Morceli, work at it. Run every day around the track. Every few weeks, time yourself again. Some day you might set a new world's record.

QUESTIONS FOR SET A WORLD'S RECORD

1. Who set a world's record in running in 1994?

   _____

   _____

2. How fast did Morceli run?

   _____

   _____

3. When you take the test, how many times do you run around the track?

   _____

   _____

4. What number do you multiply your time by?

   _____

   _____

5. What is the first thing you must think about before you run?

   _____

   _____

6. What is the last thing you do to find out how fast you ran the mile?

   _____

   _____

7. Do you think Noureddine Morceli set a world's record the first time he ran? What did he have to do to learn how to run fast?

   _____

   _____

8. The story says, "Don't run if you have an illness that gets worse if you exercise." What can happen to people who are not healthy when they run?

   _____

   _____

9. If you practice running every day, what will happen to your running speed?

_____

_____

10. The story stated that you must work hard to learn to run fast. What do you think made Morceli work so hard to set a world's record?

_____

_____

11. Write a title for the story. Use as few words as possible.

_____

_____

12. In 1980, Sebastian Coe ran the mile in 3 minutes 49.4 seconds. How much faster was Morceli than Coe? Why do you think Morceli ran faster?

_____

_____

13. Summarize the steps you should take to train yourself to run faster than you do now.

_____

_____

14. Lisa does not run as fast as her friend John. Lisa and John want to run the mile faster than anyone in the world. Lisa runs every morning before school and every night. John started to run every day, but then he started to play video games instead. At the end of one year, which person will run the fastest? Why do you think so?

_____

_____

15. The story said, "Morceli ran one mile in 3 minutes and 44.39 seconds." Is this statement a fact or an opinion? How can you prove your answer?

_____

_____

16.

_____

_____

Name _____   Date _____

GLENN CUNNINGHAM

ABOUT THE STORY

Glenn Cunningham suffered severe burns as a child. Doctors thought he would never walk again. Cunningham went on to run, setting world records in both the indoor and outdoor mile.

PREVIEW WORDS

Glenn Cunningham	exercised	terrible
usually	world's record	muscles
indoor	outdoor	

BOOKS TO READ

The Physically Disabled, Connie Baron (Crestwood House, 1988).

On Our Own Terms: Children Living With Physical Handicaps, Thomas Bergman (Gareth Stevens Children's Books, 1988).

Carol Johnston: The One Armed Gymnast, Pete Donovan (Childrens Press, 1982).

Franklin Delano Roosevelt, Russell Freedman (Clarion Books, 1990).

The Story of Stevie Wonder, James Haskins (Lothrop, Lee & Shepard, 1976).

The Value of Facing a Challenge: The Story of Terry Fox, Ann Donegan Johnson (Value Communications, 1983).

All the Way Back: A Story of Courage, Anne V. McGravie (Scott, Foresman, 1982).

The Power of Overcoming: Featuring the Story of Helen Keller, Virginia Swenson and Lawrence Tamblyn (Eagle Systems International, 1981).

Our Teacher's in a Wheelchair, Mary E. Powers (A. Whitman, 1986).

Ride the Red Cycle, Harriette Gillem Robinet (Houghton Mifflin, 1980).

Sundiata: Lion King of Mali, David Wisniewski (Clarion Books, 1992).

VIDEOS

Fantastic: The Wonderful World of Sports and Travel, Gallaudet University Press, 1989. Length: 30 minutes.

The Miracle Worker, (the story of Helen Keller) MGM/UA Home Video, 1992. Length: 107 minutes.

CDS, RECORDS, AND CASSETTES

Tradition (CD: Violin music), Itzhak Perlman (Angel Records, 1987).

Stevie Wonder's Greatest Hits, (CD) Stevie Wonder (Motown, 1991).

INTRODUCTORY ACTIVITIES

DAY ONE

Objective: The students will look at ways in which people adapt their lives when stricken by ill-
nesses, handicaps or disasters. They will learn about the life of Turlough Carolan.

Curriculum subject: Language Arts

Turlough Carolan
Materials

◆ Records, cassettes or CDs of music by Turlough Carolan. Some examples are:

Celtic Dreams: Music of Turlough O'Carolan on the Hammered Dulcimer, Vol. 3, Joemy
Wilson (Dargason Music, 1989).

The Music of Turlough O'Carolan: Patrick Ball - Celtic Harp, Patrick Ball (Fortuna Records,
1982).

O'Carolan's Dream: Patrick Ball - Celtic Harp, vol. IV, Patrick Ball (Fortuna Records, 1989).

Procedure

◆ Begin playing recordings of music by O'Carolan as the students come into the classroom.

◆ Teacher: Today we're going to learn about a man named Turlough Carolan[1], also known
as O'Carolan. As I read the story about his life, think about what you can learn
from his experiences.

◆ Read the following biography to the class.

Turlough Carolan was born in Ireland in 1670. He grew up working with his father on
a farm owned by Mrs. McDermott Roe. Everyday Turlough worked in the sunshine. He plant-
ed seeds in the bright colors of spring. He watched over the seedlings as they grew in the red
of summer. With the golds of fall, he harvested the crops. And in the white chill of winter, he
prepared the farm for the next planting. His family was proud of the son who would someday
become a fine farmer.

One day, when Turlough was eighteen years old, he became sick with smallpox. Turlough ran a high fever, and remained sick in bed for many days. To the joy of his father, Turlough lived; however, the illness left Turlough blind. Turlough could never become a farmer.
How would Turlough take care of himself? What could Turlough do with his life?

(Ask the students to consider the questions. Discuss their answers.)

Mrs. McDermott Roe knew Turlough needed to learn a trade. She gave him a harp, paid
for his lessons, and provided him with a horse and a guide. Like other blind harpers, Turlough
began traveling from house to house throughout Ireland, playing his harp for rich land owners.

Unfortunately, Turlough was not a good harper. Most musicians began their studies as
young children. Turlough began late in life.

Turlough did not give up. He began writing music. His songs were gentle and elegant.
No one in Ireland wrote such beautiful music. Turlough Carolan died in 1738 at the age of 68.

---

[1] *Complete Collection of the Much Admired Old Irish Tunes: The Original and Genuine Compositions of Carolan, The Cel-
ebrated Harper and Composer (1670–1738),* pp. 2–6. Cork, Ireland: Ossian Publications, 1984.

In his lifetime, he wrote over two hundred songs. Today, many Irishmen call him "Ireland's national composer."

◆ Teacher: What did you learn from Turlough Carolan's life? What does the story tell you about working out problems in your own life? (Discuss the answers.)

◆ Teacher: Does anyone know someone like Turlough Carolan? Do you know someone who overcame a problem—a disability or illness, or someone who survived a disaster?

◆ Discuss people in their community who worked to overcome problems in their lives. Maybe they saw a salesperson in a wheelchair or a mentally disabled person working at a restaurant. Do they feel different about these people after hearing the story of Turlough Carolan? Why?

DAY TWO

Objective: The students will meet someone who has overcome disaster or a disability to contribute to the community. They will discuss how this person accomplished his or her goals. The students can also watch and discuss the film *The Miracle Worker.*
Curriculum subject: Language Arts

Ask someone to come to class who contributes to the students' community and has overcome hardships. For example, invite someone injured in a car accident, a stroke victim, or a disabled veteran. The person must be comfortable discussing what happened and what she or he did to get her or his life back on track. What does this person have to share with the students that might inspire them if they too face extreme hardship? End with a question-and-answer session.

Students can watch the film *The Miracle Worker.* Before the film begins, tell the students to watch how Helen Keller worked to overcome her disabilities. After the film, discuss what happened to Helen. What did her life story teach them?

DAY THREE

Story Lesson
Follow the *Presenting the Story Lesson* instructions in the Introduction. Each story lesson follows the same procedure; however, say the following in step 4:
"The title of the story we're reading today is *Glenn Cunningham.* What do you think this story is about?"

EXTENSION ACTIVITY

◆ Break the class into groups of three to four students. Be sure to place learning disabled students in groups of students you know will cooperate and work with them.

◆ Write the following names on index cards. Write one name on each card. Give each group one card.

Names:
1. Steven Hawking
2. Ludwig van Beethoven

3. Helen Keller

4. Charles Proteus Steinmetz

5. Demosthenes

6. Franklin D. Roosevelt

7. Stevie Wonder

8. Itzhak Perlman

9. Nelson Mandela

10. Phillis Wheatley

◆ Go to the library or make reference books available. The students research the lives of the people on their cards. Ask the students to learn what happened to the people that put obstacles in their way. How did they overcome the obstacles? Did they change the paths they had chosen, or did they work around the obstacles in their work? What did these people accomplish? What do their lives teach the students about tackling problems of their own?

◆ Each group writes a short story about their person. Everyone in the group must actively participate.

◆ Finally, the groups draw pictures of the person they read about, showing what special thing the person did. Share the stories with the class.

GLENN CUNNINGHAM

Glenn Cunningham was born in 1909. He liked to run and play. Glenn was like any other child until one terrible day. At the age of eight, a fire burned his leg.

Glenn's burns were not like the small burns people usually get. His burns were very deep. The fire burned away the toes on his left foot. It also burned off many of his leg muscles. The doctors told his mother that Glenn would never walk.

Glenn wanted to run and play again, so he worked very hard. He exercised even when it hurt. Slowly Glenn learned to walk, but he wanted more. Glenn wanted to run. Do you think he ever learned to run?

Yes, Glenn began to run. Not only did he run, he ran very fast. At the age of 29, Glenn set the world's record in both the indoor and outdoor mile.

QUESTIONS FOR GLENN CUNNINGHAM

1. Who is the main character of the story?

   _____

   _____

2. How old was Glenn when he was burned?

   _____

   _____

3. Why did the doctors tell Glenn's mother that he would never walk again?

   _____

   _____

4. How old was Glenn Cunningham when he set the world's record for running?

   _____

   _____

5. What did Glenn have to do before he could walk again?

   _____

   _____

6. What did Glenn learn to do after he could walk?

   _____

   _____

7. Glenn Cunningham worked hard to do something everyone else said was impossible. What one word best describes Glenn?

   _____

   _____

8. Have you ever tried to do something you thought was hard? What does Glenn Cunningham's story tell you about doing something that is hard for you?

   _____

   _____

9. When people read this story, they might decide to do things they thought were impossible. In what ways could this change their lives?

_____

_____

10. Glenn wanted to run and play again. Why do you think he worked to run faster than anyone else?

_____

_____

11. Write a title for this story. Use as few words as possible.

_____

_____

12. Sarah didn't read as well as the other children in her class. Her grades were always low. Some of her classmates teased her. Sarah tried to do better, but soon she gave up. "Why should I try?" she said. "Everyone's right. I'll never learn to read." How is Sarah's attitude different from Glenn Cunningham's? What might Glenn tell her about learning to read? What might Glenn Cunningham tell her classmates?

_____

_____

13. Tell about the things Glenn Cunningham had to do to walk and run again.

_____

_____

14. The doctors told Glenn Cunningham's mother that her son would never walk again. How might the story have ended if Glenn believed what they said and gave up?

_____

_____

15. The doctors told Glenn's mother that he would never walk again. Was this a fact or the doctors' opinion? How can you prove your answer?

_____

_____

16.

_____

_____

Name _____   Date _____

HOME FOR THE SUMMER

ABOUT THE STORY

This story describes an experiment on bird migration performed by Stephen and John Emlen. The Emlens focused on birds called *buntings,* which migrate at night. They set out to learn how these small birds navigate in the dark.

PREVIEW WORDS

north	buntings	south
planetarium	John Emlen	Stephen Emlen
ink pad	ceiling	

BOOKS TO READ

Keepers of the Earth: Native American Stories and Environmental Activities for Children, Michael J. Caduto and Joseph Bruchac (Fulcrum Publishing, 1989).

Keepers of the Night: Native American Stories and Nocturnal Activities for Children, Michael J. Caduto and Joseph Bruchac (Fulcrum Publishing, 1994).

Insect Travelers, John Kaufmann (Morrow, 1972).

Mysteries of Migration, Robert M. McClung (Garrard, 1983).

Rescue of the Stranded Whales, Kenneth Mallory and Andrea Conley (Simon & Schuster, 1989).

Tree of Birds, Susan Meddaugh (Houghton Mifflin, 1990).

Animal Migration, Nancy J. Nielsen (Franklin Watts, 1991).

Animal Movement, The Animal Kingdom, Malcolm Penny (The Bookwright Press, 1987).

The Whales Go By, Fred B. Phleger (Random House, 1959).

Animal Journeys, Theodore Rowland-Entwistle (Random House Beginner Books, 1987).

VIDEO

Hans Christian Andersen, *The Ugly Duckling,* Rabbit Ears Productions and Random House Home Video, 1986. Length: 28 minutes. *Ask the students what happened to the Ugly Duckling when he did not migrate with the other birds. Why didn't the Ugly Duckling see the swans during the winter?

INTRODUCTORY ACTIVITIES

DAY ONE

Objective: The students will learn about an experiment on animal migration. They will form a hypothesis based on the results.

Curriculum subject: Science or Language Arts

Teacher: Many types of animals are on the move every year. These animals live in one home
            all summer. In the fall, they move to a new home. Sometimes they travel thousands
            of miles. We call this movement *migration*.

            Birds, butterflies, and whales travel long distances when they migrate. Scientists be-
            lieve dinosaurs also migrated.

            Scientists wonder how these animals find their way as they travel. People use maps.
            How do animals know where to go? (Discuss this question with the class.) Some sci-
            entists perform experiments to learn more about migration.

            One experiment showed that even cats can find their way home after traveling many
            miles. A group of scientists took several cats from their hometown. They put the
            cats in dark crates and loaded them on a truck. None of the cats could see where
            they were going.

            The truck traveled many miles from the cats' home. They drove along curving roads
            and took confusing turns.

            The truck stopped in a faraway town. They unloaded the cats one at a time. Each
            cat was put in a maze with twenty-eight exits. The scientists watched the cats move
            through the maze. Most of the cats chose the exit that pointed in the direction of
            their hometown. Why did the cats do this? (Matthieu Ricard, *The Mystery of Ani-
            mal Migration*, 194, Hiil & Wang, 1969)

        Break the class into groups of four to five students. Ask the students to draw pictures
of the cat experiment. As they draw, the students should discuss what happened.

        Ask each group to develop a theory or hypothesis on the outcome of the experiment.
Why did the cats choose the path pointing home? Is this a behavior that could help a cat? Why
do you think so?

        Finally, the groups will share their ideas with the class.

DAY TWO

Objective: (Experiment) The students will test a human's ability to determine direction when
            taken on an erratic path while blindfolded. They will record and discuss results.
Curriculum subject: Science or Language Arts

Materials

◆ one blindfold for every two students

◆ paper and pencil to record the results

* *Take the proper precautions and care when leading blindfolded students around the
school.*

Procedure

◆ Review yesterday's lesson.

◆ Teacher: Do you think you could do what the cats did? Today I'll blindfold you. We will
               go out of the classroom, and wander around the schoolyard. Could you point
               to our classroom without looking? (Discuss the answers.)

◆ Divide the class into groups of two. Blindfold one student in each group. The partner will
   carefully lead the blindfolded student.

◆ Line up the students in pairs and lead them out of the classroom. Take an erratic path and backtrack to add to the confusion.

◆ At the end of the walk, tell the blindfolded students to point in the direction of the classroom. *Do not take off the blindfolds.*

◆ Note how many students were correct and how many were wrong.

◆ Remove the blindfolds and return to class.

◆ Repeat the experiment, blindfolding the other student.

◆ Write the results on the chalkboard. Discuss what happened. Was it hard to know where the classroom was when you were blindfolded? Why do you think so?

DAY THREE

Story Lesson

Follow the *Presenting the Story Lesson* instructions in the Introduction. Each story lesson follows the same procedure; however, say the following in step 4:

"The title of the story we're reading today is *Home for the Summer*. What do you think this story is about?" If the students answer "migration" ask, "What do you already know about migration?"

EXTENSION ACTIVITIES

1. In this activity, the students will write a short description of an animal that migrates. They will draw a map of the migration pattern.

◆ Teacher:

Animals migrate in many different ways. Some, like the buntings and bats, migrate at night. Other animals, like the Monarch butterfly, travel long distances, spending their entire lives flying to a new home. Many extinct animals, like the dinosaurs, also migrated. Whales even swim from their summer to winter homes.

Today you will work in groups of three or four. Choose an animal you would like to write about. Try to pick an animal no one else is working on. Read about your animal and its migration. Your group will write a story about your animal. (Write the following on the board.)

You will tell:

1. The name of your animal

2. Why your animal migrates

3. Where your animal migrates

4. How your animal migrates

5. How many miles it travels

After you finish your story, draw a map that shows the path your animal takes on its migration.

◆ Mount each story and map on one piece of colorful construction paper. Mount the story on one side, and the map on the other. Leave a small portion of the construction paper showing around the edge.

2. The students will make a mobile of a migrating animal. They will use the mobile to display the story written in Extension Activity 1. Continue to work in the same groups as in Extension Activity 1.

Migration Mobile
Materials

◆ one hanger for each mobile

◆ string

◆ construction paper

◆ nature magazines

◆ scissors

◆ story and map from Extension Activity 1

Procedure

◆ Cut out four to six photographs of animals the student wrote about in Extension Activity 1 from the nature magazines. Cut the photographs around the shapes of the animals.

◆ Glue each picture to a piece of construction paper. Trim the paper about ¼″ from the edge of the picture.

◆ Punch holes at the top of each animal picture.

◆ Tie each animal picture to the end of a string 6″ to 8″ long.

◆ Tie the other end of each string along the bar of the hanger.

◆ Tie a 10″ string at the center of the hanger. Punch a hole in the top of the story written during Extension Activity 1. Tie it to the end of the center string.

◆ Hang the mobiles in the classroom, library, or cafeteria.

Example:

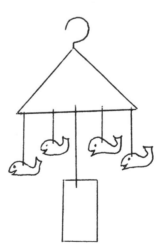

3. *Keepers of the Earth: Native American Stories and Environmental Activities,* by Michael J. Caduto and Joseph Bruchac, is an extensive resource for teachers. The activity "Migration: By Day and By Night," page 161, coordinates with *Home for the Summer.*

HOME FOR THE SUMMER

Many birds fly south in the winter, then return to the north in the summer. How do they return without getting lost?

Stephen Emlen and his father, John Emlen, studied birds called buntings. The buntings fly only at night, so how do the birds know where they are going?

The Emlens made a round cage for each bird. The white paper sides sloped to the center of the cage. The bird stood on an ink pad on the bottom. When the bird tried to fly, it slid down the paper, leaving an ink line.

The Emlens took their birds to the planetarium. This is a place where tiny lights shine on the ceiling. The lights move just like real stars.

The men left the birds to watch the stars. Later, they looked at the marks on the white paper. Every bird made a line pointing north.

The Emlens think they know why. The buntings know that the stars turn around the North Star. The birds follow the North Star in the summer to find their way home.

QUESTIONS FOR HOME FOR THE SUMMER

1. Where do birds fly in the summer?

   _____

   _____

2. What was the name of the birds that the Emlens studied?

   _____

   _____

3. What did these birds do at night?

   _____

   _____

4. What did the buntings follow to find their way north?

   _____

   _____

5. What was the first thing the Emlens did in their experiment?

   _____

   _____

6. At the end of the experiment, what did the Emlens look at?

   _____

   _____

7. The story does not name the Emlens' job. After reading the story, what do you believe is the name of the Emlens' job?

   _____

   _____

8. Read the first paragraph again. All the birds in the cages made lines pointing north. What season of the year was it at the time of the experiment?

   _____

   _____

9. The experiment tries to answer a question: How do birds return to the same place every summer without getting lost? Do you think more experiments will be done to try to answer this question? Why do you think so?

_____

_____

10. The Emlens had a reason for doing this experiment. Why might it be important to learn how birds travel so far without getting lost?

_____

_____

11. Write a title for this story. Use as few words as possible.

_____

_____

12. Geese are birds that fly in the daytime. They fly north for the summer, and south for the winter. How are geese and buntings alike? How are they different?

_____

_____

13. In a few words, tell about the Emlens' experiment.

_____

_____

14. Reread the last paragraph of the story. What do you think would happen if it were cloudy for several weeks during the time the buntings fly north?

_____

_____

15. The Emlens said that the buntings followed the North Star when flying north. Is this a fact or is it their opinion? Why do you think so?

_____

_____

16.

_____

_____

Name _____   Date _____

JAPAN'S KITES

ABOUT THE STORY

The story tells about the tradition of kites in Japan. The students learn how they can make kites.

PREVIEW WORDS

butterflies	dragons	Japan
different	frame	finally
imagine	anything	

BOOKS TO READ

Nature Crafts for Kids, Gwen Diehn and Terry Krautwurst (Sterling Pub., 1992).

Why Kites Fly, Don Dwiggins (Childrens Press, 1976).

Fishing for Angels: The Magic of Kites, David Evans (Annick Press, 1991).

Catch the Wind: All About Kites, Gail Gibbons (Little, Brown, 1989).

Jimmy and Joe Fly a Kite, Sally Glendinning (Garrard, 1970).

A Kite for Bennie, Genevieve Gray (McGraw-Hill, 1972).

Kites on the Wind: Easy-to-Make Kites That Fly Without Sticks, Emery J. Kelly (Lerner Publications, 1991).

Rabbit's Birthday Kite, Maryann MacDonald (Bantam Books, 1991).

The Ultimate Kite Book, Paul and Helene Morgan (Simon & Schuster, 1992).

Dragon Kite of the Autumn Moon, Valerie Reddix (Lothrop, Lee & Shepard, 1992).

The Missing Ball of String, Nancy L. Robison (Garrard, 1977).

Kites and Flying Objects, Denny Robson (Gloucester Press, 1992).

Experimenting With Air and Flight, Ormiston H. Walker (Franklin Watts, 1989).

The Emperor and the Kite, Jane Yolen (Philomel Books, 1988).

VIDEO

Adventures in Arts and Crafts: Making and Flying Kites, Making Masks, Making Puppets, Troll Video, 1986. Length: 44 minutes.

CDS, RECORDS, AND CASSETTES

The Disney Collection: Best-Loved Songs From Disney Motion Pictures, Television, and Theme Parks, Original Soundtrack Recordings (CD), Disneyland Records and Tapes, 1991. (Includes "Let's Go Fly a Kite.")

INTRODUCTORY ACTIVITIES

DAY ONE

Objective: The students will listen to a story about kites. They will make a kite bulletin board.
Curriculum subject: Art

Read the story *Dragon Kite of the Autumn Moon,* by Valerie Reddix to the class. Ask where the story took place. Why do you think the author chose this location?

Bulletin Board Kites

Before beginning the lesson, cover a bulletin board with sky-blue paper. Cut white paper to make large white clouds, and yellow paper for the sun. Arrange a sky view on the bulletin board.

Materials

◆ four straws per student
◆ brightly colored construction paper
◆ crayons, glitter, stickers, and so forth to decorate kites
◆ string

Procedure

◆ Give each student four straws.
◆ The student cuts two pieces of construction paper, following the pattern shown.

13 inches long

3 inches	3 inches	3 inches	3 inches	1 inch

3 inches wide

◆ Decorate the paper with crayon drawings, glitter, stickers, or construction paper designs. Do not decorate the 1" section.
◆ Fold the paper along the dotted lines.
◆ Glue the 1" flap under the opposite edge to form a block. (Make two blocks.)
◆ Glue one end of each straw to an inside corner of the two blocks to make a box kite.
◆ Tie a string on one straw to make the kite string.
◆ Staple one side of the box kite to the bulletin board. The opposite side of the kite stands off the board to make a three-dimensional design.
◆ Attach the end of the string to the bottom of the bulletin board.

DAY TWO

Story Lesson

Follow the *Presenting the Story Lesson* instructions in the Introduction. Each story lesson follows the same procedure; however, say the following in step 4:

"The title of the story we're reading today is *Japan's Kites*. What do you think this story is about? What do you already know about kites?"

EXTENSION ACTIVITIES

1. Following a pattern, the students will make a simple kite. Many books in the library give clear instructions for kite making. For older students, I suggest *Making Kites: How to Build and Fly Your Very Own Kites—From Simple Sleds to Complex Stunters* by Rhoda Baker and Miles Denyer (Secaucus, NJ: Chartwell Books, Inc., 1993). This book shows pictures of many different kites.

   For younger students, try Emery J. Kelly's book, *Kites on the Wind: Easy-To-Make Kites That Fly Without Sticks* These kites are simple to make. The illustrations by Jennifer Hagerman include easy-to-copy, full-size patterns.

2. The students will write poems about the kites they made in Extension Activity 1. The students write poems describing their kites in flight. How will it feel to have the wind pull on the kite? Glue the poems to the fronts of the kites.

   Guide the older students through longer poems. The younger students write short poems. For example, "My bright red kite ... flies like rocket fire through the blue sky." Display the "poem kites" in the classroom.

3. Group students into sets of two. Take the students and their kites to an open field. The students take turns holding their partner's kite for launch.

JAPAN'S KITES

The sky is full of giant butterflies and dragons. Bright colors fly across the skies of Japan. May is the month for kites.

In Japan, many people enjoy making kites. The kites are different shapes, sizes, and colors. Some are so big that six people must hold the strings. Others are as small as postcards.

Would you like to make a kite? First, make a wood frame. The wood cannot be heavy, or the kite will not fly. Next, cover the frame with paper.

Finally, make a picture on your kite. You can make a bat, a bird, or anything you like.

Read about the many ways to make kites. Make kites in every shape and color you can imagine. Soon your friends will want to make kites, too.

QUESTIONS FOR JAPAN'S KITES

1. What is the name of the country where the story takes place?

   _____

   _____

2. What is a kite frame made of?

   _____

   _____

3. What is a kite frame covered with?

   _____

   _____

4. Which month is Japan's month for kites?

   _____

   _____

5. When you make a kite, what do you do <u>first</u>?

   _____

   _____

6. What is the <u>last</u> thing you do when you make a kite?

   _____

   _____

7. Do you think it would cost a lot of money to make a kite? Why do you think so?

   _____

   _____

8. The story tells us to read about the many ways to make kites. How will this help you to be a better kite maker?

   _____

   _____

9. Will people always enjoy making kites? Why do you think so?

_____

_____

10. Why do you think the Japanese make so many different types of kites?

_____

_____

11. Write a title that best describes the story. Use as few words as possible.

_____

_____

12. Look at a picture of a box kite and a common diamond-shaped kite. How are the two kites alike? How are they different?

_____

_____

13. In a few words, tell how to make a kite.

_____

_____

14. After reading this story, do you want to make a kite? Why do you feel this way?

_____

_____

15. The story said, "In Japan, many people enjoy making kites." Is this sentence a fact or an opinion? How can you prove your answer?

_____

_____

16.

_____

_____

Name _____   Date _____

TRAMP'S CODE

ABOUT THE STORY

This story tells about a secret code used by hobos in France. Tramps traveling from house to house left picture messages written in chalk near the homes they visited. How did the police solve the mystery of the Tramp's Code?

PREVIEW WORDS

Tramp's Code	France	chalk
strange	signs	meant
appeared	beware	prison
important	offers	coins

BOOKS TO READ

Top Secret! Codes to Crack, Burton Albert, Jr. (A. Whitman, 1987).

Secret Writing: Codes and Messages, Eugene H. Baker (Child's World: Childrens Press, 1980).

Computer Overbyte: Plus Two More Codebreakers, Andrew Bromberg (Greenwillow Books, 1982).

The Bloodhound Gang's Secret Code Book: With Five Stories, Sid Fleischman (Random House/Children's Television Workshop, 1983).

Codes, Ciphers, and Secret Writing, Martin Gardner (Simon & Schuster, 1972).

The Ghostwriter Detective Guide: Tools and Tricks of the Trade, Susan Lurie (Bantam Books, 1992).

Codes, Nigel Nelson (Thomson Learning, 1994).

How to Write Codes and Send Secret Messages, John Peterson (Four Winds, 1970).

The Code and Cipher Book, Jane Sarnoff and Reynold Ruffins (Scribner, 1975).

Encyclopedia of Espionage: Codes and Ciphers, Peter Way (USA Danbury, 1977).

Codes and Mystery Messages, Cameron Yerian (Childrens Press, 1975).

VIDEO

Look What I Found: Making Codes and Solving Mysteries (Intervideo, 1993). Length: 45 minutes.

INTRODUCTORY ACTIVITIES

DAY ONE

Objective: The students will work in a group to break a secret code.
Curriculum subject: Language Arts

Before class, prepare index cards with the following numbers written on them. Make a card for each student. Be sure to place the spaces correctly.

7 15 15 4 23 15 18 11!   4 15   14 15 20   20 1 12 11.
19 8 15 23   13 5   20 8 9 19   16 1 16 5 18.
25 15 21' 12 12   7 5 20   1   18 5 23 1 18 4.

Teacher: This week we'll learn about codes. There are many kinds of codes. Who can tell me what a secret code is? What does it mean when someone says, "I cracked a secret code?" Do you think you could crack a secret code?
Get into groups of 3 to 4 people. I'll give each person a card. The numbers on the card are really a secret code. If you break the code, you can read the message.

Hand out the cards. As the students show you their answers, give them stickers, pencils, or other reward for breaking the code. As they wait for other students to finish, tell them to create a similar secret code of their own.

Code

A	B	C	D	E	F	G	H	I	J	K	L	M	N	O
1	2	3	4	5	6	7	8	9	10	11	12	13	14	15

P	Q	R	S	T	U	V	W	X	Y	Z
16	17	18	19	20	21	22	23	24	25	26

Solution

Good work! Do not talk.

Show me this paper. You'll get a reward.

DAY TWO

Story Lesson
Follow the *Presenting the Story Lesson* instructions in the Introduction. Each story lesson follows the same procedure; however, say the following in step 4:
"The title of the story we're reading today is *Tramp's Code*. What do you think the story is about? What do you already know about codes?"

EXTENSION ACTIVITIES

1. In this activity the students learn about Morse Code, and how people use sound and lights in codes.

Materials

◆ A poster of Morse Code

```
A . __              F .. __ .        K __ . __        P . __ __ .       U .. __
B __ ...            G __ __ .        L . __ ..        Q __ __ . __      V ... __
C __ . __ .         H ....           M __ __          R . __ .          W . __ __
D __ ..             I ..             N __ .           S ...             X __ .. __
E .                 J . __ __ __     O __ __ __       T __              Y __ . __ __
                                                                       Z __ __ ..

PERIOD . __ . __ . __          COMMA __ __ .. __ __
```

◆ Pencils to knock Morse Code on the desks
◆ A flashlight
◆ A whistle

Procedure

(If possible, ask a speaker to come to class to demonstrate Morse Code.)

◆ Teacher:

There are many types of codes. One famous code is a code of sound. It's called Morse Code.

Samuel Finley Breese Morse invented Morse Code in 1835. Morse lived when there were no telephones. He found that if you stretched wires between towns, you could send electrical knocks over the wires. If you assigned special knocks to each letter of the alphabet, you could send messages.

The poster shows the knocks Morse used in his code. The dots are short knocks. The dashes are long knocks.

An S.O.S. means there is trouble and send help. S.O.S. stands for Save Our Ship. S.O.S. sounds like this. (Knock out S.O.S. with a pencil on a desk.)

If you don't have something to knock on, you can use a whistle. Who can show us how to send an S.O.S. using the whistle? If you don't have a whistle, you can use a flashlight. Can anyone show us how to send an S.O.S. using a flashlight?

Break into groups of three to four people. Think of a unique way to send a secret message. You can use sound, paper, or light. You might even come up with something no one has thought of. Write out your code and be ready to demonstrate it for the class.

(Give the students time to invent a code. Call one group at a time to demonstrate their code.)

2. Invite someone who knows sign language or braille to class. Ask the person to bring equipment that helps in reading and writing braille. Some cities have groups who sign to music. Discuss how braille and sign language help people to communicate.

◆ Teacher:

> Are braille and sign language codes? Why do you think so?

3. The students will write a fictional story in which the characters use codes.

◆ Teacher:

> Who can tell me about the codes we learned about this week? How are these codes used? Do you know about other codes we haven't talked about?

> Today you'll write a story about someone who uses codes. The person can be a spy or someone who needs to get a message to a friend. Tell what the code is and how your character used the code. If you'd like, you can make the story end with a mystery about what the coded message said.

(After the students finish the stories, ask volunteers to share the stories with the class.)

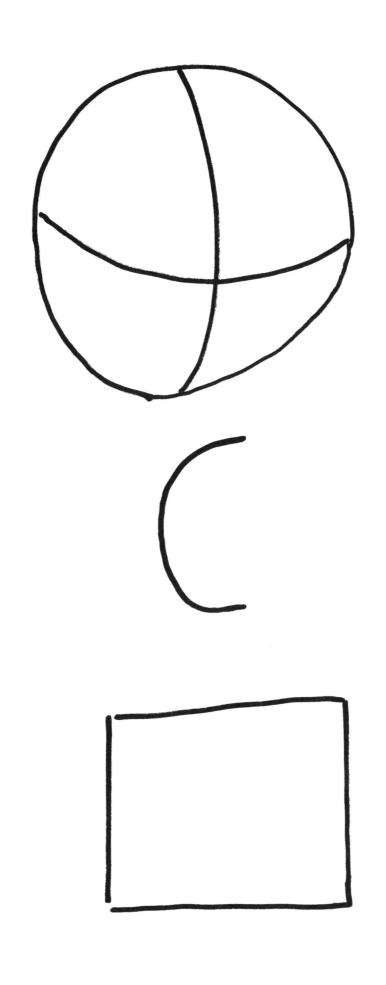

TRAMP'S CODE

Everyone in France knew about the strange signs written with chalk. The signs appeared on homes the day after a visit from a tramp. No one knew what the marks meant. They called the signs "Tramp's Code."

One day, the police arrested a young tramp. In his pocket they found a paper. It showed each sign and its meaning. The man had not lived on the road for long. He needed his notes to learn the signs.

This is what the police learned. When a tramp visited a house, he left a mark on the door or wall. This mark told the next tramp about the people living in the house.

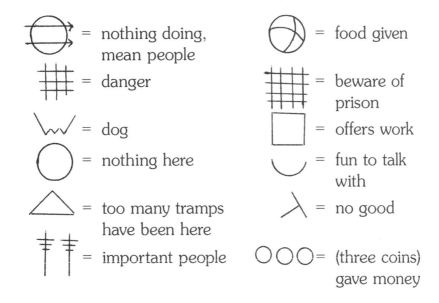

QUESTIONS FOR TRAMP'S CODE

1. Where did the story take place?

   _____

   _____

2. When did the signs appear on the houses?

   _____

   _____

3. What were the signs called?

   _____

   _____

4. What did the police find in the pocket of the young tramp?

   _____

   _____

5. Did the strange signs appear on homes before or after a tramp's visit?

   _____

   _____

6. When the story began, did the people of France know what the signs meant?

   _____

   _____

7. How do you think the people felt about the signs before they learned what they meant?

   _____

   _____

8. Read the first paragraph again. Do you think the people wanted to learn what the signs meant? Why do you think so?

   _____

   _____

9. If the police had never found the notes in the tramp's pocket, what other ways might they have cracked the code?

_____

_____

10. Why do you think the tramps kept their code a secret?

_____

_____

11. What would be a good title for this story? Use as few words as possible.

_____

_____

12. How are the drawings and meanings of the "Tramp's Code" pictures for "nothing doing, mean people" and "nothing here" alike? How are they different?

_____

_____

13. In a few words, tell how the tramps in France used their secret code to send messages to one another.

_____

_____

14. At the end of the story, everyone in France knew what the signs of the "Tramp's Code" meant. Do you think this changed the way the tramps sent messages? Why do you think so?

_____

_____

15. The story said, "Everyone in France knew about the strange signs written with chalk." Is this statement a fact or an opinion? How can you prove your answer?

_____

_____

16.

_____

_____

Name _____ Date _____

THE STANLEY STEAMER

ABOUT THE STORY

Identical twins, F.E. and F.O. Stanley, invented the Stanley Steamer in the early 1900s. The Stanley Steamer was a steam-driven car.

> *If possible, display models of steam engine trains, steamboats, and other steam-driven implements in the classroom throughout the week.

PREVIEW WORDS

noisy	steam	pollution
identical	electricity	throttle
pedal	backward	seconds
F.E. and F.O. Stanley	invented	

BOOKS TO READ

Worthington Botts and the Steam Machine, by Betty Baker (Macmillan, 1981).

A Telling of the Tales: Five Stories (includes the story of John Henry), William J. Brooke (Harper & Row, 1990).

Mike Mulligan and His Steam Shovel, by Virginia Lee Burton (Weston Woods, 1939).

Weird Wheels, Alain Chirinian (Messner, 1989).

The Man Who Transformed the World: James Watt, William D. Crane (Julian Messner, 1963)

The Automobile, Arthur N. Evans (Lerner Publications, 1985).

Energy, Robin McKie (Hampstead, 1989).

American Tall Tales (includes the story of John Henry), Mary Pope Osborne (Alfred A. Knopf, 1990).

The Marshall Cavendish Science Project Book of Water, Steve Parker (Marshall Cavendish Corporation, 1986).

Pictorial History of Steam Power, J.T. Van Riemsdijk (Octopus, 1980).

The Age of Steam, Jonathan Rutland (Random House, 1987).

Huck Scarry's Steam Train Journey, Huck Scarry (Collins-World, 1979).

The Steam Engine, Beatrice Siegel (Walker, 1986).

Look Out! Here Comes the Stanley Steamer, K.C. Tessendorf (Atheneum, 1984).

175 Science Experiments to Amuse and Amaze Your Friends: Experiments! Tricks! Things to Make!, Brenda Walpole (Random House, 1988).

VIDEO

John Henry, American Heroes and Legends Series, Rabbit Ears Productions, 1992. Length: 30 minutes.

INTRODUCTORY ACTIVITIES

DAY ONE

Objective: The students will conduct an experiment involving steam power. They will demonstrate how water expands as it vaporizes into steam. The students will discuss how this power can move objects.

Curriculum subject: Science

The Power of Steam

Note: Use caution when dealing with hot water, candles, and steam.

Teacher: People understood the power of steam over 2,000 years ago. Leonardo da Vinci described a steam-powered gun in the late 1400s. It was not until the 1600s that inventors used steam engines to move water. Steam engines pumped water out of mines. Miners needed to get rain water out of the mines so they could work. Soon people used steam engines to move boats, trains, and even cars. How can the steam from ordinary hot water move things? Do you have any ideas? (Allow the students to speculate.) Let's do an experiment.

Instructions for two similar experiments about building model steam boats are in the following books:

The Marshall Cavendish Science Project Book of Water, Steve Parker. Experiment: *Full Steam Ahead!*, p. 23.

175 Science Experiments to Amuse and Amaze Your Friends: Experiments! Tricks! Things to Make!, Brenda Walpole. Experiment: *Make a Steam Boat*, p. 127. Diagram of a steam engine, p. 126.

Teacher: Why did the boat move when the water changed to steam?

Answer: When water is a liquid, it takes up less room. If you change water to steam, it will take up more space. The steam forces itself out of the cigar tube through the only exit. Enough force builds up to move the model.

DAY TWO

Objective: The students will discuss how steam engines work. They will determine if steam engines would be an adequate form of power today.

Curriculum subject: Science or Language Arts

Review the experiment performed on Day One. Ask someone with an understanding of steam engines to talk to the class. Even a member of a model train club should have extensive knowledge of steam engines. The speaker should tell how steam engines were important in history. Are steam engines used today? Should we begin to look at steam engines as a power source? Why do you think so? End with a question-and-answer session.

DAY THREE

Story Lesson

Follow the *Presenting the Story Lesson* instructions in the Introduction. Each story lesson follows the same procedure; however, say the following in step 4:

"The title of the story we're reading today is *The Stanley Steamer*. What do you think this story is about? What do you already know about steam engines?"

EXTENSION ACTIVITIES

1. In this activity, the students look for other objects that use steam power. They also demonstrate an understanding of the purpose of the steam-powered object.

◆ Teacher:

We've looked at several things that use steam power. Can you name any? (Students list as many as possible. Write their list on the board.) Choose your favorite steam-powered machine. You can use one we just listed, or find something you like better. Draw a picture of someone using it. Write a story telling how the machine works, and why you like it.

(Pair insecure students with those who are more outgoing. Let volunteers share their stories. Display the pictures and stories around the room.)

◆ Teacher:

Tomorrow you'll draw your own invention. Try to think of something you would like to invent that could use steam power. Be ready to draw a picture and write about your invention.

2. Continuing yesterday's activity, the students invent their own steam-powered machines.

◆ Teacher:

Yesterday we looked at many steam-powered machines. Can anyone tell me some? Today it's your turn to invent something that uses steam power. Does anyone have ideas?

(Discuss what their inventions are, and how they work.)

◆ Teacher:

Now, draw a picture of your invention. After you finish, write a story about it. Tell how it uses steam power, and why your invention is needed.

(If a student seems apprehensive, pair him or her with other students who can discuss ideas. The students develop the idea together. When everyone finishes, ask volunteers to share their papers. Display the papers around the room.)

THE STANLEY STEAMER

Today, most cars run on gas. The motors are noisy, and make air pollution. People are now looking at quiet and clean electricity or sun power to make cars go. Perhaps we should use steam again. Yes, again.

In the early 1900s, F.E. and F.O. Stanley invented a car called the Stanley Steamer. The men were identical twins. This quiet car ran on steam from hot water.

The car had a stick, called the throttle, and two pedals. You pushed the throttle to go. One pedal made the car stop. The other made the car go backward.

The steamer was the fastest car of its time. No car could go as fast uphill. On a flat road, it could go one mile in 28 ½ seconds. With a speed of 120 miles an hour, it held the world's record from 1906 to 1910.

QUESTIONS FOR THE STANLEY STEAMER

1. Who made the Stanley Steamer?

   _____

   _____

2. What did you push to make the car go?

   _____

   _____

3. How fast did the Stanley Steamer go on a flat road?

   _____

   _____

4. In what years did the Stanley Steamer hold the world's record for speed?

   _____

   _____

5. In 1899, Henry Ford began to make his Model T, a car powered by gasoline. Which car was the first to be made, Ford's Model T or the Stanley Steamer?

   _____

   _____

6. What did you have to do before the Stanley Steamer would go?

   _____

   _____

7. You know that teachers teach, and doctors help sick people. What job name best tells what the Stanley brothers did?

   _____

   _____

8. Read the first paragraph of the story again. In what ways are motors that run on steam better than those that run on gas?

   _____

   _____

9. In the future, will cars use gas to make them run? Why do you think so?

_____

_____

10. Why are people looking for new ways to make cars go?

_____

_____

11. What title would best tell about the story? Use as few words as possible.

_____

_____

12. Compare steam-powered cars to gas-powered cars. Which one do you believe is the best way to make cars go? Why do you think so?

_____

_____

13. Tell how you would make the Stanley Steamer go forward, backward, and stop.

_____

_____

14. Cars that run on gas make pollution called carbon monoxide. They are also very noisy. Think about the cars that drive on the busy streets where you live. How would the streets look and sound different if everyone drove a Stanley Steamer?

_____

_____

15. The story said, "The (Stanley) steamer was the fastest car of its time." Is this a fact or an opinion? How can you prove your answer?

_____

_____

16.

_____

_____

Name _____ Date _____

ALBINO

ABOUT THE STORY

This story explains what albino means. The story discusses the occurrence of albinism in plants, animals, and people.

PREVIEW WORDS

albino	squirrels	snakes
10,000	because	

BOOKS TO READ

They Came From DNA, Billy Aronson (Scientific American Books for Young Readers, 1993).

How Did We Find Out About Genes, Isaac Asimov (Walker, 1983).

White Rabbit's Color Book, Alan Baker (Kingfisher Books, 1994).

What Makes You What You Are: A First Look at Genetics, Sandy Bornstein (J. Messner, 1989).

Heredity, Dennis B. Fradin (Childrens Press, 1987).

Rabbits: Everything About Purchase Care, Nutrition and Diseases, Helga Fritzsche (Barron's, 1983).

The White Horse, Edith Thacher Hurd (Harper & Row, 1970).

Grandfather's Nose: Why We Look Alike and Different, Dorothy Hinshaw Patent (Franklin Watts, 1989).

Guinea Pigs: All About Them, Alvin and Virginia Silverstein (Lothrop, Lee & Shepard, 1972).

Hamsters: All About Them, Alvin and Virginia Silverstein (Lothrop, Lee & Shepard, 1974).

Mouse Paint, Ellen Stoll Walsh (Harcourt Brace Jovanovich, 1989).

VIDEO

The Wondrous World of Weird Animals, (MPI Home Video, 1993). Series: Videosaurus. Length: 32 minutes.

INTRODUCTORY ACTIVITIES

DAY ONE

Objective: The students will visually compare an albino animal to a nonalbino. They will draw and write about the comparison.

Curriculum subject: Science or Language Arts

If the school district allows, keep an albino pet in the classroom. Consider selecting a mouse, hamster, or guinea pig. Also, keep a nonalbino animal of the same species for comparison. Discuss how the albino animal is alike and different from the nonalbino (compare/contrast). Break the class into small groups. Instruct each group to draw pictures of the albino and nonalbino animals. Include as much detail of the differences and similarities as possible. After drawing the pictures, the groups will write short compare/contrast essays about the animals. Ask volunteers to share their observations with the class.

DAY TWO

Story Lesson

Follow the *Presenting the Story Lesson* instructions in the Introduction. Each story lesson follows the same procedure; however, say the following in step 4:

"The title of the story we're reading today is *Albino*. What do you think this story is about? What do you already know about albinism?"

EXTENSION ACTIVITIES

1. The students will determine which is the most popular pet, albino or nonalbino. They will record the results on a bar graph.

Materials

◆ Poster board
◆ Green and red markers

Procedure

◆ Prepare the poster board before class. Follow the example below.

	10		
S	9		
T	8		
U	7		
D	6		
E	5		
N	4		
T	3		
S	2		
	1		
	0		
		LIKE ALBINO	LIKE NONALBINO

(The numbers represent the number of students in the class.)

◆ Teacher:

Today you'll have the opportunity to vote for your favorite pet. Everyone will have a vote. When we're done, we'll know exactly how many of us like albino pets, and how many like nonalbino pets.

When I call your name, come to the poster. If you like albino pets, color the next square above "like albino" with red. If you like nonalbino pets, color the next square above "like nonalbino" with green. (Help the students as they mark the graph.)

You have all marked your choices. Together, we made a bar graph. What does our bar graph tell us? (Discuss the answers.)

Now we need a name for our bar graph. What can we call this bar graph? (Discuss the answers and write the chosen name on the line at the top of the graph.)

Is a bar graph a good way to show information? Why do you think so? Can you think of other topics we could show on a bar graph? (Examples: Boys and Girls in Our Class, Hair Color in Our Class, etc.)

◆ Assign a bar graph for homework. The students will ask ten people if they own an albino pet. The students will put the information into a bar graph and name the bar graph.

2. In this activity, the students discuss why there are few albinos in the wild, yet pet stores stock many albino animals (drawing conclusions). Display the graph the students created in Extension Activity 1. Discuss which pets are more popular, albino or nonalbino.

◆ Teacher:

Think about the last time you went into a pet shop. Did you see several albino pets offered for sale? Why do you think the pet stores stock so many albino pets? (Discuss the answers. Encourage the students to base their conclusions on the bar graph they made in Extension Activity 1 and their homework survey.)

Think about the last time you went to the zoo. Maybe you went for a walk away from the city. Did you see as many albino animals in the wild as you did in the pet store? Why do you think there are fewer albino animals in the wild? (Discuss the answer.)

◆ Break the students into groups. Ask them to draw a picture of two animals in the wild. The students will draw animals of the same species, making one albino. Next, they will write a short essay in which they answer the question, "Why are there fewer albino animals in the wild?" Tell the students to base their conclusions on their observations. Any conclusions that are reasonable, if they are not fully correct, should be considered appropriate answers. (Pet owners are more likely to choose the more popular albino animal. Albinos in the wild are easy to see. Predators attack the animals who can not hide effectively. They do not pass their genes on to offspring.)

◆ Display their pictures and essays around the room.

3. Invite a speaker with knowledge of albinos to the class. A veterinarian, a speaker from the zoo, or a pet breeder would have information about albinos. Ask the speaker to show pictures and discuss albinism. How often does albinism occur? What causes albinism? Where can students go to see unique albino animals?

After the discussion, break the class into groups of three to four students. Each group will write a news article about albino animals. Suggest the following topics, or let the students choose their own.

◆ Unique Albino Animals

◆ Albinos in the Wild

◆ What Causes Albinism?

◆ Albinos as Pets

Each group will read their news article. Finally, conduct a vote to choose the students' favorite article. Submit the article to a local newspaper for publication.

ALBINO

The next time you go to the pet store, ask to see the mice. Most pet stores have white mice. They have white hair with pink feet, tails, and eyes. We call these mice albino.

Albino means that the body has no color. Even the eyes have no color. The eyes are pink because you are seeing what is behind the missing color. The brown, blue, or green color of other eyes covers the pink.

Mice are not the only living things that are albino. In fact, any animal or plant can be albino. Albino plants often die. Plants need the green color to help them make food.

In the animal world, there are albino birds, squirrels, snakes, deer, and insects. The white color of albino animals can cause problems. A wild white mouse hiding in the leaves is easier to see than a brown mouse. Other animals, like owls, who eat mice see the white mouse first.

There are also albino people. One out of every 10,000 people is albino.

QUESTIONS FOR ALBINO

1. What does albino mean?

   _____

   _____

2. If an albino animal has no color, why are its eyes pink?

   _____

   _____

3. Why do albino plants often die?

   _____

   _____

4. Can people be albino?

   _____

   _____

5. What is the first albino animal the story tells you about?

   _____

   _____

6. What is the last type of albino the story tells about?

   _____

   _____

7. Is a white dog with brown eyes an albino? Why?

   _____

   _____

8. The story tells us that most pet stores sell albino mice. Why do you think that so many stores have albino mice?

   _____

   _____

9. During your lifetime, is it likely that you will meet an albino person? Why do you think so?

_____

_____

10. The story tells us that an albino has no color. What do you think might cause this to happen?

_____

_____

11. What would be a good title for this story? Use as few words as possible.

_____

_____

12. How are an albino mouse and a brown mouse alike? How are they different?

_____

_____

13. In a few words, explain what albino means.

_____

_____

14. Imagine that you meet a person who is an albino. How would you feel when you saw her or him? Would you feel any different about meeting an albino person than you would anyone else?

_____

_____

15. The story said, "One out of every 10,000 people is albino." Is this a fact or an opinion? How can you prove your answer?

_____

_____

16.

_____

_____

Name _____ Date _____

WHITE BUFFALO CALF WOMAN

ABOUT THE STORY

This story tells about the myth of the White Buffalo Calf Woman. In 1994, a white buffalo calf was born. Native Americans believe this calf is the fulfillment of the White Buffalo Calf Woman's promise.

PREVIEW WORDS

White Buffalo Calf Woman	Sioux	buffalo
Native Americans	million	Woo'pe
Miracle		

BOOKS TO READ

The Sacred Path: Spells, Prayers and Power Songs of the American Indians, edited by John Bierhorst (William Morrow and Company, 1983).

Flying With the Eagle, Racing the Great Bear: Stories From Native North America, Joseph Bruchac (Bridgewater Press, 1993).

People of the Buffalo: How the Plains Indians Lived, Maria Campbell (Douglas & McIntyre, 1983).

Keepers of the Animals: Native American Stories and Wildlife Activities for Children, Michael J. Caduto and Joseph Bruchac (Fulcrum Publishing, 1991).

Keepers of the Earth: Native American Stories and Environmental Activities for Children, Michael J. Caduto and Joseph Bruchac (Fulcrum Publishing, 1988).

Keepers of the Night: Native American Stories and Nocturnal Activities for Children, Michael J. Caduto and Joseph Bruchac (Fulcrum Publishing, 1994).

Buffalo Woman, Paul Goble (Bradbury Press, 1984).

Buffalo and Indians on the Great Plains, Noel Grisham (Eakin, 1985).

Coyote and the Laughing Butterflies, Harriet Peck Taylor (Macmillan Books for Young Readers, 1995).

Buffalo Moon, G. Clifton Wisler (Dutton, 1984).

CDS, RECORDS, AND CASSETTES

Dream Catchers (CD), Kevin Locke (Earth Beat, 1992). Songs of Indians of North America.

INTRODUCTORY ACTIVITIES

DAY ONE

Objective: The students will learn about the relationship between the buffalo and Native Americans. They will discuss and write about this relationship.

Curriculum subject: History or Language Arts

Invite an expert in Native American life and folklore to speak to the class. A storyteller might also know Native American myths. Ask the speaker to tell about buffalo folklore. Why were buffalo such an important part of Native American life? Is the buffalo a common character in Native American myth? Why does it play such an important role? End with a question-and-answer session.

(For the teacher's reference only, watch the video *Joseph Campbell and The Power of Myth,* With Bill Moyers, Program 3: "The First Storytellers" (Mystic Fire Video, 1989). The abstract concepts would confuse children; however, this video gives the teacher insight into the buffalo myths.)

Ask the speaker to tell or read a Native American folktale that centers around buffalo.

DAY TWO

Objective: The students will listen to the story *Buffalo Woman* by Paul Goble. They will write
a folktale.
Curriculum subject: Language Arts

Read the story *Buffalo Woman* by Paul Goble to the class. Discuss the moral, "We are all related." Did the folktale explain how animals and people are related better than a scientific explanation? Why do you think so?

Write a Folktale

Teacher: Folktales teach us about life in ways a scientific explanation can not. The story *Buffalo Woman* teaches us that everyone, animals and people, is related. We all exist together. Can you think of a lesson you could teach through a folktale?
(Discuss how a folktale talks about things the storyteller knows about. Maybe they can write about the responsibilities you have for your pet, caring for the environment, being part of a strong family, or fulfilling an obligation.)

Break the class into groups of three to four students. Together they will decide on a topic and write a folktale. Finally, each student draws a picture to illustrate the story. One student draws the beginning, another student the middle and another the end (sequencing).

DAY THREE

Story Lesson
Follow the *Presenting the Story Lesson* instructions in the Introduction. Each story lesson follows the same procedure; however, say the following in step 4:
"The title of the story we're reading today is *White Buffalo Calf Woman.* What do you think this story is about? What do you already know about buffalo folktales?"

EXTENSION ACTIVITIES

1. In this activity, the students make a "Circle of Life." They will learn that the buffalo is an important part of the Native Americans' "Circle of Life." The following is a modified version of "Earth Circle of Life" from *Keepers of the Earth: Native American Stories and Environmental Activities for Children* by Michael J. Caduto and Joseph Bruchac, p. 189.

◆ Teacher:

> Native Americans respect and honor the buffalo. They once depended on buffalo for food and clothing; however, they felt the responsibility for taking the life of the animal who kept them alive. Native Americans honored the buffalo in dance and rituals of thanksgiving. Animals, plants, and people live together and support one another. This "giving of themselves" makes a "Circle of Life." According to Native Americans, if you take from the circle, you must give something in return. Nothing is wasted, and you must demonstrate respectful thankfulness to the giver.

Circle of Life
Materials

◆ a large circle cut from bulletin board paper

◆ drawing paper

◆ crayons

◆ scissors

◆ glue

◆ large drawing of a sun

Procedure

◆ Hand out drawing paper to each student.

◆ Ask the students to think of an animal, plant, or product of the Earth (e.g., water) that they need to use in order to survive.

◆ The students draw, color, and cut out a picture of the subject they chose.

◆ Lay the large paper circle on the floor.

◆ The students stand around the circle, holding their pictures.

◆ The students take turns telling about what they drew. What do they need that animal, plant, or element for? How does it help people to survive? Why should we be thankful for what the animal, plant, or element gives to us?

◆ Glue the picture to the edge of the circle in front of the student.

◆ Continue around the circle, giving each student a turn.

◆ The teacher glues a picture of a buffalo on the edge of the circle in front of him or her. He or she tells the students again about the importance of the buffalo; the meat fed them and the hide kept them warm. Native Americans believed that if they gave thanks and respected the buffalo, it would continue to give its life for their sake.

◆ Glue the picture of the sun in the center of the circle. Discuss how the sun keeps all the things in the Circle of Life alive.

◆ Hang the circle on a bulletin board entitled "The Circle of Life."

2. Follow the directions for the Circle Dance. The dance can be found in:

Keepers of the Animals: Native American Stories and Wildlife Activities for Children, Michael J. Caduto and Joseph Bruchac, pp. 46–47.

3. Michael J. Caduto and Joseph Bruchac wrote several books on Native American stories and activities. Each book has activities and resources to help students experience the rich culture of Native Americans.

WHITE BUFFALO CALF WOMAN

Long ago, three Sioux hunters found a white buffalo calf. The animal had red horns. Its eyes were bright pink. Suddenly, the buffalo turned into a beautiful woman.

"Go home to your people," she said. "Get ready for my visit."

Four days later the White Buffalo Calf Woman returned. She gave the Sioux a holy pipe and Woo'pe, the Sioux laws.

The White Buffalo Calf Woman said, "One day I will come back and bring peace to the world. All people will live together in kindness."

In the late summer of 1994, a white buffalo calf was born. Only one out of every 10 million buffalo is white. This rare buffalo's name is Miracle.

To hundreds of Native Americans, Miracle is the White Buffalo Calf Woman. She is a sign that peace and kindness is coming to all people.

Where is the White Buffalo Calf Woman's holy pipe? The Sioux kept it all these years to be ready for her second visit.

QUESTIONS FOR WHITE BUFFALO CALF WOMAN

1. What color were the white buffalo calf's eyes?

   _____

   _____

2. What did the buffalo turn into?

   _____

   _____

3. What is the name of the rare buffalo calf born in 1994?

   _____

   _____

4. Who is Miracle to hundreds of Native Americans?

   _____

   _____

5. What did the White Buffalo Calf Woman give the Sioux on her first visit?

   _____

   _____

6. What did the White Buffalo Calf Woman say she would bring on her second visit?

   _____

   _____

7. Look at the picture of Miracle. What color are her eyes? What color were the White Buffalo Calf Woman's eyes? Which one is an albino? How can you prove your answer?

   _____

   _____

8. Did the Sioux believe that the White Buffalo Calf Woman would come back? Why do you think so?

   _____

   _____

9. Hundreds of Native Americans think Miracle is the White Buffalo Calf Woman. Will the people of the world begin to live in peace and kindness? Why do you think so?

_____

_____

10. Why did the Sioux keep the White Buffalo Calf Woman's holy pipe?

_____

_____

11. Write a title for this story. Use as few words as possible.

_____

_____

12. Read the story Buffalo Woman by Paul Goble. How is this story like White Buffalo Calf Woman? How is it different?

_____

_____

13. In a few words, tell about the first visit from the White Buffalo Calf Woman.

_____

_____

14. Imagine that everyone believed that peace and kindness is coming to all people. How would this effect the way people act towards each other? Why do you think so?

_____

_____

15. The story said, "She (Miracle) is a sign that peace and kindness will soon come to all people." Is this a fact or an opinion? How can you prove your answer?

_____

_____

16.

_____

_____

Name _____   Date _____

THE HUBBLE SPACE TELESCOPE

ABOUT THE STORY

Edwin P. Hubble learned that the universe is made up of many galaxies with star systems. He also learned that the universe is growing. The space telescope, which looks for answers to questions raised by Hubble's discoveries, is called the Hubble Space Telescope.

PREVIEW WORDS

Edwin P. Hubble	universe	galaxies
solar system	Milky Way	telescope
Hubble Space Telescope	planets	Earth

BOOKS TO READ

Lenses! Take a Closer Look, Siegfried Aust (Lerner Publications Co., 1991).

Telescopes, Lionel Bender (Gloucester Press, 1991).

Astronomy, Boy Scouts of America (Boy Scouts of America, 1992, ©1971).

Space Telescope, Franklyn Mansfield Branley (Crowell, 1985).

Telescopes and Observatories, Heather Couper and Nigel Henbest (Franklin Watts, 1987).

The New Astronomy: Probing the Secrets of Space, Fred D'Ignazio (Franklin Watts, 1982).

Space Telescope, Dennis B. Fradin (Childrens Press, 1987).

Stars, Michael George (Creative Education, Inc., 1991).

The Space Telescope, Christopher Lampton (Franklin Watts, 1987).

Telescope Makers: From Galileo to the Space Age, Barbara Land (Thomas Y. Crowell Co., 1968).

A Young Astronomer's Guide to the Night Sky, Michael R. Porcellino (Tab Books, 1991).

The Third Planet: Exploring the Earth From Space, Sally Ride (Crown, 1994).

How Far Is a Star?, Sydney Craft Rozen (Carolrhoda Books, 1992).

The Amateur Astronomer: Explorations and Investigations, Fred Schaef (Franklin Watts, 1994).

Space Words: A Dictionary, Seymour Simon (HarperCollins, 1991).

Voyager, Gregory Vogt (Millbrook Press, 1991).

Photo Fun: An Idea Book for Shutterbugs, David Webster (Franklin Watts, 1973).

Microscopes and Telescopes, Fred Wilkin (Childrens Press, 1983).

Science for Kids: 39 Easy Astronomy Experiments, Robert W. Wood (TAB Books, 1991).

PRIOR TO THE LESSON

Several weeks before the lesson, contact NASA's Johnson Space Center. Inquire into the availablity of photographs from the Hubble Space Telescope for educational use. Decorate the classroom with these amazing photographs.

> National Aeronautics and Space Administration
> Lyndon B. Johnson Space Center
> 2101 NASA Road 1
> Houston, TX 77058-3696

Prepare for a trip to your local planetarium. Tell the guide that your class is learning about the Hubble Space Telescope. This lesson week can be moved to a date which corresponds to your scheduled planetarium field trip.

VIDEOS

Mr. Know-It-Owl Presents: Space, Concord Video, 1987.

America's Space Adventure: To Be an Astronaut, KVC Home Video, 1988. Length: 45 minutes.

SOFTWARE

Where in Space Is Carmen San Diego? (Broderbund, 1993).

Odyssey, 1996 (Astromedia Corp., 1996).

INTRODUCTORY ACTIVITIES

DAY ONE

Objective: The students will listen to a story about the space telescope.

Curriculum subject: Science

Teacher: Throughout the week, we'll learn about the Hubble Space Telescope. We'll learn about its history and its name, and see images sent back to Earth from the telescope.

Today, we'll listen to a story written about the space telescope before the space shuttle took it into orbit. As I read the story, make a list of goals NASA and astronomers hope the telescope will meet. Later, we'll learn if the space telescope is living up to these goals.

Read the story *Space Telescope* by Dennis B. Fradin (Chicago: Childrens Press, 1987) to the class. As you read the story, point out the objectives astronomers hope the Hubble Space Telescope will meet. After the lesson, the students will discuss and list the goals of the space telescope. Write the list on chart paper. Later, the students will look at pictures sent back from the telescope, and discuss the value of the telescope.

DAY TWO

Story Lesson

Follow the *Presenting the Story Lesson* instructions in the Introduction. Each story lesson follows the same procedure; however, say the following in step 4:

"The title of the story we're reading today is *The Hubble Space Telescope.* What do you think the story is about? What do you already know about the space telescope?"

EXTENSION ACTIVITIES

1. The students will visit a planetarium, and ask questions about the Hubble Space Telescope.

◆ Before leaving the school, the students will prepare a question list. The students should write three questions they would like to ask the guide at the planetarium. Most of these questions should apply to the Hubble Space Telescope.

◆ While at the planetarium, encourage the students to find answers to all their questions.

2. The students will discuss the goals of the Hubble Space Telescope, and whether those goals were met.

◆ Display and discuss photographs from the Hubble Space Telescope.

◆ Display the chart paper from Day One which lists the goals of the space telescope.

Teacher: Look at the goals of the space telescope we wrote earlier. Do you think the telescope is living up to these goals? Why do you feel this way? Has the space telescope revealed more about our universe than you expected? What did the space telescope teach you that you didn't know before?

3. Hold an "Astronomy Party."

◆ Hold a nighttime "Astronomy Party" on a PTA night. Choose a night when the moon will not be out during the party. This will improve visibility.

◆ The students will write invitations to school administrators, parents and other classes to join them for an "Astronomy Party."

◆ Set up the party in a carnival format. People can move from booth to booth looking at the science experiments, telescopes and binoculars to learn about the night sky.

◆ Invite local astronomy clubs to bring telescopes, and help the students learn about astronomy. To locate an Astronomical League (a federation of astronomical societies, a non-profit organization) in your area, contact:

The Astronomical League
2112 Kingfisher Lane East
Rolling Meadows, IL 60008-2735

◆ Set up cameras to photograph the night sky. Suggested activities for photographing stars are in:

Couper, Heather and Nigel Henbest, *Space Scientist:Telescopes and Observatories,* pp. 26–67. New York: Franklin Watts, 1987.

Webster, David, *Photo Fun; An Idea Book for Shutterbugs,* pp. 28–45. New York: Franklin Watts, Inc., 1973.

Wood, Robert W., *Science for Kids: 39 Easy Astronomy Experiments,* pp. 90–93. Blue Ridge Summit, PA: TAB Books, 1991.

◆ Prepare experiments in astronomy. Sources for astronomy experiments include:

Porcellin, Michael R., *A Young Astronomer's Guide to the Night Sky.* Blue Ridge Summit, PA: TAB Books, 1991.

Wood, Robert W., *Science for Kids: 39 Easy Astronomy Experiments,* pp. 90–93. Blue Ridge Summit, PA: TAB Books, 1991.

Death of an Ordinary Star · Egg Nebula

Hubble Space Telescope · WFPC2

THE HUBBLE SPACE TELESCOPE

Our earth circles around a star we call the sun. The Earth, Sun and other planets make up our solar system. Our solar system sits on the outside arm of a galaxy called the Milky Way. There are more stars than you can count in the Milky Way.

Edwin P. Hubble learned there are many galaxies out in space. Like our Milky Way, the galaxies hold star systems.

These galaxies float in a place called the universe. Hubble learned that the universe is growing. It is getting bigger.

Hubble made people think about the universe in a different way. If there are many galaxies with star systems, are there planets around the stars? Could there be life on some of these planets?

If the universe is growing, will it ever stop growing? If it stops growing, what will happen next? Maybe the universe will begin to get smaller.

High above the earth, a telescope looks out into space. It is finding hundreds of galaxies. It is looking for signs of a growing universe. We call it the Hubble Space Telescope.

QUESTIONS FOR THE HUBBLE SPACE TELESCOPE

1. Where does our solar system sit?

   _____

   _____

2. Name two things that Edwin P. Hubble learned.

   _____

   _____

3. What is the name of the telescope in the story?

   _____

   _____

4. Where is the Hubble Space Telescope?

   _____

   _____

5. What did the story tell about first: galaxies, or the universe?

   _____

   _____

6. What might happen after the universe stops growing?

   _____

   _____

7. What one word best describes the things that Edwin Hubble learned about the universe?

   _____

   _____

8. Why was the space telescope named the Hubble Space Telescope?

   _____

   _____

9. Will the Hubble Space Telescope help people find the answers to the questions in the story? Why do you feel this way?

_____

_____

10. Why did the things that Edwin Hubble learned make people ask new questions?

_____

_____

11. Write a title for the story. Use as few words as possible.

_____

_____

12. How is the Hubble Space Telescope like telescopes on Earth? How is it different?

_____

_____

13. In only a few words, tell about the things Edwin P. Hubble learned.

_____

_____

14. How will the Hubble Space Telescope change the way people study the universe?

_____

_____

15. The story said, "Maybe the universe will begin to get smaller." Is this a fact or someone's opinion? Why do you feel this way?

_____

_____

16.

_____

_____

Name _____   Date _____

©1997 The Center for Applied Research in Education

JULES VERNE

ABOUT THE STORY

This story tells about the first science fiction writer, Jules Verne. It discusses how Verne studied a subject before he wrote about it.

PREVIEW WORDS

Jules Verne	France	Captain Nemo
submarine	science fiction	

Around the World in Eighty Days

Journey to the Center of the Earth

20,000 Leagues Under the Sea

BOOKS TO READ

The Brain on Quartz Mountain, Margaret Anderson (Knopf, 1982).

Mutants, Isaac Asimov (Raintree, 1982).

Science Fiction, Science Fact, Isaac Asimov (Gareth Stevens, 1989).

Space Cats, Steven Kroll (Holiday House, 1979).

The Giver, Lois Lowry (Houghton Mifflin, 1993).

An Album of Great Science Fiction Films, Frank Manchel (Franklin Watts, 1982).

Space Case, Edward Marshall (Dial Press, 1980).

Merry Christmas, Space Case, James Marshall (Dial Books for
Young Readers, 1986).

The Drought on Ziax II, John Morressy (Walker, 1978).

Guys From Space, Daniel Manus Pinkwater (Macmillan, 1989).

Who Said There's No Man on the Moon?: A Story of Jules Verne, Robert M. Quackenbush
(Simon & Schuster Books for Young Readers, 1989.)

Alistair in Outer Space, Marilyn Sadler (Prentice Hall Books for Young Readers, 1984).

Alistair's Time Machine, Marilyn Sadler (Prentice Hall, 1986).

Around the World in Eighty Days, Jules Verne (Dell, 1984).

A Journey to the Center of the Earth, Jules Verne (Airmont Books, 1965).

A Long Vacation, Jules Verne (Holt, Rinehart & Winston, 1976).

The Mysterious Island, Jules Verne (Watermill Press, 1983).

Twenty Thousand Leagues Under the Sea, Jules Verne (Pendulum Press, 1973).

June 29, 1999, David Wiesner (Clarion Books, 1992).

VIDEOS

New Explorers: Science and Star Trek, Kurtis Productions, 1994. Available through Public
Media, Inc. with teacher's guide at 1-800-621-0660. Length: 60 minutes.

20,000 Leagues Under the Sea, Walt Disney's Studio Film Collection, Walt Disney Home
Video, 1991. Length: 127 minutes.

INTRODUCTORY ACTIVITIES

DAY ONE

Objective: The students will listen to and discuss the book *Science Fiction, Science Fact* by Isaac Asimov. They will discuss how science fiction writers research their subject before they write.

Curriculum subject: Reading or Language Arts

Read *Science Fiction, Science Fact* by Isaac Asimov to the class. Discuss how science fiction writers must understand the science behind their story.

Teacher: If you want to write a story about a space station on Saturn, what must you learn first? Where are some places you could find this information?

Look for information about the planet Saturn. You might find it in a book or a movie, or from someone who knows about Saturn. Bring the information to class on Thursday (Extension Activity 1). Be ready to talk about building a space station. Imagine what it would be like to live on the space station. What space creatures might you meet there?

On Friday (Extension Activity 3), we'll have an Alien Pageant. Look for things around your house that might make an alien costume. An empty dish detergent bottle could be a space phone. Strips of colored paper could be alien hair. Don't go out and buy a costume. You must create it from things you find around the house.

DAY TWO

Objective: The students will watch the movie *New Explorers: Science and Star Trek,* a PBS series. They will discuss the scientific facts used by *Star Trek* writers.

Curriculum subject: Science or Language Arts

Video: New Explorers: Science and Star Trek, a PBS series (Fall 1995). If the video is not loaned through your local library or PBS station, order the film at Public Media, Inc., 1-800-621-0660.

Teacher: Yesterday we discussed how science fiction writers must study science before they write a story. The *Star Trek* series also based many of its creations on science fact. Watch the movie. Be ready to tell me about *Star Trek* creations that the writers based on science fact or scientific theory.

After the movie, talk about what the writers for *Star Trek* must know when they write an episode. What *Star Trek* ideas might we see in the future?

DAY THREE

Show the film *20,000 Leagues Under the Sea* by Jules Verne before reading the story.
Story Lesson
Follow the *Presenting the Story Lesson* instructions in the Introduction. Each story lesson follows the same procedure; however, say the following in step 4:

"The title of the story we're reading today is called *Jules Verne.* What do you think this story is about? What do you already know about Jules Verne?"

Remind the students to bring in information about Saturn tomorrow (Extension Activity 1). Also, Friday (Extension Activity 3) is Alien Pageant Day. Tell the students to keep working on their costumes and be ready to wear them to class.

EXTENSION ACTIVITIES

1. Review the information about Saturn that the students brought to class. Working with the entire class, write a description of a space station on Saturn. Write the description on a poster that can be displayed in the room. Include information about inventions needed to travel to Saturn. What would the people need to wear and eat to live on the space station? Describe aliens who might visit the station. The students can then draw pictures or make models of the space station.

2. Each student will write a description of the alien she or he will be on Friday (Extension Activity 3). Where does the alien live? What inventions does it need to live on its planet or to visit Earth? Why does it look the way it does? Be sure to name the alien.

3. Alien Pageant Day:

◆ The students dress in alien costumes. Each student reads the description of his or her alien to the class. After each story, students can ask questions such as: What does your alien eat? Why does your alien eat that? Why does your alien have long fingers?

◆ Lay out a long piece of bulletin board paper. The students will work together to draw the inside of an alien space ship. Include sleeping quarters, showers, eating areas. Remember to base the drawings on science fact. Hang the picture around the room to give the appearance that the students are riding in a space ship.

◆ Alien Lunch:

Bring food to school that looks like an alien lunch. Room mothers might enjoy helping. Make green gelatin with fruit cocktail inside. Peanut butter sandwiches with purple dots of food coloring spotting the bread are space sandwiches. Alien ice cream drink is lime sherbet in lemon-lime soda. Use odd-shaped glasses and colorful paper plates.

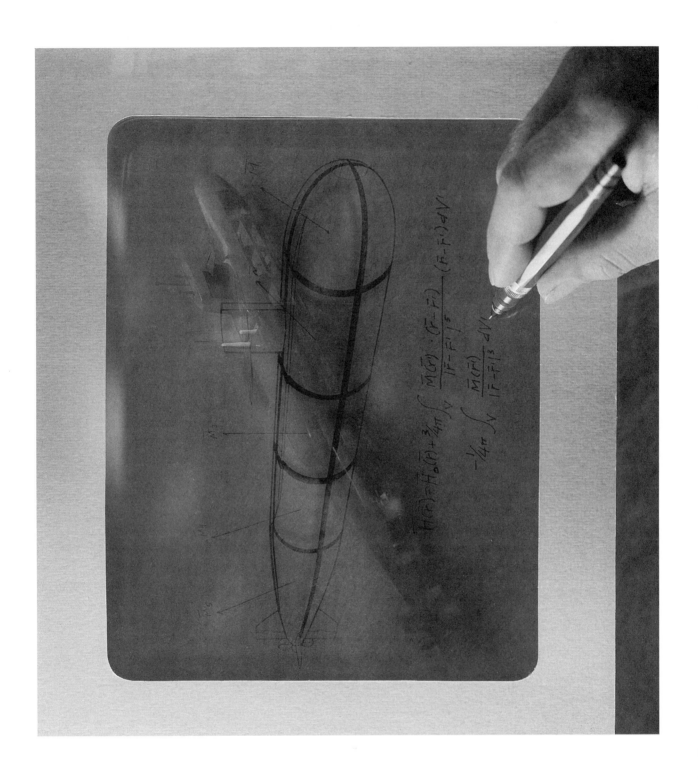

JULES VERNE

Jules Verne was born in 1828. He always wanted to see the world. When he was twelve, Verne tried to sail far away. His father found him, and took him back home to France.

Verne never traveled far from home. How could he make his dream to see the world come true? He wrote—wonderful stories about places he would never go.

His story *Around the World in Eighty Days* took him and his readers to far-off places. He read many books to learn what the world looked like.

Verne also learned about Earth. Then he took his readers on *A Journey to the Center of the Earth.*

20,000 Leagues Under the Sea told about Captain Nemo who lived in a submarine. It would be 80 years before people made a real submarine.

Jules Verne was the first science fiction writer. Today, there are many science fiction writers. They take us on trips we can see only in our dreams.

QUESTIONS FOR JULES VERNE

1. How old was Verne when he tried to sail far away?

   _____

   _____

2. Name three stories written by Jules Verne.

   _____

   _____

3. Did Verne ever travel far from home?

   _____

   _____

4. Who was the first science fiction writer?

   _____

   _____

5. What did Verne learn about before he wrote <u>Journey to the Center of the Earth</u>?

   _____

   _____

6. What was invented 80 years after Verne wrote <u>20,000 Leagues Under the Sea</u>?

   _____

   _____

7. Why are Jules Verne's stories called science fiction?

   _____

   _____

8. Did people like to read Jules Verne's stories? Why do you think so?

   _____

   _____

9. Will people enjoy reading science fiction stories in the future? Why do you think so?

_____

_____

10. Why did Jules Verne write about places he never visited?

_____

_____

11. Write a title for this story. Use as few words as possible.

_____

_____

12. How are <u>Journey to the Center of the Earth</u> and <u>20,000 Leagues Under the Sea</u> alike? How are they different?

_____

_____

13. In your own words, tell how Jules Verne wrote <u>Around the World in Eighty Days.</u>

_____

_____

14. What effect have Jules Verne's stories had on writers today?

_____

_____

15. The story said, "Jules Verne was the first science fiction writer." Is this a fact or an opinion? How can you prove your answer?

_____

_____

16.

_____

_____

Name _____ Date _____

TEAMWORK

ABOUT THE STORY

This story tells about people and dolphins working together to herd fish to shore. This partnership works for the best interest of both the dolphins and the people.

PREVIEW WORDS

important	shore	diet
cowboys	dolphins	herd
tribe	months	favorite

BOOKS TO READ

Whales of the World, June Behrens (Childrens Press, 1987).

The Several Tricks of Edgar Dolphin, Nathaniel Benchley (Harper & Row, 1970).

D Is for Dolphin, Janet Biondi (Windom Books, 1991).

Splash, the Dolphin, Cynthia Overbeck (Carolrhoda Books, 1976).

Nine True Dolphin Stories, Margaret Davidson (Hastings House, 1974).

The Girl Who Danced With Dolphins, Frank De Saix (Farrar, Straus & Giroux, 1991).

In Dolphin Time, Diane Farris (Maxell Macmillan International, 1994).

The Way of the Dolphin, Michael W. Fox (Acropolis Books, 1981).

Riding With the Dolphins: The Equinox Guide to Dolphins and Porpoises, Erich Hoyt (Camden House, 1992).

Island of the Blue Dolphins, Scott O'Dell (Houghton Mifflin, 1990).

The Bottlenose Dolphin, William R. Sanford and Carl R. Green (Crestwood House, 1987).

A Dolphin Goes to School: The Story of Squirt, a Trained Dolphin, Elizabeth Simpson Smith (Morrow, 1986).

Killer Whales and Dolphins Play, Don Arthur Torgersen (Childrens Press, 1982).

Dolphin's First Day: The Story of a Bottlenose Dolphin, Kathleen Weidner Zoehfeld (Soundprints, 1994).

VIDEOS

Deep Sea Dive, Columbia Tristar Home Video, 1994. Length: 30 minutes.

Spouts Ahoy!, Marty Stouffer Productions, 1992. Length: 30 minutes.

CDS, RECORDS, AND CASSETTES

What's in the Sea: Vocal and Music (Cassette), Lois Skiera-Zuck (Kimbo Educational, 1990).

INTRODUCTORY ACTIVITIES

DAY ONE AND CONTINUED THROUGHOUT THE WEEK

Objective: The students will research the large variety of dolphins and porpoises. They will make a model of a dolphin or porpoise.

Curriculum subject: Art or Science

Dolphin and Porpoise Models

Introduction:

There are a large variety of dolphins and porpoises. The book *Riding With the Dolphins: The Equinox Guide to Dolphins and Porpoises* by Erich Hoyt describes these varieties in detail. The photographs show students clear views of each animal.

Materials

- Riding With the Dolphins
- papier mâché (flour and water)
- long balloons
- gesso
- nontoxic paints
- brushes
- string
- paper clips
- masking tape
- cardboard

Instructions

1. Write the following names of porpoises and dolphins on small pieces of paper. Put the names in a bag. Each student reaches in the bag and pulls out a name. This is the model the student will make.

   Porpoises: Dall's, Harbour, Vaquita, Finless

   River Dolphins: Boto, Baiji, Ganges Susu, Bhulan

   Oceanic Dolphins: Rough-Toothed, Tucuxi, Atlantic Hump-Backed, Common, Bottlenose, Pantropical Spotted, Spinner, Striped, Atlantic Spotted, Clymene, Fraser's, Pacific White-Sided, Atlantic White-Sided, White-Beaked, Northern Right Whale, Risso's, Melon-Headed Whale, Pygmy Killer Whale, False Killer Whale, Orca (Killer Whale), Long-Finned Pilot Whale, Short-Finned Pilot Whale

2. Hang this poster in front of the class. Each student makes his or her papier mâché.

Papier Mâché

1. Soak sheets of newspaper overnight.
2. Mix 2 tablespoons of flour with 2 to 3 tablespoons of cold water.
3. Mix together until the paste is smooth.
4. Ask your teacher to quickly pour in a little boiling water.
5. Stir until the paste is thick and shiny.

3. Blow up a long balloon. Each student refers to a picture of her or his animal to determine how long to make the balloon. The balloon must match the proportions of the animal. Some bodies are slender and long. Shorter, stouter bodies need less air in the balloon.

4. Dip the wet newspaper into the paste. Cover the balloon with the pasted newspaper (papier mâché).

5. Let the model dry overnight.

6. Cut out cardboard shapes of fins and tails. Tape the fins and tail to the body with masking tape.

7. Bend a paper clip so one hook lies perpendicular to the other. Tape one hook to the top of the body while the other hook points up.

8. Cover the model with paper mâché. Leave exposed the paper clip hook that points up. Let the model dry overnight.

9. Paint the entire body with gesso. Let the model dry overnight.

10. Following the photographs in the reference book, paint the markings of the dolphin or porpoise onto the model. Let the model dry overnight.

11. Tie a string to the hook and hang the model from the ceiling.

DAY TWO

Objective: The students will read a story about a trained dolphin. They will discuss how dolphins learn tricks.

Curriculum subject: Reading or Language Arts

1. Read the story *A Dolphin Goes to School: The Story of Squirt, a Trained Dolphin,* by Elizabeth Simpson Smith to the class.

2. Discuss how Squirt learned tricks. Why do you think Squirt learned these tricks? Can dolphins learn to do other things?

3. Read *Riding With the Dolphins: The Equinox Guide to Dolphins and Porpoises* by Erich Hoyt, pp. 52–53. The author tells stories about "friendly dolphins." Can you think of other ways dolphins might work with people?

DAY THREE

Story Lesson

Follow the *Presenting the Story Lesson* instructions in the Introduction. Each story lesson follows the same procedure; however, say the following in step 4:

"The title of the story we're reading today is *Teamwork.* What do you think the story is about?" If the students mention dolphins, ask: "What do you already know about dolphins?"

EXTENSION ACTIVITIES

1. The students write a fictional story about training a dolphin.

◆ Teacher:

This week we have learned about dolphins and porpoises. We saw how dolphins work with people, and how dolphins learn to do tricks. If you could train a dolphin, what would you teach it to do? How would you teach the dolphin to do it?

Draw a picture of what you would train your dolphin to do. Write a story telling about your dolphin. Explain why and how you trained your dolphin.

2. As a class project, write to the Center for Marine Conservation for more information about dolphins and porpoises.

◆ Center for Marine Conservation
P.O. Box 96003
Washington, DC 20077-7172

TEAMWORK

Fish are an important part of our diet. You have seen people fishing with nets and poles. Have you ever seen people fish with dolphins?

There is a tribe of people who fish with dolphins. When the time is right, the men stand on the shore. They beat the ocean water with heavy sticks.

Far off shore, the dolphins hear the beating sticks, and answer the call. Like swimming cowboys, the dolphins round up schools of fish. The dolphins herd the fish toward the beating sound.

From the shore, the men see hundreds of fish coming toward them. They quickly run out in the water with their nets. The dolphins drive the fish into the nets. When the fishing is over, the tribe has fish to last for months. What do the dolphins get for their work? They get an easy meal of their favorite food, fish.

QUESTIONS FOR TEAMWORK

1. What does the tribe in the story fish with?

   _____

   _____

2. How do the men of the tribe call the dolphins?

   _____

   _____

3. What do the dolphins do when they hear the call?

   _____

   _____

4. What do the dolphins get for their work?

   _____

   _____

5. What is the first thing the men do when they want the dolphins to bring the fish?

   _____

   _____

6. What do the men do after they see the fish coming toward them?

   _____

   _____

7. This story shows that dolphins are smart animals. What information in the story tells you that this is true?

   _____

   _____

8. When the fishing begins, why can't the fish get away?

   _____

   _____

9. Do you think the teamwork between the dolphins and the tribe will continue? Why do you think so?

_____

_____

10. Why do you think the dolphins help the men of the tribe?

_____

_____

11. Write a title that tells about the story. Use as few words as possible.

_____

_____

12. Compare fishing with nets and dolphins to fishing with fishing poles. How are the two alike? How are they different?

_____

_____

13. In your own words, tell how the tribe and the dolphins work together to catch fish.

_____

_____

14. Imagine a day when the dolphins no longer live near the shore where the tribe lives. How will the tribe's way of fishing change?

_____

_____

15. The story says, "There is a tribe of people who fish with dolphins." Is this a fact or an opinion? How can you prove your answer?

_____

_____

16.

_____

_____

Name _____   Date _____

JACKIE TORRENCE

ABOUT THE STORY

This story tells about the life of Jackie Torrence. Jackie had a speech impediment as a child. She grew up to become a popular storyteller.

PREVIEW WORDS

Jackie Torrence	overweight	grandmother
great-grandparents	national treasure	slaves
Mrs. Lancaster		

BOOKS TO READ

Storytelling: Art and Technique, Augusta Baker and Ellin Greene (Bowker, 1977).

Crazy Gibberish and Other Story Hour Stretches (From a Storyteller's Bag of Tricks), Naomi Baltuck (Linnet Books, 1993).

Spinning Stories: An Introduction to Storytelling Skills, Vicky L. Crosson and Jay C. Stailey (Texas State Library, 1988).

Every Child a Storyteller: A Handbook of Ideas, Harriet R. Kinghorn and Mary Helen Pelton (Teacher Ideas Press, 1991).

I Dream a World: Portraits of Black Women Who Changed America, Brian Lanker (Stewart, Tabori & Chang, 1989).

Storytelling Folklore Sourcebook, Norma J. Livo and Sandra A. Rietz (Libraries Unlimited, 1991).

Look Back and See: Twenty Lively Tales for Gentle Tellers, Margaret Read MacDonald (H.W. Wilson Co., 1991).

The Storyteller's Start-Up Book: Finding, Learning, Performing, and Using Folktales Including Twelve Tellable Tales, Margaret Read MacDonald (August House, 1993).

Best-Loved Stories Told at the National Storytelling Festival: 20th Anniversary Edition, selected by the National Association for the Preservation and Perpetuation of Storytelling (National Storytelling Press, 1991).

More Best-Loved Stories Told at the National Storytelling Festival: 20th Anniversary Edition, selected by the National Association for the Preservation and Perpetuation of Storytelling (National Storytelling Press, 1991).

The Story Vine: A Source Book of Unusual and Easy-to-Tell Stories From Around the World, Anne Pellowski (Macmillan, 1984).

Multicultural Folktales: Stories to Tell Young Children, Judy Sierra and Robert Kaminski (Oryx Press, 1991).

Storytelling Made Easy With Puppets, Jan M. Van Schuyver (Oryx Press, 1993).

African-American Folktales for Young Readers: Including Favorite Stories From African and African-American Storytellers, collected and edited by Richard and Judy Dockrey Young (August House, 1993).

VIDEO

Stories at Sundown: An Evening of Storytelling in Sante Fe, Joe Hayes at the Wheelwright Museum, Trails West Publishing, 1988 (P.O. Box 8619, Santa Fe, NM 87504-8619). Length: 45 minutes.

CDS, RECORDS, AND CASSETTES

Graveyard Tales (cassette), National Association for the Preservation and Perpetuatin of Storytelling, 1984. Includes *The Monkey's Paw* told by Jackie Torrence.

Homespun Tales: A Country-Flavor Collection (cassette), National Association for the Preservation and Perpetuation of Storytelling, 1986. Includes *Wiley and the Hairy Man* told by Jackie Torrence.

Tales for Scary Times (record), Jackie Torrence (Earwig Music Co., 1985).

Tales of Fools and Wise Folk (cassette), National Association for the Preservation and Perpetuation of Storytelling, 1991. Includes *Jack and the Northwest Wind* told by Jackie Torrence.

INTRODUCTORY ACTIVITIES

DAY ONE

Objective: The students will listen to a story told by Jackie Torrence. They will describe what makes Jackie Torrence a good storyteller.
Curriculum subject: Reading or Language Arts

Before beginning this week's lessons, talk to other teachers at the school. Explain that you will have a Storytelling Festival on Friday (Extension Activity 3). Arrange a time when you can send students to their classes to tell stories.

Teacher: Today we will listen to a story told by Jackie Torrence. Jackie Torrence is a popular storyteller. After the story, we will talk about what Jackie Torrence does that makes her a good storyteller.

Listen to the story "Wiley and the Hairy Man," told by Jackie Torrence. The story is recorded on *Homespun Tales: A Country-Flavor Collection* from the series *A Festival of Stories.* For more information about Jackie Torrence, other storytellers and storytelling, call the association at 1-800-525-4514, Monday through Friday, 9 A.M. until 5 P.M. ET.

After listening to the story, write "Reasons Why Jackie Torrence Is a Good Storyteller" on the board.

Teacher: Let's list five reasons why Jackie Torrence is a good storyteller. (Ask students to give their input.) How could listening to Jackie Torrence tell a story help you to become a storyteller? During the week, we'll learn more about storytelling. On Friday, we'll have our own Storytelling Festival. Working in groups, you'll go to other classes and tell stories you have practiced.

DAY TWO

Story Lesson

Follow the *Presenting the Story Lesson* instructions in the Introduction. Each story lesson follows the same procedure; however, say the following in step 4:

"The title of the story we're reading today is *Jackie Torrence*. What do you think the story is about? What do you already know about Jackie Torrence?"

*The class will listen to the story *Elvira and Henry* as told by Jackie Torrence on *Tales for Scary Times*.

EXTENSION ACTIVITIES

1. Listen to the story "Jack and the Northwest Wind," as told by Jackie Torrence. The story is recorded on *Tales of Fools and Wise Folk*. Display books about storytelling (see *Books to Read* list).

◆ Teacher:

Friday we'll have a Storytelling Festival. You'll go as a group to other classes and tell stories. You've listened to stories told by Jackie Torrence. She's a good example of tone of voice. Notice how she changes her voice for different characters. She slows down when she wants to add suspense. She speeds up when she wants to show excitement. Sometimes she stops and makes you hold your breath, wondering what will come next.

The book *The Story Vine: A Source Book of Unusual and Easy-to-Tell Stories From Around the World,* by Anne Pellowski teaches you more ways to tell a story. You can use string stories, picture-drawing stories, stories with dolls, finger-play stories, riddling, or stories using musical instruments.

You can use this book and other references to get ideas about a story you want to tell. If you need to, you can go to the library and look at picture books. They are good sources for good, short stories.

Today you must choose a story and start practicing. We'll practice again tomorrow.

2. The class will listen to the stories "Lydia" and "Shoes" as told by Jackie Torrence on *Tales for Scary Times*. The students continue to practice in their groups on the stories they chose yesterday.

3. The class will listen to the story "The Golden Arm" as told by Jackie Torrence on *Tales for Scary Times*. Review what makes Jackie Torrence a good storyteller.

The students must rehearse their stories in front of their own class before going to other classes.

Send the groups to other classes to share their stories. When they return, discuss the experience.

Did the children like their stories?

Did they enjoy telling their stories?

What went well?

What didn't go well?

Would they like to have another Storytelling Festival?

Why would, or wouldn't, they?

JACKIE TORRENCE

When Jackie Torrence was a little girl, the children laughed at her. Her teeth did not grow and she could not talk. Jackie was also overweight.

Jackie's happiest times were with her grandmother. Jackie sat in her grandmother's arms and talked. She learned about her African family. She learned about her great-grandparents who lived as slaves. Jackie came from a proud past.

When Jackie was fourteen years old, a teacher named Mrs. Lancaster saw something special in Jackie. Mrs. Lancaster taught Jackie to talk. Day and night they practiced. Mrs. Lancaster said, "In Jackie I found an eagle among my chickens."

When Jackie was older, she worked in a library. One day her boss asked her to tell the children a story. Could she do it?

The children loved Jackie's story. Soon other people heard about the Story Lady. They wanted to hear her stories, too.

Jackie tells stories all over America and around the world. Mrs. Lancaster's eagle grew up to become a national treasure.

QUESTIONS FOR JACKIE TORRENCE

1. When did Jackie have her happiest times as a child?

   _____

   _____

2. What did Jackie learn from her grandmother?

   _____

   _____

3. What did Mrs. Lancaster say about Jackie?

   _____

   _____

4. When Jackie was older, where did she work?

   _____

   _____

5. Who talked to Jackie before she met Mrs. Lancaster?

   _____

   _____

6. What happened after other people heard about the Story Lady?

   _____

   _____

7. What did Mrs. Lancaster mean when she said, "In Jackie I found an eagle among my chickens?"

   _____

   _____

8. Did Mrs. Lancaster teach Jackie to speak well? Why do you think so?

   _____

   _____

9. Think about children who are laughed at in your neighborhood or school. Could they grow up to do great things like Jackie Torrence? Why do you think so?

_____

_____

10. Why did the children laugh at Jackie when she was a little girl?

_____

_____

11. Write a title that tells about the story. Use as few words as possible.

_____

_____

12. How did children feel about Jackie when she was a little girl? How do children feel about Jackie today? Why do you think they treat her differently now?

_____

_____

13. In your own words, tell how Jackie Torrence became a storyteller.

_____

_____

14. How did Jackie's grandmother and Mrs. Lancaster help Jackie to become a storyteller?

_____

_____

15. Mrs. Lancaster said, "In Jackie I found an eagle among my chickens." Is this a fact or Mrs. Lancaster's opinion? Why do you think so?

_____

_____

16.

_____

_____

Name _____   Date _____

READING LEVEL 2
BIBLIOGRAPHY

"Albinism," *The Audubon Nature Encyclopedia* (1973), 1, 23–26, 76–79.

"Automobiles," *Our Wonderful World: An Encyclopedic Anthology for the Entire Family* (1962), 6, 73.

Bisignani, J.D., *Japan Handbook* (2nd ed.), pp. 66, 77. Chico, California: Moon Publications, 1983.

Cousteau, Jacques-Yves and Philippe Diolé, *Dolphins,* The Undersea Discoveries of Jacques-Yves Cousteau, pp. 203–220. Garden City, NY: Doubleday & Company, 1975.

d'Agapeyeff, Alexander, "Code Sounds and Signs," *Our Wonderful World: An Encyclopedic Anthology for the Entire Family* (1962), 1, 209.

De Gregorio, George, "Track and Field," *The Americana Annual: 1994,* p. 511.

Garvey, Megan, "Seeking Miracle, the Great White Hope," *Fort Worth Star-Telegram,* Sept. 25, 1994, p. 7AA.

Lanker, Brian, *I Dream a World: Portraits of Black Women Who Changed America,* pp. 124–125. New York, NY: Stewart, Tabori & Chang, 1989.

Mead, Chris, *Bird Migration,* pp. 128–129. New York: Facts on File Publications, 1983.

"A Novel Bird Cage," *Nature/Science Annual* (1978), Alexandria, VA: Time/Life Books, pp. 54–55.

Quackenbush, Robert, *Who Said There's No Man on the Moon?: A Story of Jules Verne.* New York, NY: Prentice Hall, 1985.

Robinson, Leif J., "The Hubble Space Telescope," *The Americana Annual* (1991), 130–131. Canada: Grolier Enterprises, Inc., 1991.

Simon, Seymour, *Our Solar System.* New York, NY: Morrow Junior Books, 1992.

Tesar, Jenny, "Ever-Broadening Applications," *The Americana Annual: 1992,* p. 198.

Tessendorf, K.C., *Look Out! Here Comes the Stanley Steamer.* New York, NY: Atheneum, 1984.

"Two Strikes Against Them," *Our Wonderful World: An Encyclopedic Anthology for the Entire Family* (1962), 7, 156–157.

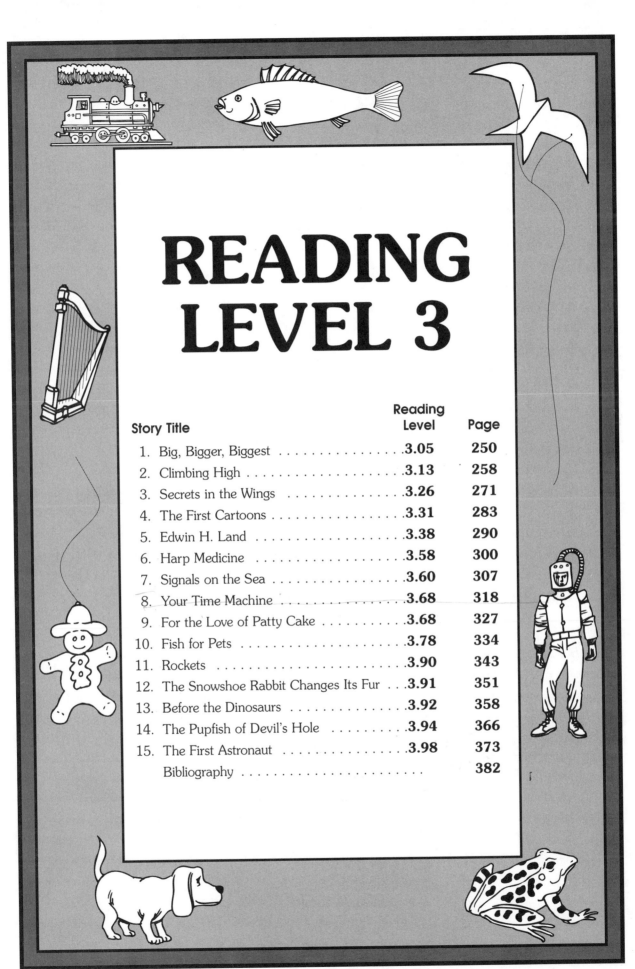

READING LEVEL 3

BIG, BIGGER, BIGGEST

ABOUT THE STORY

This story tells about whales. It describes the size of killer whales, humpback whales, and blue whales.

> *Play the cassette *Sounds and Songs of the Humpback Whales* (Special Music Co., 1989) as the students enter and leave the classroom, and as they do their work.

PREVIEW WORDS

elephant	whales	Earth
Shamu	killer whale	humpback whale
blue whale		

BOOKS TO READ

Whale, Judy Allen (Candlewick Press, 1993).

Orca Song, Michael C. Armour (Soundprints, 1994).

The Fish That Wasn't, Paul Borovsky (Hyperion Books for Children, 1994).

Baby Whales Drink Milk, Barbara Juster Esbensen (HarperCollins, 1994).

Arctic Whales and Whaling, Bobbie Kalman and Ken Faris (Crabtree Publishing, 1994).

World Water Watch, Michelle Koch (Greenwillow Books, 1993).

Waiting for the Whales, Sheryl McFarlane (Philomel Books, 1993).

Songs in the Silence, Catherine Frey Murphy (Macmillan, 1994).

Killer Whales, Dorothy Hinshaw Patent (Holiday House, 1993).

Whales, Nomads of the Sea, Helen Roney Sattler (Lothrop, Lee & Shepard Books, 1987).

VIDEOS

Deep Sea Dive (Columbia Tristar Home Video, 1994). Length: 30 minutes.

Gift of the Whales (Miramar, 1989). Length: 30 minutes.

Orca Whales and Mermaid Tales (Discovery Program Enterprises, 1993). Length: 25 minutes.

Spouts Ahoy! (Marty Stouffer Productions, 1992). Length: 30 minutes.

CDS, RECORDS, AND CASSETTES

Grandpa Art Sings About Sea Creatures (cassette), Arthur Custer (Sun Group, 1993).

Sing a Whale Song (cassette), Tom Chapin and John Forster (Random House, 1993).

Baleena the Blue Whale: Adventures of Wild Animals (cassette and book set), story adaptation by Robert H. Hunt (Society for Visual Education, Inc., 1978).

Sounds and Songs of the Humpback Whales (cassette) Special Music Co., 1989.

INTRODUCTORY ACTIVITIES

DAY ONE

Objective: The students will make a scale drawing of a whale.
Curriculum subject: Science

Watch the film *Spouts Ahoy!* before the lesson.

Growing Up Wild: Spouts Ahoy!, Time-Life Video, 1992. Length: 30 minutes.

(Before beginning this activity, find a large area such as a blacktop. The blacktop must be at least 100 feet long.)

Break the class into four groups. Assign one of the following whales to each group: blue whale, killer whale, humpback whale, sperm whale. Take the students to the library. Each group will find information about their whale. They will make a drawing of the whale and write down its measurements. How long is its body? How tall is it from belly to back? How long and wide is its tail? How long are its fins? Return to class, where the students will write a short description of their whale.

Whale Drawings
Materials

- plenty of sidewalk chalk for all four groups
- tape measures
- measurements and pictures of the assigned whales
- written descriptions of the whales

Procedures

1. Take the students to the blacktop. They need their descriptions, pictures, and measurements of their assigned whales.
2. Using tape measures and sidewalk chalk, the students draw life-size pictures of the whales on the blacktop.
3. When the students finish drawing the pictures, they will read their descriptions of the whales to the class as they stand next to their drawings.

DAY TWO

Before the story lesson, play the cassette and book set *Baleena the Blue Whale.*
Story Lesson
Follow the *Presenting the Story Lesson* instructions in the Introduction. Each story lesson follows the same procedure; however, say the following in step 4:

"The title of the story we're reading today is *Big, Bigger, Biggest.* What do you think the story is about?" If the students say whales, ask, "What do you already know about whales?"

EXTENSION ACTIVITES

1. Read the story "The Gift of the Whale," from *Keepers of the Animals: Native American Stories and Wildlife Activities for Children* by Michael J. Caduto and Joseph Bruchac (Fulcrum Publishing, 1991), p. 205. Discuss the story. How did the Inupiaq people feel about the whales? Why did the Inupiaq people show respect to the Bowhead Whale? How did they show this respect? How did the Great Spirit feel about the Bowhead Whale? Why do you think so?

◆ Teacher:

What can you learn about hunting from the story "The Gift of the Whale"? If hunters kill many whales without respecting the animal, what might happen?

Write a folktale about whales. In your folktale, tell how this mammal, a type of animal that usually lives on the land, came to live in the water. Remember, this is a folktale. It does not need to include scientific fact.

2. The students will explore discoveries about prehistoric whales. They will look for ways whales evolved to become mammals that live in the oceans.

◆ Teacher:

How long do you think whales have lived on Earth? In 1991, scientists called paleontologists, people who study fossils, made an amazing discovery. These paleontologists worked in Egypt. They dug for fossils in the desert. In a rock they found a 40-million-year-old whale fossil. The whale had feet. Never before had scientists seen an ancient whale with back legs.

◆ Break into groups of three to four students. Discuss what this fossil means to the history of whale development. Why did the whale have legs? Where did it live? Why don't whales have legs now?

◆ When you finish your discussion, write a story telling about your ideas. Draw a picture of this ancient whale on large drawing paper.

◆ The students share their papers with the rest of the class. Display the pictures and stories on the walls of the classroom.

3. The students will research adaptations whales made when they became creatures of the sea. They will compare a whale to mammals living on land, and explain how the similarities point to a whale ancestor that lived on land.

◆ Teacher:

Yesterday we learned about an ancient whale that walked on legs. This whale lived on land. Over time it moved into the oceans where whales live now. Like people, dogs, elephants, and any animal that feeds its babies mother's milk, whales are mammals. Listen to how whales changed as they moved from the land to the oceans.

◆ Read *Whales, Nomads of the Sea* by Helen Roney Sattler pp. 15–16 to the class. Discuss the adaptation whales made when they became ocean dwellers.

◆ Teacher:

How are whales like mammals living on land? How are they different? Let's make a chart showing how whales and land mammals are alike and how they are different.

Whales	Land Mammals
SIMILARITIES	
Breathes through nostrils	Breathes through nostrils
Hip and leg bones	Hip and leg bones
Babies drink mother's milk	Babies drink mother's milk
Hair (bristles on head and chin)	Hair
DIFFERENCES	
Able to drink salt water	Cannot drink salt water
Nostrils on top of head	Nostrils on the face
Fins	Arms and legs

(List other attributes the students name.)

◆ Teacher:

Write a story comparing whales to mammals living on land. Tell how these animals are alike and how they are different. Explain how the similarities point to a whale ancestor that lived on land.

4. Listen to the book and cassette set *Sing a Whale Song* by Tom Chapin and John Forster.

BIG, BIGGER, BIGGEST

If you have seen an elephant, you know that elephants are very big. Elephants are the largest animals that live on land. Do you know what animal is bigger than an elephant? Yes, whales are the biggest animals living on Earth.

Shamu, the famous killer whale, is a big animal. Killer whales are 15 to 20 feet long. They make the people around them look small, but killer whales are small. Yes, they are among the smaller whales.

Humpback whales are bigger than killer whales. They grow to 35 to 50 feet. If six tall men swam in a close line, they might be as long as a humpback whale.

The biggest whale is the blue whale. Blue whales are about 100 feet long. They are the biggest animals on Earth. One blue whale is about as big as ten elephants.

People study whales. These people count whales, measure whales, and learn what whales eat and where whales live. Maybe some day you will study whales, too.

QUESTIONS FOR BIG, BIGGER, BIGGEST

1. What is the name of the famous killer whale?

   _____

   _____

2. How big are killer whales?

   _____

   _____

3. How big are humpback whales?

   _____

   _____

4. What is the name of the whale that grows to 100 feet?

   _____

   _____

5. What is the first whale named in the story?

   _____

   _____

6. What is the last whale named in the story?

   _____

   _____

7. Would you like to study whales? Why do you feel this way?

   _____

   _____

8. The story tells us that people study whales. What reason might people have for studying whales?

   _____

   _____

9. Humpback whales may become extinct. This means that there would be no humpback whales alive on Earth. How would studying these whales save them? Do you think people will save the humpback whales?

_____

_____

10. Why do you think whales grow to be so much bigger than any animal living on the land?

_____

_____

11. What would be a good name for this story? Use as few words as possible.

_____

_____

12. How are a blue whale and a killer whale alike? How are they different?

_____

_____

13. In your own words, tell what you learned about killer whales, humpback whales, and blue whales.

_____

_____

14. If people do not take care of the whales, many will die. If all the blue whales die, they will become extinct. What would happen if the blue whales became extinct? Do you think our world would change? If you said yes, how would it change? If you said no, why would it not change?

_____

_____

15. People do not know what lives in the deepest parts of the ocean. We do not have the special machines that could take us to the bottom of the sea.
    The story says, "Blue whales are the largest animals on Earth." Is this a fact or an opinion? Why do you think so?

_____

_____

16.

_____

_____

Name _____   Date _____

CLIMBING HIGH

ABOUT THE STORY

This story tells about Annie S. Peck. Annie climbed Mount Huascaran in Peru. She was the first person to climb such a high mountain in the Americas.

THE WEEK OF THE LESSON

Read chapters from *I'm Going to Be Famous,* by Tom Birdseye (New York: Holiday House, 1986) daily to the class. The story tells how Arlo Moore tries to break records he finds in *The Guinness Book of World Records.*

PREVIEW WORDS

Annie S. Peck	Mount Huascaran	college
Americas	Peru	Mount Madison

BOOKS TO READ

Record Breakers of Pro Sports, Nathan Aaseng (Lerner Publications Co., 1987).

I'm Going to Be Famous, Tom Birdseye (Holiday House, 1986).

Famous Firsts in Baseball, Joseph J. Cook (Putnam, 1971).

Olympic Games in Ancient Greece, Shirley Glubok and Alfred Tamarin (Harper & Row, 1976).

Famous Firsts of Black Americans, Sibyl Hancock (Pelican Publishing, 1983).

Record Breakers of the Air, Rupert Matthews (Troll Associates, 1990).

Record Breakers of the Land, Rupert Matthews (Troll Associates, 1990).

Record Breakers of the Sea, Rupert Matthews (Troll Associates, 1990).

The Glorious Flight: Across the Channel With Louis Blériot, Alice and Martin Provensen (Viking, 1983).

Amelia Earhart, Blythe Randolph (Franklin Watts, 1987).

VIDEO

Record Breakers of Sport, HBO Video, 1990. Length: 51 minutes.

INTRODUCTORY ACTIVITIES

DAY ONE

Objective: The students will learn about famous firsts in history.

Curriculum subject: History

Fabulous Famous Firsts: The Game
Materials

◆ copies of famous first questions and answers

◆ construction paper

◆ 10 feet of bulletin board paper

◆ glue sticks and markers

> **Note:** If you want to keep the game board and playing cards for several years, laminate them before the students play the game.

Procedure

1. Lay out the bulletin board paper. Using a marker, divide it into 10 one-foot sections. This makes a life-size game board. Mark the first square START, and the last square FINISH.

2. Glue famous first questions and answers pages to the front of construction paper, using glue sticks. Cut them out along the dotted lines. These are the playing cards.

3. Divide the class into two teams. Assign one person from each team to stand on the word START.

4. Draw a card from the playing cards. Read the question to Team One. As a group they decide on an answer. If they are right, their team member moves forward one square on the game board. Pull the next card for Team Two.

5. If Team One answers incorrectly, Team Two tries to answer the question. If Team Two gives the correct answer, their team member moves forward one square. No player ever moves backward.

6. If both teams are incorrect, read the answer. Pull another card from the deck, and continue the game, returning to Team One for the answer.

7. Continue until the winning team reaches FINISH.

DAY TWO

Story Lesson

Follow the *Presenting the Story Lesson* instructions in the Introduction. Each story lesson follows the same procedure; however, say the following in step 4:

"The title of the story we're reading today is *Climbing High*. What do you think this story is about?"

In 1896, Georges Méliès' movie
camera accidentally jammed.
When he later looked at the
film he saw a bus change into
a car. What was it?

————

The first movie special
effect.

On February 12, 1931,
Pope Pius XI spoke to the
world. What was it?

————

The first radio address
from a pope.

Funnies on Parade was
published in 1933.
What was it?

————

The first comic book.

On April 30, 1939,
President Roosevelt
opened the World's Fair.
What was it?

————

The first regular
television service in the
United States (NBC).

On July 20, 1969,
Neil Armstrong said, "That's one
small step for a man, one
giant leap for mankind."
What was it?

————

The first words spoken
on the moon.

On December 17, 1903,
Orville Wright traveled
120 feet in 12 seconds.
What was it?

————

The first airplane
flight.

On July 21, 1969, President Nixon talked to Neil Armstrong 240,000 miles away.
What was it?
————

The first phone call to the moon.

On March 10, 1876, Alexander Graham Bell said, "Mr. Watson, come here, I want you."
What was it?
————

The first phone call.

On February 2, 1893, William Dickson filmed Fred Ott sneezing.
What was it?

————

The first filmed close-up.

On January 17, 1949, CBS aired the television show *The Goldbergs*. What was it?
————

The first TV situation comedy (sitcom).

On January 1, 1914, the Benoist Company began flights between Tampa, Florida, and St. Petersburg. What was it?
————

The first regular airline service.

In 1921, 16-year-old Margaret Gorman won an award.
What was it?
————

The first Miss America title.

On May 21, 1927, Charles
Lindbergh landed his plane,
Spirit of St. Louis, outside
Paris. What was it?

————

The first solo flight over the
Atlantic Ocean.

The Marble Dry Goods
opened in New York in
1848.
What was it?

————

The first department
store.

In 1889, Mrs. W.A. Cockran
made a machine to wash, rinse
and dry dishes.
What was it?

————

The first dishwasher.

A Table Alphabetical
was published in London
in 1604.
What was it?

————

The first dictionary.

In 1751, John Newbery
published *The Young Gentleman
and Lady's Golden Library.*
What was it?

————

The first children's magazine.

The 100-seat
Vitascope Hall
opened on June 26, 1896.
Tickets were 10 cents.
What was it?

————

The first movie theater.

On January 12, 1967, the Green
Bay Packers defeated the
Kansas City Chiefs, 35 to 10.
What was it?

———

The first Superbowl.

On May 5, 1961, Alan B.
Shepard, Jr., rode
114 miles in the air at
5,181 miles per hour.
What was it?

———

The first American to
travel into space.

In October, 1876, Boston
lawyer Gardiner Hubbard spoke
to Thomas Watson by phone for
over three hours.
What was it?

———

The first long-distance phone
call.

In 1889, Dr. Herman
Hollerith built this
machine to count the
American population
(census). What was it?

———

The first electronic
computer.

In 1948, movie-theater owners
Maurice and Richard McDonald
opened a self-service
restaurant. What was it?

———

The first McDonalds.

In 1955, 65-year-old
Harland Sanders
persuaded restaurant
owners to serve his
chicken. What was it?

———

The first Kentucky Fried
Chicken restaurant.

In 1769, Nicholas Joseph Cugnot rode 2 miles per hour in a steam-driven car. What was it?

———

The first self-propelled car ride and the first auto accident. Cugnot hit a wall.

In 1924, two single-engine, open-cockpit planes flew 25,345 miles in 363 hours and 7 minutes. What was it?

———

The first flight around the world.

In 1849, Dr. Elizabeth Blackwell earned her medical degree. What was she?

———

The first American woman doctor.

In 776 B.C., athletes met for athletic competitions. What was it?

———

The first Olympics

In 1893, Whitcomb Judson demonstrated the slide fastener he called the "Clasp Locker or Unlocker of Shoes." What was it?

———

The first zipper.

In 1922, the movie *The Power of Love* opened in theaters. The audience wore special polarized glasses. What was it?

———

The first 3-D movie.

EXTENSION ACTIVITIES

1. In this activity, the students will research and write a book about famous firsts.

Famous First Books
Materials

◆ construction paper

◆ loose notebook paper

◆ plain white drawing paper

◆ stapler

◆ markers and crayons

Procedure

◆ Staple paper, starting with two pages of drawing paper, between two pages of construction paper. Alternate one page of notebook paper and one page of drawing paper. Continue until there are ten pages of notebook paper. End with a notebook paper page.

◆ The students choose the topic they want to write about. For example, famous firsts in football, famous firsts in space, famous firsts in women's sports, automobile famous firsts.

◆ On scratch paper, the students write about ten famous firsts under their topic. They must include the who, what, when, where, and why of the event. Provide research materials and trips to the library.

◆ On the first page of the books, the students write the names of their books (e.g., Famous Firsts in Space) and their names (by John Smith). Include the name of the school and the date.

◆ Open the books to the first notebook page. The students write the final draft of their first story. On the drawing paper page facing the story, the students draw a picture of the famous first.

◆ Continue writing about one famous first on each notebook paper page, while illustrating the event on the facing drawing paper page.

◆ Share and display the books.

2. The students write about a famous first each student would like to accomplish.

◆ Teacher:

We learned about many famous firsts this week. We saw how Annie S. Peck was the first person to climb the highest mountain in the Americas. We talked about famous firsts in space, inventions, and sports.

What famous first would you like to do? Maybe you want to be the first person to talk to aliens from another planet. Perhaps you want to be the first person to live in a house at the bottom of the ocean.

(Write on the board: What would you do? When would you do it? Where would you do it? Why would you do it?)

◆ Teacher:

Think about what you would like to do. Write a story about your dream. Remember to answer the questions on the board. (Discuss the questions.) When you finish, draw and color a picture of you doing your famous first.

(Mount each picture and story on a large piece of construction paper. Display them around the room.)

CLIMBING HIGH

Annie S. Peck was born in 1850. When Annie was a little girl, she enjoyed playing sports; however, her brothers didn't like to play with her.

"Girls can't play sports," they would say. "Go play with your dolls!"

Annie knew she was as good as the boys. She ran as fast. She learned as fast. Most of all, she climbed better than anyone she knew.

When Annie grew up, she found that people thought women were not as good as men. Annie decided to show the world what wonderful things women could do. First, she graduated from college. Very few women went to college then.

Next, Annie began to climb mountains. One day, Annie climbed Mount Huascaran in Peru. She was the first person to climb such a high mountain in the Americas. Peru later named part of the mountain after her.

Annie went on to climb many mountains. At the age of 82, Annie climbed Mount Madison. Annie Peck died in 1935.

QUESTIONS FOR CLIMBING HIGH

1. Who is the main character of the story?

_____

_____

2. In what year was Annie S. Peck born?

_____

_____

3. What did Annie's brothers tell her when she wanted to play sports with them?

_____

_____

4. What was the name of the mountain in Peru that Annie climbed?

_____

_____

5. What was the first thing Annie did to show what wonderful things women could do?

_____

_____

6. What did she do next?

_____

_____

7. What one word would best describe Annie Peck?

_____

_____

8. How did Annie Peck feel about herself?

_____

_____

9. Do you think women will continue to try to do as well as men in the future? Why do you think so?

_____

_____

10. What happened to Annie to make her want to do such amazing things?

_____

_____

11. Write a title for this story. Use as few words as possible.

_____

_____

12. Sally Ride was the first American woman to fly into space. She rode in the space shuttle. How are Sally Ride and Annie Peck alike? How are they different?

_____

_____

13. In your own words, tell about the special things Annie Peck did.

_____

_____

14. Annie Peck was the first person to climb Mount Huascaran. She climbed many other mountains, too. She continued to climb at the age of 82. How might men think differently about women when they hear what Annie did?

_____

_____

15. The story said, "Annie Peck was the first person to climb Mount Huascaran." Is this statement a fact or an opinion? How can you prove your answer?

_____

_____

16.

_____

_____

Name _____   Date _____

SECRETS IN THE WINGS

ABOUT THE STORY

In 1914, German spies sent secret information about France's military capabilities to the German government. Pictures drawn in sketches of butterfly wings mapped out France's forts, bridges, and roads.

PRIOR TO THE LESSON

Complete *Tramp's Code* (Story 8 of Reading Level 2, page 188) the week before this story. If the students have already read *Tramp's Code,* review the story and activities. Discuss how people send secret messages.

PREVIEW WORDS

Germany	closer	France
patterns	studied	bridges
butterflies		

BOOKS TO READ

Codes and Ciphers: Hundreds of Unusual and Secret Ways to Send Messages, Christina Ashton (Betterway Books, 1993).

Confederate Spy Stories, Katherine Little Bakeless (Lippincott, 1973).

The Three Investigators in the Mystery of the Trail of Terror, M.V. Carey (Random House, 1984).

The Sign Painter's Secret: The Story of a Revolutionary Girl, Dorothy and Thomas Hoobler (Silver Burdett Press, 1991).

Spies, Spies, Spies, Barbara Nolan (Franklin Watts, Inc., 1965).

Spy for the Confederacy: Rose O'Neal Greenhow, Jeanette Covert Nolan (Julian Messner, 1960).

Code Games, Norvin Pallas (Sterling Publishing, 1971).

Behind Rebel Lines: The Incredible Story of Emma Edmonds, Civil War Spy, Seymour Reit (Harcourt Brace Jovanovich, 1988).

Encyclopedia Brown and the Case of the Two Spies, Donald J. Sobol (Delacorte, 1994).

Encyclopedia Brown's Book of Wacky Spies, Donald J. Sobol (Morrow, 1984).

Spies, Hazel Songhurst (Random House, 1994).

Agent K-13: The Super Spy, Bob Teague (Doubleday & Co., 1974).

The Encyclopedia of Espionage: Codes and Ciphers, Peter Way (The Danbury Press, 1977).

INTRODUCTORY ACTIVITIES

DAY ONE

Objective: The students will look for hidden messages in a drawing. They will discuss how the artist incorporated the message into the picture. They will create pictures with hidden messages.

Curriculum subject: Language Arts or Art

Before beginning the lesson, enlarge Picture Ia or copy it onto a transparency. The picture contains a secret message that says, "You found me."

Teacher: As you learned in the story *Tramp's Code,* people use codes to send secret messages. During times of war, spies use secret codes to send messages to their government. They might tell how many people are in the enemy's army. Maybe they'd tell about a secret weapon.

One of the oldest ways to send secret messages is through pictures. These picture messages are part of a family of codes called *steganography.*

Look at this picture (Picture Ia). It looks like a simple child's drawing; however, there's a message hidden in it. Can you find it?

Key:

The letters YOU are in the flower on the hat.

The letters FOUND are on her face.

(F on right side of the head, O as the right ear, U as the mouth, N as the nose, and D as the left ear and hair.)

The letters ME are in the shoes (M on the right sock and E as the left shoe lace).

Answer: YOU FOUND ME.

Teacher: Can you make a picture with a secret message hidden inside? Draw a picture, then trade it with your neighbors. Can they decode your message?

DAY TWO

Story Lesson

Follow the *Presenting the Story Lesson* instructions in the Introduction. Each story lesson follows the same procedure; however, say the following in step 4:

"The title of the story we're reading today is *Secrets in the Wings.* What do you think the story is about?" If the students say secret messages in pictures, ask, "What do you already know about secret messages in pictures?"

EXTENSION ACTIVITIES

1. The students plot coordinates on a grid to decode secret messages. They will create their own graph messages for other students to solve.

Picture Ia

Graph Messages
Materials

◆ graph message example (copy onto a transparency for overhead projectors)

◆ graph paper

Graph Message

Plot the cordinates ($\rightarrow$, $\uparrow$):

○

(13,8), (5,3), (5,6), (20,2)

□

(13,6), (5,10)

△

(20,8), (15,5), (13,2), (15,1), (18,2), (18,5), (15,10), (23,9)

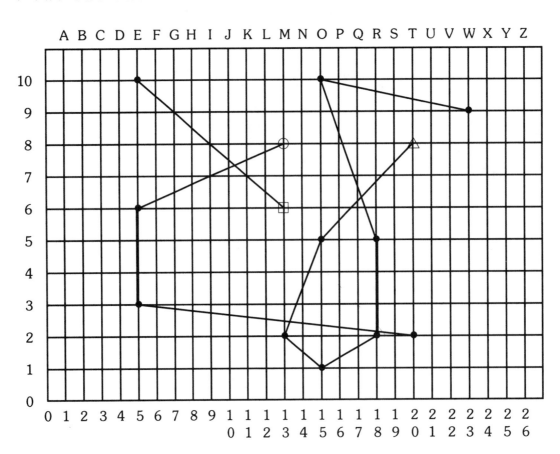

ANSWER:

_ _ _ _   _ _   _ _ _ _ _ _ _ _ .

Procedure

◆ Display the Graph Message example on the board.

◆ Each set of coordinates is one word. The first word is marked with a ○, the second with a □ and the last word with a △.

◆ Ask the students to read the first set of coordinates under the ○. Demonstrate how to find the coordinates by moving across the bottom of the graph 13 lines, and moving up the graph 8 lines. This is the first letter of the first word, so circle it. Repeat the procedure for every set of coordinates under the ○.Connect the dots after plotting each coordinate. Stop connecting the dots at the end of the word.

◆ Ask the students to read the first set of coordinates under the □. Demonstrate how to plot the coordinates. This is the first letter of the second word, so draw a square around it. Repeat the procedure for every set of coordinates under the □. Connect the dots after each coordinate is plotted. Stop connecting the dots at the end of the word.

◆ Follow the same procedure for the last word marked by the △.

◆ Find the plotted point at the beginning of the message. Follow the line up to the letter it represents. Write the letter in the first space under ANSWER. Continue filling in the letters until the message is complete ("Meet me tomorrow.")

◆ Hand out graph paper. The students write the numbers 0-26 on the bottom under each line. They write the numbers 0-10 up the side of the graph paper next to each line. Write the letters of the alphabet above each line along the top of the paper.

◆ Write the following on the board. The students will plot the coordinates and read the secret message. (Answer: Read this book.)

○
(18,9), (5,1), (1,7), (4,7)

□
(20,3), (8,9), (9,7), (19,5)

△
(2,1), (15,9), (15,2), (11,1).

ANSWER:
__ __ __ __   __ __ __ __   __ __ __ __.

◆ Each student will make his or her own graph message. They will share their messages with a neighbor, who will decode it. A message of three words works well for this type of code.

2. The students will make a paper chain that hides their names in Morse Code.

Morse Code Chain

◆ Teacher:

We talked about many types of secret codes this week. Spies might write their messages in pictures or secret writings. But how do they get their message to the people they want to talk to? One way to send the message is not to write it at all. If the spy could hide the message in clear sight where no one would suspect a secret code, he or she could smuggle out the message.

Some spies knitted secret codes into sweaters. If you knew the code, you could look at the pattern of the knit and read the message.

Today we're going to make a secret code chain. The chain will spell out your name in Morse Code. You can wear the chain as a necklace or belt. Maybe you could decorate your backpack. No one would know the code except someone in our class.

Materials

◆ precut colored paper. Before class, cut thin paper into 4" by 1½" rectangles of red, green, white, and yellow.
◆ one crayon of any color
◆ Morse Code chart

Procedure

◆ Display the Morse Code chart. Discuss how the dots and dashes represent letters and punctuation marks.

Morse Code Chart

A . __	F . . __ .	K __ . __	P . __ __ .	U . . __
B __ . . .	G __ __ .	L . __ . .	Q __ __ . __	V . . . __
C __ . __ .	H	M __ __	R . __ .	W . __ __
D __ . .	I . .	N __ .	S . . .	X __ . . __
E .	J . __ __ __	O __ __ __	T __	Y __ . __ __
				Z __ __ . .

PERIOD . __ . __ . __   COMMA __ __ . . __ __

◆ To make the secret code chain, you need four colors of paper. Red for the dashes, green for the dots, white for spaces between letters and yellow for spaces between words or names.
◆ Make the chains like gum wrapper chains. Follow the diagram on the next page.

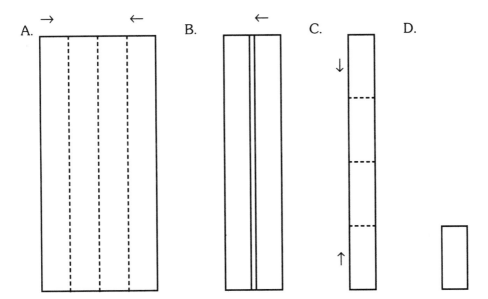

A. Fold the paper in fourths (at the dotted lines). Open the paper and lay it flat on the desk. Fold outside edges to center fold.

B. Fold right side over left so that the raw edges are inside the folds.

C. Fold the paper in fourths (at the dotted lines). Open the folds you just made. Fold the bottom section up and the top section down.

D. Fold the center fold down so that the raw edges are inside the folds.

◆ Write your name on a piece of paper.

◆ Using red for all the dashes, green for all the dots, white for spaces between the letters, and yellow for spaces between the words, begin folding the paper you need.

   Connect the links, or folded paper, of the chain. Slide the legs of the first link through the loops of the legs of the second link. Slide the second link down to the bottom of the first link's legs. The legs of the second link stick out.

◆ Slide the legs of the third link through the legs of the second. The legs of the third link stick out.

◆ Continue making the chain until your name is spelled out.

◆ Draw a dot on the front of the beginning of the chain so that the reader knows where to start.

   The ● tells the reader that this is the first letter. This chain sections spells __ ... or the letter B.

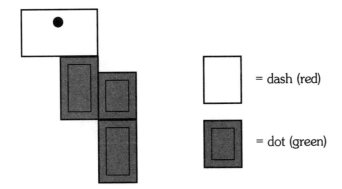

☐ = dash (red)

▨ = dot (green)

◆ Each student shows his or her chain to a neighbor. Can the neighbor read the chain?

3. Supply several books on secret codes (see *Books to Read* list). The students will make a secret message using a code from a book or from their imaginations. Share the secret messages. Can the students break someone else's secret code?

SECRETS IN THE WINGS

In 1914, Germany and France went to war. A few years before the war, the French army saw many Germans walking around France with butterfly nets.

The Germans said that they studied butterflies. They drew pictures of the wings of the butterflies. The Germans then sent the pictures back to Germany for closer study.

"Why are the Germans studying France's butterflies?" the French army asked.

The French took some of the pictures away from the Germans. The French army looked closely at each picture. There was something strange about the patterns on the wings. They were really tiny maps. The maps showed where to find France's forts, bridges, and roads. The maps even showed the number of France's guns.

QUESTIONS FOR SECRETS IN THE WINGS

1. What happened to France and Germany in 1914?

    _____

    _____

2. What were the Germans collecting?

    _____

    _____

3. Where did the Germans send their butterfly pictures?

    _____

    _____

4. What did the French army find on the pictures of butterfly wings?

    _____

    _____

5. Which happened first—the war between Germany and France, or the drawing of the butterfly wing maps?

    _____

    _____

6. What was the first thing the French army did to learn what the Germans were doing?

    _____

    _____

7. What one word would describe the Germans who invented the butterfly wing maps?

    _____

    _____

8. Why didn't the Germans make regular maps instead of hiding the maps in pictures of butterflies?

    _____

    _____

9. What might have happened if the French army had not discovered the butterfly wing maps?

_____

_____

10. Why did Germany want the butterfly wing maps?

_____

_____

11. Write a title for this story. Use as few words as possible.

_____

_____

12. Look at a picture of a butterfly wing. Look at a road map. How are the designs on butterfly wings like the designs on maps? How are they different?

_____

_____

13. In your own words, tell how the Germans secretly made maps of France.

_____

_____

14. At the time of the story, France thought Germany was a friendly nation. How did France's feelings about Germany change after they found the maps on butterfly wings?

_____

_____

15. The French army looked at the pictures of the butterfly wings. The story said, "There was something strange about the patterns on the wings. They were really tiny maps."
Is this a fact or an opinion? Why do you think so?

_____

_____

16. _____

_____

Name _____ Date _____

THE FIRST CARTOONS

ABOUT THE STORY

This story tells about the first animated cartoons, *Drama Among the Puppets* and *Gertie the Dinosaur.* The author describes the look and theme of these animated cartoons.

BEFORE THE LESSON WEEK

During this lesson week, the students make animated films. Look for teachers who will allow your class to show their film. If several teachers work on the same project this week, prepare an Animated Film Festival. At the Animated Film Festival, the various classes meet to share their films.

PREVIEW WORDS

cartoon	drawing	Émile Cohl
Winsor McCay	France	dinosaur
drama	Gertie	background
make-believe		

BOOKS TO READ

Make Your Own Animated Movies and Videotapes: Film and Video Techniques from the Yellow Ball Workshop, Yvonne Anderson (Little, Brown, 1991).

Making Pictures Move, Harry Helfman (William Morrow, 1969).

Animation: How to Draw Your Own Flipbooks and Other Fun Ways to Make Cartoons Move, Patrick Jenkins (Addison-Wesley, 1991).

Bill Peet: An Autobiography, Bill Peet (Houghton Mifflin, 1989).

The Animated Film, Ralph Stephenson (A.S. Barnes & Co., 1973).

Disney's Art of Animation: From Mickey Mouse to Beauty and the Beast, Bob Thomas (Hyperion, 1991).

VIDEOS

Computer Animation Festival, Vol. 2.0, BMG Video, 1994. Length: 58 minutes.

State of the Art of Computer Animation: A Spectacular Showcase of the Most Dramatic Synthetic Imagery Ever Created, Pacific Arts Video, 1988. Length: 75 minutes.

Raymond Briggs' The Snowman, Snowman Enterprises, Ltd., 1982. Length: 26 minutes.

INTRODUCTORY ACTIVITIES

DAY ONE

Objective: The students will watch an award-winning or award-nominated animated movie. They will discuss what made the movie worthy of an award or an award nomination. Finally, they will write a critique of the movie.

Curriculum subject: Language Arts or Art

Show an award-winning or award-nominated animated movie. An example of a quality movie is *Raymond Briggs' The Snowman*. Nominated for an Academy Award, *The Snowman* has no dialogue. The students can focus their attention on the animation.

Before the movie begins, tell the students the movie won or was nominated for an award.

Teacher: Before we watch this movie, let's think about what makes quality animation. As we watch this movie, what should we look for that will tell us that the animation is better than most?

After the movie, we'll discuss the animation. Be ready to tell me your opinion of the animation. The people who nominated this movie for an award thought it was very good. You might not agree. You'll discuss whether the animation was especially good, and why you feel the way you do. You might want to take notes as you watch.

Show the movie. After the movie is over, discuss the quality of the animation. Acting as critics, the students write a critique of the animation. They must explain why they feel the way they do about the movie.

Finally, set up two chairs in front of the class. Call on volunteers in pairs to read their critiques as if they were famous critics, like Siskel and Ebert.

DAY TWO

Story Lesson

Follow the *Presenting the Story Lesson* instructions in the Introduction. Each story lesson follows the same procedure; however, say the following in step 4:

"The title of the story we're reading today is *The First Cartoons*. What do you think the story is about? What do you already know about cartoons?"

EXTENSION ACTIVITIES

1. Before this activity, read *Make Your Own Animated Movies and Videotapes: Film and Video Techniques from the Yellow Ball Workshop* by Yvonne Andersen. Choose the technique your class will use for making an animated movie. Base your choice on the equipment and time available to you. The length of time to prepare the film depends on the technique you choose.

   Today the students prepare a story and storyboard. The storyboard helps the students plan what the movie will look like (see pp. 83–88 of *Make Your Own Animated Movies and Videotapes*).

   As a group, choose a story such as *Snow White,* or write a class story. Help the students prepare a storyboard based on their story. The students then choose the type of animation that would best tell their story: clay animation, flat animation, and so on.

   Throughout the week, the students continue making their animated movie. It might take several days to complete the film.

2. When the students finish their animated film, show the film to your class. The students practice presenting and showing the film. Next, your students show their film to another class. If several classes participate in this activity, bring the students together for an Animated Film Festival.

3. Show *State of the Art of Computer Animation: A Spectacular Showcase of the Most Dramatic Synthetic Imagery Ever Created.* This video contains a collection of short, computer-animated films. Several are monotonous for highly distractable students, and some of these films are not suitable for younger students. I recommend watching this film beforehand. Reset your video player's counter and note the number of the titles you want to show your class. When showing the film to the students, fast-forward the film to the counter numbers of the titles you want your students to see.

Some of the more engaging works are:

◆ *Stanley and Stella in Breaking the Ice*

◆ *Chromosaurus*

◆ *The Adventures of André & Wally B.*

◆ *Simulation Excellence*

◆ How computer animation created a commercial to promote the use of cans (no title)

◆ *L.A., The Movie,* a computer-mapped fly-over of Los Angeles

◆ *Peppy*

◆ *Boom, Boom, Boom*

◆ *Voyager 2 Encounters Neptune (August 24, 1988)* NASA

◆ *Speeder*

Discuss the films. Ask the students to imagine animated movies twenty years from now. What will they look like? How will these films be different from the animated films we see today?

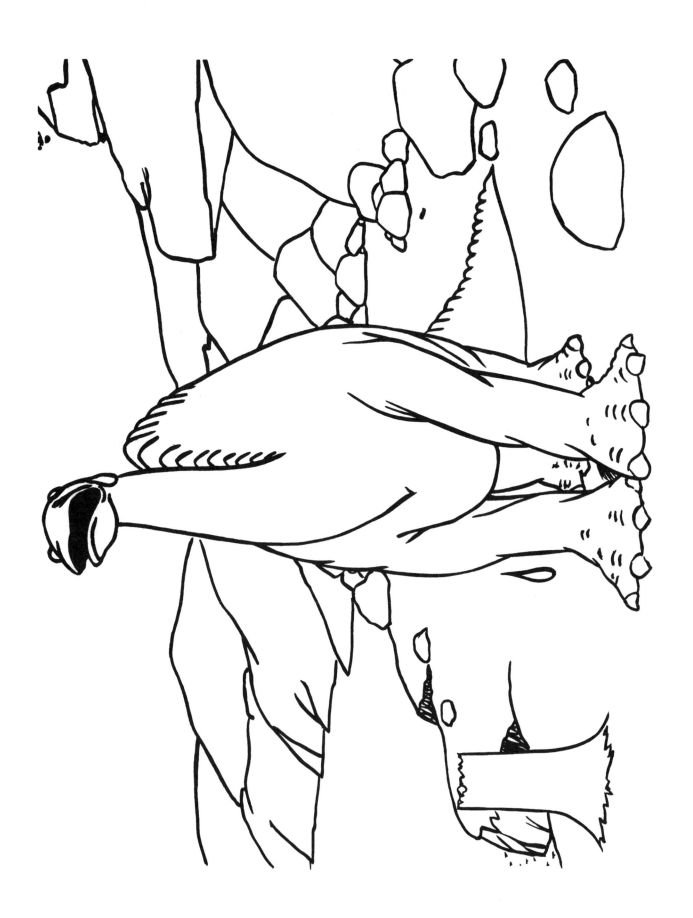

THE FIRST CARTOONS

Today we see cartoons about super people and talking animals. We never stop and think about the first cartoon.

Émile Cohl of France made the first cartoon in 1908. He called his five minute movie *Drama Among the Puppets.* The puppets looked like drawings made by little children. The lines were white on a black background. There was no sound to make the puppets talk. An American, Winsor McCay, made the second cartoon in 1909. The cartoon was *Gertie the Dinosaur.* Gertie was a simple drawing. In this cartoon, there were background pictures. Gertie walked in a make-believe dinosaur world. Still, there was no sound. Mr. McCay drew 10,000 pictures to make Gertie come to life.

Today you might run home from school to see cartoons. If you do, stop and think about Gertie. Maybe you will someday see the dinosaur who started it all.

QUESTIONS FOR THE FIRST CARTOONS

1. Who made the first cartoon?

   _____

   _____

2. In what year was the cartoon <u>Drama Among the Puppets</u> made?

   _____

   _____

3. In what year was the cartoon <u>Gertie the Dinosaur</u> made?

   _____

   _____

4. Who was the main character of the second cartoon?

   _____

   _____

5. In what country was the first cartoon made, France or America?

   _____

   _____

6. Which cartoon was made first, <u>Gertie the Dinosaur</u> or <u>Drama Among the Puppets</u>?

   _____

   _____

7. Do you think <u>Gertie the Dinosaur</u> was a better cartoon than <u>Drama Among the Puppets</u>? Why do you think so?

   _____

   _____

8. The story tells us that the drawings for the first cartoon were very simple. Why do you think Émile Cohl started with simple pictures?

   _____

   _____

9. The story tells us that the second cartoon improved the art of cartoon making. Do you think that the cartoons of tomorrow will be better than those of today? In what ways do you think they will be better?

_____

_____

10. Why do you think cartoon makers continue to try to improve their art?

_____

_____

11. Write a title for the story. Use as few words as possible.

_____

_____

12. How are the two cartoons, <u>Drama Among the Puppets</u> and <u>Gertie the Dinosaur,</u> alike? How are they different?

_____

_____

13. In your own words, tell what you learned about the cartoon <u>Drama Among the Puppets.</u>

_____

_____

14. When Cohl and McCay made the first cartoons, people did not know how to put sound into movies. How do you think cartoons changed when sound was added? Did this make the cartoons better? Why do you think so?

_____

_____

15. Which cartoon is better, <u>Drama Among the Puppets</u> or <u>Gertie the Dinosaur</u>? Is your answer a fact or an opinion? Why do you think so?

_____

_____

16.

_____

_____

Name _____   Date _____

EDWIN H. LAND

ABOUT THE STORY

This story tells about Edwin H. Land and his invention, "instant photography." Land invented 533 ways to use a camera.

PREVIEW WORDS

Edwin H. Land	Polaroid	invented
inventions	pilots	company
instant photography	created	

BOOKS TO READ

Herbert Binhs and the Flying Tricycle, Caroline Castle and Peter Weevers (Dial Books for Young Readers, 1987).

The Trouble With Dad, Babette Cole (Putnam, 1986).

Almost Famous, David Getz (Henry Holt, 1992).

Dr An Wang: Computer Pioneer, Jim Hargrove (Childrens Press, 1993).

Outward Dreams; Black Inventors and Their Inventions, James Haskins (Walker, 1991).

The Inventor Through History, Peter Lafferty and Julian Wheele (Thomson Learning, 1993).

Hello, Alexander Graham Bell Speaking, Cynthia Copeland Lewis (Dillon Press, 1991).

The Family Minus, Fernando Krahn (Parents' Magazine Press, 1977).

Animal Inventors, Thane Maynard (Franklin Watts, 1991).

Click! A Story About George Eastman, Barbara Mitchell (Carolrhoda Books, 1986).

Dear Dr. Bell—Your Friend, Helen Keller, Judith St. George (Putnam's Sons, 1992).

David Bushnell and His Turtle: The Story of America's First Submarine, June Swanson (Atheneum, 1991).

The Real McCoy: The Life of an African-American Inventor, Wendy Towle (Scholastic, 1992).

Brainstorm! The Stories of Twenty American Kid Inventors, Tom Tucker (Farrar, Straus and Giroux, 1995).

Mothers of Invention. From the Bra to the Bomb: Forgotten Women and Their Unforgettable Ideas (William Morrow, 1988).

VIDEO

Legacy of Genius: The Story of Thomas Alva Edison, PBS Video, 1979. Length: 59 minutes.

INTRODUCTORY ACTIVITIES

DAY ONE

Objective: The students will learn about inventors and their inventions. They will make a time line of inventions.

Curriculum subject: Science or History

Teacher: This week we'll learn about inventors and their inventions. Inventors are people who see a problem and invent something that solves the problem. Does anyone know the name of an inventor? What did he or she invent? What problem did the invention solve?

Today we're going to make a time line of inventors. A time line is a drawing that shows events that happened in history. These events are laid out in the order in which they happened. On our "Time Line of Inventors," we'll draw inventions in the order in which the inventors created them.

Time Line of Inventors
Materials

◆ white bulletin board paper, cut in half lengthwise

◆ pencils, crayons, markers

◆ glue and glue sticks

◆ construction paper scraps

◆ Odds and Ends Box—contains yarn, paper towel rolls, egg cartons, milk cartons, glitter, and so forth

Procedure

1. Write the following names and inventions on index cards. Make one card for each student. Randomly hand out one card to each student.

1. 250 B.C.
   Water-raising screw
   Archimedes
   Problem solved:

2. 1450
   Moveable letter
      printing
   Johann Gutenberg
   Problem solved:

3. 1590
   Compound microscope
   Zacharias Janssen
   Problem solved:

4. 1609
   Telescope
   Galileo Galilei
   Problem solved:

5. 1642
   Adding machine
   Blaise Pascal
   Problem solved:

6. 1714
   Typewriter
   Henry Mill
   Problem solved:

7. 1714
   Thermometer
   Gabriel Daniel Fahrenheit
   Problem solved:

8. 1776
   Submarine
   "Bushnell's Turtle"
      David Bushnell
   Problem solved:

9. 1780
   Bifocal lens
   Benjamin Franklin
   Problem solved:

11. 1800
    Electric battery
    Alessandro Volta
    Problem solved:

13. 1805
    Life preserver
    John Edwards
    Problem solved:

15. 1829
    Braille printing (1829)
    Louis Braille
    Problem solved:

17. 1844
    Usable rubber (1844)
    Charles Goodyear
    Problem solved:

19. 1853
    Condensed milk (1853)
    Gail Borden
    Problem solved:

21. 1872
    Lubricating cup or
       drip cup
    Elijah McCoy "The Real McCoy"
    Problem solved:

23. 1879
    Electric light bulb
    Thomas Alva Edison
    Problem solved:

25. 1923
    Automatic traffic signal
    Garrett Morgan
    Problem solved:

27. 1947
    Space helmet
    Alice Chatham
    Problem solved:

10. 1793–1794
    Cotton gin
    Eli Whitney
    Problem solved:

12. 1804–1805
    Preserved food
       tin cans
    Nicholas (François)
       Appert
    Problem solved:

14. 1824
    Steam locomotive
    George Stephenson
    Problem solved:

16. 1832
    Electric telegraph
    Samuel F.B. Morse
    Problem solved:

18. 1846
    Improved sewing
       machine
    Elias Howe
    Problem solved:

20. 1758
    Refrigerator
    William Cullen
    Problem solved:

22. 1876
    Telephone
    Alexander Graham
       Bell
    Problem solved:

24. 1869
    Paper-bag machine
    Margaret Knight
    Problem solved:

26. 1924
    Popsicle
    Frank W. Epperson
    Problem solved

28. 1953
    Automatic flight
       control
    Irmgard Flugge-Lotz
    Problem solved:

29. 1955
   Computer magnetic memory
     cores
   Dr. An Wang
   Problem solved:

30. 1986
   Voice-controlled
     wheelchair
   Martine Kempf
   Problem solved:

2. Cut a long piece of white bulletin board paper in half lengthwise. Tape the short ends together to make a long banner. It should be long enough to divide into 2-foot sections for each student in the class. A class of 15 students needs a 30-foot-long banner. Draw a line down every 2 feet of the banner to section off the students' work areas.

3. Assign each student a banner section according to the date of the invention on the student's card. For example, Archimedes' water-raising screw (250 B.C.) goes in the first section. Martine Kempf's voice-controlled wheelchair (1986) goes in the last section.

   *Plan the layout of each section to leave room for a one-page story about each inventor (DAY TWO).

4. Using black markers, the students write the date of the invention at the top of their section. Under the date they write the name of the invention and the inventor.

5. Next, they draw a picture of the invention. Yarns, glitter, paper towel rolls, and so on add decoration to the invention.

6. Finally, under the picture the students write "Problem solved:" with a short explanation of the problem solved by the invention.

DAY TWO

Objective: The students will write a short report about an inventor.
Curriculum subject: Language Arts, Science, or History

Review yesterday's assignment. Discuss the inventors and inventions the students drew on the banner. Notice how many of the inventors still have their names on the products they invented. For example, we still see volts on batteries (Volta), Goodyear on rubber tires, Bell for Bell Telephone, Fahrenheit on thermometers.

Today the students write about the inventor they drew on the banner. Help the students find and read the information they need to write their reports. The completed report must fit on only one side of one paper.

Special reference books about minority, child, and women inventors might be too difficult for some students to read. Research the inventors before class. Be prepared to offer the information to the students. Some reference books include:

Hargrove, Jim. *Dr. An Wang: Computer Pioneer.*

Haskins, Jim. *Outward Dreams: Black Inventors and Their Inventions.* (Elijah McCoy, Garrett Morgan)

Tucker, Tom. *Brainstorm! The Stories of Twenty American Kid Inventors.* (Frank W. Epperson)

Vare, Ethlie Ann and Greg Ptacek. *Mothers of Invention. From the Bra to the Bomb: Forgotten Women and Their Unforgettable Ideas.* (Margaret Knight, Alice Chatham, Martine Kempf, Irmgard Flugge-Lotz)

After the students finish the reports, share them with the class. Mount the papers on colorful construction paper with glue sticks. Glue the report in the appropriate section of the "Time Line of Inventors."

DAY THREE

Before reading the story, take photographs of the students next to their "Time Line of Inventors," using a Polaroid camera. Ask them why we call the photographs "instant photography."
Story Lesson
Follow the *Presenting the Story Lesson* instructions in the Introduction. Each story lesson follows the same procedure; however, say the following in step 4:

"The title of the story we're reading today is *Edwin H. Land.* What do you think the story is about?" If the students call Land an inventor, ask, "What do you already know about inventors?"

EXTENSION ACTIVITIES

1. Discuss how inventors create things to solve a problem. Walk through the "Time Line of Inventors," talking about the problems the inventions solved.

◆ Teacher:

Can any of you think of a problem you would like to solve with an invention? Maybe you're tired of making your bed or combing your hair. (Call on volunteers to name the problems they would like to solve with an invention.)

Today you're going to design a make-believe invention to solve a problem. Before you make your design, you must write a description of your invention. First, tell about the problem you have. Next, tell about your invention. How will your invention solve the problem? What special things does your invention do? Finally, you'll draw a picture of your invention. Be as creative as you can.

Tomorrow you'll build a model of your invention using papier mâché. Bring anything you might need to make your model. For example, you might use an empty bleach bottle, box, milk carton, or paper towel roll.

◆ Remind the students to bring what they need to make their models before they leave the class for the day. Soak newspaper for papier mâché overnight. Prepare the paste before the students arrive for class the next day. Keep the paste in an air-tight container.

Papier Mâché

1. Soak sheets of newspaper overnight.

2. Mix 2 tablespoons of flour with 2 to 3 tablespoons of cold water.

3. Mix together until the paste is smooth.

4. Ask your teacher to quickly pour in a little boiling water.

5. Stir until the paste is thick and shiny.

2. The students use the items they brought to class to create models of their inventions.

◆ Tape or glue together the parts to form the basic shape of the model.

◆ Dip the wet newspaper into the paste. Cover the model with the pasted newspaper.

◆ Let the model dry overnight or over the weekend.

◆ Paint the model.

◆ Share the models with the class. The students will read their descriptions of each invention to the class and tell about how it solves their problem.

EDWIN H. LAND

One day, Edwin H. Land took a picture of his three-year-old daughter. Then his daughter asked a question that would change his life.

"May I see my picture now?"

"No," explained her father. "First, I must take enough pictures to fill the roll of film. Next, I take the film to a man who makes pictures from the film. Finally, I will go back to the man days later to get your picture. You can see it when I bring it home."

"How long will that take?" she asked.

"I have no idea," said Land.

Land kept thinking about his daughter's question. In one hour he invented a way to take a picture and see it minutes later. He called it "instant photography."

In 1937, Land created his own company, Polaroid. Over the next 45 years, Land invented 533 ways to use a camera. Some of his inventions are glasses that let you see at night and cameras that let pilots take pictures high above the ground.

QUESTIONS FOR EDWIN H. LAND

1. What did Edwin H. Land call his new way of taking pictures?

   _____

   _____

2. What is the name of Edwin H. Land's company?

   _____

   _____

3. Name one of Edwin H. Land's inventions.

   _____

   _____

4. In what year did Edwin H. Land start his company, Polaroid?

   _____

   _____

5. What was the first thing Land had to do before his daughter could see her picture?

   _____

   _____

6. What was the last thing Land had to do before his daughter could see her picture?

   _____

   _____

7. What one word best describes Edwin H. Land?

   _____

   _____

8. How did Edwin H. Land's life change after his daughter asked to see her picture?

   _____

   _____

9. What type of camera invention do you think Polaroid should make next?

_____

_____

10. Edwin H. Land was an inventor. Would you like to be an inventor? Why do you feel this way?

_____

_____

11. Write a title for the story. Use as few words as possible.

_____

_____

12. A Polaroid camera sends out a photograph from the camera just after a picture is taken. If you use other cameras, you must take the film to a special place where someone turns the film into pictures. How is a Polaroid camera like other cameras? How is it different?

_____

_____

13. In your own words, tell what happened in Mr. Land's life that made him want to invent "instant photography."

_____

_____

14. How do you think Mr. Land's life changed after he invented "instant photography?"

_____

_____

15. The story tells us that Edwin H. Land was an inventor. Is this a fact or an opinion? Why do you think so?

_____

_____

16.

_____

_____

Name _____   Date _____

HARP MEDICINE

ABOUT THE STORY

This is an old story about a man healed by harp music. Today we know that following a doctor's directions and listening to music helps people heal faster.

PREVIEW WORDS

medicine	harp	heard
beautiful	morning	surprise
directions	listen	faster

THROUGHOUT THE WEEK—Decorate the classroom with pictures of instruments and musicians. Play harp music as the students enter and leave the classroom, and as they do their work (see *CDs, Records, and Cassettes* list).

Read each day from the Newbery Medal book *Adam of the Road* by Elizabeth Janet Gray. (New York: The Viking Press, 1960.)

BOOKS TO READ

Truthful Harp, Lloyd Alexander (Holt, Rinehart and Winston, 1967).

Music Crafts for Kids: The How-To Book of Music Discovery, Noel Fiarotta and Phyllis Fiarotta (Sterling Publishing, 1993).

American Indian Music and Musical Instruments With Instructions for Making Instruments, George S. Fichter (McKay, 1978).

Music, Carol Greene (Childrens Press, 1983).

Pages of Music, Tony Johnston (Putnam's Sons, 1988).

The Cat's Midsummer Jamboree, David Kherdian (Philomel Books, 1990).

The Ballad of the Harp-Weaver, Edna St. Vincent Millay (Philomel Books, 1991).

VIDEO

The Little Band. James Sage (American School Publishers: Macmillan/McGraw-Hill School Publishing Company, 1992.) Length: 7 minutes.

CDS, RECORDS, AND CASSETTES

Music Is a Miracle (book and cassette), Patrick Hyde (HarperCollins, 1994).

African Tribal Music and Dances (CD), Laserlight, 1993.

The Celtic Harp: Chieftains (CD), RCA Victor, 1993.

Patrick Ball: Celtic Harp, The Music of Turlough Carolan, (CD), Fortuna Records, 1982.

Patrick Ball: Celtic Harp, Volume II, From a Distant Time, (CD), Fortuna Records, 1982.

Patrick Ball: Celtic Harp, Volume III, Secret Isles, (CD), Fortuna Records, 1985.

Patrick Ball: Celtic Harp, fiona, (CD), Celestial Harmonies, 1993.

Patrick Ball: Celtic Harp, Volume IV, O'Carolan's Dream, (CD), Fortuna Records, 1989.

INTRODUCTORY ACTIVITIES

DAY ONE

Objective: The students will watch the film *The Little Band* and discuss how the music affected the villagers. The students will conduct an experiment on the effects of music on their peers.

Curriculum subject: Language Arts, Music or Science

Teacher: Today we will watch a movie called *The Little Band*. In the story, you will see a little band march through a village. How do the villagers change after the band marches by? Why do the villagers change?

Show the video *The Little Band,* based on the book by James Sage.

Teacher: What did the little band do? Did they say anything to the people in the village? Did the people change after the little band marched through the village? Why do you think so? Does music change the way people feel or act in real life? Let's do an experiment. I've invited three classes to come to our room and watch the video *The Little Band*. When the first class comes in we'll not play any music. The class will come in, sit down and watch the video. For the second class, we'll play exciting music while they come in and as they leave. The last class will hear soft harp music as they come in and leave. Watch how the classes act. Will the classes who hear music act different from the class that doesn't hear music? Will the class that hears exciting music act different from the class that hears soft music?

Conduct the experiment, watching each class carefully. Between classes, ask your students if they noticed differences in the way each class behaved. Why did the classes behave the way they did?

Throughout the week, play quiet harp music while your students enter and leave class, and as they work. At the end of the week, ask the students if they worked and felt better when the music was playing. Why do they feel this way?

Patrick Ball is a harper who plays the traditional wire-strung Celtic harp. He has several recordings of Irish music (see *CDs, Records, and Cassettes* list).

DAY TWO

Story Lesson

Follow the *Presenting the Story Lesson* instructions in the Introduction. Each story lesson follows the same procedure; however, say the following in step 4:

"The title of the story we're reading today is *Harp Medicine*. What do you think the story is about? What do you already know about the harp?"

EXTENSION ACTIVITIES

1. Invite a speaker who plays a folk instrument or studies folk music to come to class. Types of music might include African tribal music, Native American music, Irish music, American folk music, or Japanese music. Ask the speaker to discuss how folk music affects audiences. Does the music change the way people feel or act? Are there any stories about how music affects people?

◆ If possible, arrange a short concert of folk music. As the students listen to the music, they will draw pictures of how the music makes them feel. When folk musicians are not available, play recordings of folk music such as *African Tribal Music and Dances.*

2. Look at and discuss the pictures the students drew yesterday, showing how music makes them feel. How are the pictures alike? How are they different?

◆ Lay a large piece of bulletin board paper on the floor. The students will design a mural, based on the pictures they drew yesterday. Use bright colors and movement in the mural. Donate the mural to a local senior citizens home or other charity.

3. Teacher:

This week we learned how music affects people. How do people change when they hear music? Can you think of ways we can use music to make life better? (Some examples are playing music in hospitals, nursing homes, or the school cafeteria.)

Write a story about ways you might use music to make life better. As you write your story, answer the following questions: (Write the questions on the board.)

Who would benefit from listening to music?

What type of music would you play for them?

When would you play the music?

Where would you play the music?

Why do you think the music would help?

What do you predict will happen when the people hear the music?

◆ The students can work in groups to help students with learning disabilities gain confidence. Share the stories and display them in the classroom.

HARP MEDICINE

Harp playing is a very old art. Long ago, people said harp players could make the sick feel well again.

One story tells about a man who was very sick. This was long before doctors had good medicines. He was so sick no one thought he would get better.

A harp player heard about the man, and went to his house. All night, the harp player sat by the man's bed. The music he played was soft and beautiful. The music of the harp put the man into a deep sleep.

In the morning, the man's family came to his room. To their surprise, the man was much better.

"The music of the harp has saved me," the man said.

Today, we know that music does help people feel better. People who follow their doctor's directions, and listen to soft music, feel better faster.

QUESTIONS FOR HARP MEDICINE

1. Long ago, what did people say harp players could do?

   _____

   _____

2. What did the harp player do for the sick man?

   _____

   _____

3. What did the sick man do as he listened to the harp music?

   _____

   _____

4. How did the sick man feel in the morning?

   _____

   _____

5. What happened first in the story—the sick man felt better, or the harp player played music for the man?

   _____

   _____

6. What happened last in the story: The man said, "The music of the harp has saved me," or the harp player went to the sick man's house?

   _____

   _____

7. Why do you think the man felt better in the morning?

   _____

   _____

8. The story tells us that people who follow their doctor's directions, and listen to soft music, feel better faster. Why should people follow their doctor's directions first?

   _____

   _____

9. After reading this story, what could hospitals in the future do to help sick people feel better faster?

_____

_____

10. The harp player stayed with the man and played for him all night. Why do you think he did that?

_____

_____

11. Write a title for the story. Use as few words as possible.

_____

_____

12. Think about a time you did not feel well. Do you think you would have felt better listening to soft music, or listening to nothing at all? Why do you think so?

_____

_____

13. In your own words, tell how the harp player helped the sick man feel better.

_____

_____

14. Many restaurants, stores, and doctors' offices play soft music for their customers. They are trying to change the way people feel or act. After reading this story, how might soft music change the way people feel or act in a store?

_____

_____

15. The sick man in the story said, "The music of the harp has saved me." Is this a fact or his opinion? Why do you think so?

_____

_____

16.

_____

_____

Name _____   Date _____

SIGNALS ON THE SEA

ABOUT THE STORY

This story tells how ships use flags as signals. Sailors use these flags to write out messages to other ships.

PREVIEW WORDS

signals	captain	emergency
course	language	represent
triangle	warships	messages

THROUGHOUT THE WEEK—Obtain flags of various countries and hang them around the room. If possible, include ship flags, racing flags, old flag designs no longer in use, and so on.

BOOKS TO READ

Communication! News Travels Fast, Siegfried Aust (Lerner Publications, 1991).

Safety First! Bicycles, Eugene Baker (Creative Education, 1980).

Puff—Flash—Bang! A Book About Signals, Gail Gibbons (Morrow Junior Books, 1993).

Flag, Eyewitness Books, William Crampton (Alfred A. Knopf, 1989).

I Read Symbols, Tana Hoban (Greenwillow Books, 1983).

Flags, David Jefferis (Franklin Watts, 1985).

The Dog That Pitched a No-Hitter, Matt Christopher (Little, Brown, 1988).

The Dog That Called the Signals, Matt Christopher (Little, Brown, 1982).

The Dog That Stole Football Plays, Matt Christopher (Little, Brown, 1988).

Indian Signals and Sign Language, George Fronval (Bonanza Books, 1985).

You Can Sign: A Path to the Deaf Way, Bradley Wyant (Rushmore House Publishing, 1994).

Train Talk: An Illustrated Guide to Lights, Hand Signals, Whistles, and Other Languages of Railroading, Roger B. Yepsen (Pantheon Books, 1983).

INTRODUCTORY ACTIVITIES

DAY ONE

Objective: The students will discuss the parts of a flag and how flags are symbols of the countries they represent. They will learn about the meaning behind the flag of the United States.

Curriculum subject: History

> *Before this lesson, the teacher should refer to books about flags. *Flag* (Eyewitness Books), by William Crampton is an excellent reference.

(Display the United States flag. Draw the following diagram of a flag on the board or use an overhead projector.)

hoist →
rope

First quarter, or canton	Second quarter, or upper fly canton
Third quarter, or lower hoist canton	Fourth quarter, or lower fly canton

hoist rope → sleeve

Teacher: This week we'll learn about flags. Some flags are used as symbols for countries, states, and organizations. When people design a flag, they make it represent their ideas and goals.

Before we look at flag designs, let's look at the parts of a flag.

A flag is held on a pole by a hoist. The hoist attaches to the flag by sliding into the sleeve. The body of the flag is made up of four sections called cantons. The two cantons next to the hoist rope sleeve are called hoist cantons. However, the first quarter canton is usually called the canton. The two cantons on the outer edge of the flag are called fly cantons.

Look at the flag of the United States of America. Imagine dividing the flag into the four cantons. In which canton are the stars? (Answer: The stars are in the canton or first quarter.) Many flags have a badge or emblem in the canton or first quarter.

When the founders of the United States signed the Declaration of Independence, there were only thirteen colonies. The thirteen stripes represent these original thirteen colonies. What do you think the 50 stars in the canton represent? (Answer: The stars in the canton represent the 50 states of the Union.)

DAY TWO

Objective: The students will learn about the symbolism used on flags from other countries.

Curriculum subject: History or Language Arts

Teacher: Yesterday we talked about the flag of the United States of America. We saw how parts of the flag represented the 50 states and the thirteen original colonies. Today we'll look at flags from other countries. We'll learn how the flags tell us about the government and history of each country.

Break into groups. I'll assign a flag to each group. Using construction paper, make a model of your flag. When you finish, write a story telling which country the flag is from and what the design of the flag represents. Explain how the design tells about the country the flag represents.

[Write the following information on index cards, using one country on each card. Give one card to each group. See *Flag* by William Crampton (New York: Alfred A. Knopf, 1989.)]

◆ The United Kingdom:

1. The flag is called the Union Jack.

2. The white *x* on a blue background represent Scotland.

3. The Red cross or "plus sign" represents England. It is the English cross of St. George.

4. The red *x* represents Ireland. It is the cross of St. Patrick.

◆ Australia:

1. The canton is the United Kingdom's Union Jack. It tells that Australia is related to Britain.

2. The Commonwealth Star in the lower hoist canton stands for the joining of states or commonwealths under one government.

3. The Southern Cross on the fly cantons stands for Australia. The Southern Cross is a constellation that can be seen only in the Southern Hemisphere.

◆ Japan:

1. The flag is called the Sun-Disk Flag.

2. The white background stands for purity and integrity.

3. The red circle stands for sincerity, brightness, and warmth.

4. The entire flag is a symbol of the Japanese saying, "Akaki kiyoki tadashiki naoki makoto no kokoro," or "Bright, pure, just, and of gentle heart."

◆ China:

1. The red background stands for revolution.

2. The large yellow star in the canton stands for Communism (the type of government in China).

3. The four smaller stars stand for the four classes of the people: workers, peasants, middle class, and "patriotic capitalists."

◆ Greece:

1. The idea of the flag came from the flag of the United States.

2. The cross in the canton tells that the freedom movement began in religious groups.

3. The stripes represent the countries that were once joined with Greece in 1918, when the flag was designed.

◆ Portugal:

1. The red section stands for revolution.

2. The green section represents Prince Henry the Navigator.

3. The picture in the center shows the orbits of the planets. It is the emblem of Henry the Navigator.

4. The five blue shields in the emblem remember Alphonso Henriques. He set up Portugal as an independent kingdom.

After the students finish the flags and stories, they will share their flags and information with the class.

DAY THREE

Objective: The students will learn one way ships used flags to send messages before the invention of the radio. They will send messages using semaphore, or flag, signals.

Curriculum subject: Language Arts

Teacher: Yesterday we learned that flags can be symbols of countries. Flags tell us about the history, government, and people of the country. Did you know people also use flags to send messages?

Before radios, sailors often used semaphore or flag signals to send messages from ship to ship or from ship to shore. Today you will make flags and learn to use them to send messages.

(Using red and white construction paper, glue sticks, straws and tape, each student makes two flags as shown below. Tape the construction paper flag to the straw.)

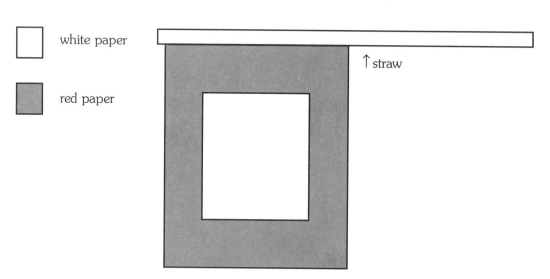

(Display diagram A from the "Semaphore or Flag Signals" page on the overhead projector.)

Semaphore or Flag Signals

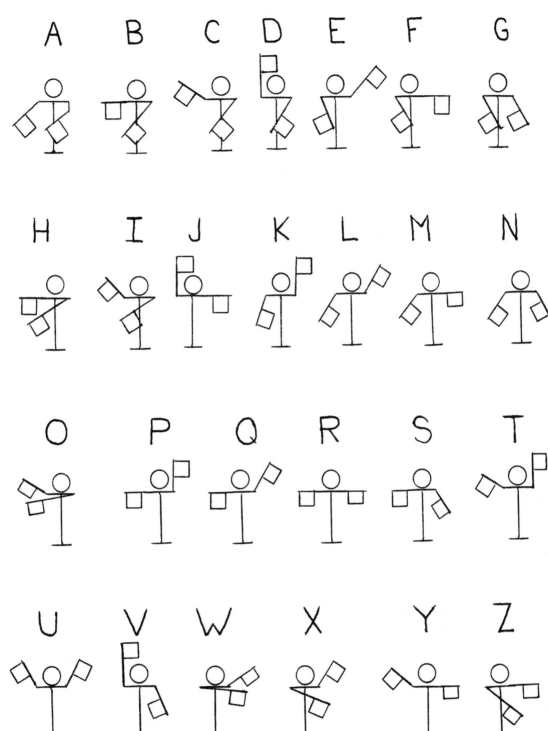

Teacher: When sailors held flags in certain positions, they made letters. Hold a flag in each
            of your hands and stand up. Look at the way the first man made the letter *A*. Using
            your flags, make the letter *A*.
            (Continue in this format throughout the alphabet.)
            Now, break into groups of four. Looking at the chart, take turns sending messages.
            See if the other people in your group can read your message. Make your message
            a short, four-word sentence.

DAY FOUR

Story Lesson

Follow the *Presenting the Story Lesson* instructions in the Introduction. Each story lesson follows the same procedure; however, say the following in step 4:

    "The title of the story we're reading today is *Signals on the Sea*. What do you think
the story is about?" If the students mention flags, ask, "What do you already know about flags?"

EXTENSION ACTIVITIES

1. Using the International Code of Signals, the students will make flags that spell out their
names.

Materials

◆ 4″ × 5″ index cards

◆ kite string

◆ hole punch

◆ crayons and markers

◆ chart of the International Code of Signals

Procedure

◆ Break the students into small groups.

◆ Distribute reference books about ships among the groups. The books must have a chart of
the International Code of Signals, which is a set of signaling flags. Most encyclopedias have
illustrations of the chart. Another source is *Ships: A History With Over 1,000 Illustrations,* by Enzo Angelucci and Attilio Cucari (New York: Greenwich House, 1975), pp.
162–163.

◆ Cut 4″ × 5″ index cards in half to make two 4″ × 2½″ flags.

◆ The students use the International Code of Signals to make flags that spell out their names.

◆ Punch a hole at the top right and bottom right corners of each flag.

◆ String the flags together, using kite string.

◆ Hang the strings of flags on a bulletin board entitled "The International Code."

2. The students will design a flag that represents their school.

◆ Teacher:

This week we learned how flags can represent ideas and send messages. Today we're going to design a flag to represent our school.

Break into groups and talk about how to design a flag to represent our school. What is the purpose of our school? What would we like people in and out of the school to think about us? What colors would best represent the school in our flag?

Draw out your designs. When you finish, we'll choose our favorite ideas and put them together into a flag design. Remember to keep the designs simple. A difficult design is sometimes impossible to sew.

Finally, the flag will be made and we'll give it to our principal with a letter telling about our flag. (Call fabric stores asking for donated materials. Ask a parent or volunteer to sew the flag. Make it large enough to fly on a flag pole.)

SIGNALS ON THE SEA

Your ship rocks softly on the calm ocean. Far off in the distance your captain sees another boat.

"Change course!" he cries. "There's an emergency on the boat ahead!"

How did your captain know the other boat was in trouble? He simply looked at the boat and knew they needed help.

Your captain saw a special flag. Ships talk to each other, using flags of all shapes and colors. Some flags stand for letters used by everyone no matter what language they speak. Other flags represent numbers. There are even flags that send special messages.

Your captain saw a triangle flag with red and white squares. It told the captain there was an emergency on board.

Some flags identify warships. In boat racing, flags tell everyone the number of minutes left before the race begins. The flags also tell what kinds of boats are in the race.

Make a set of signal flags. Can you send messages to your friend?

QUESTIONS FOR SIGNALS ON THE SEA

1. What did the captain see that told him there was an emergency on the other boat?

   _____

   _____

2. Name two things a ship's flag might stand for.

   _____

   _____

3. What does the emergency flag look like?

   _____

   _____

4. What do flags tell people in boat races?

   _____

   _____

5. What did your captain say after he saw another ship?

   _____

   _____

6. What do flags tell boat racers before the race begins?

   _____

   _____

7. Why do you think sailors made flag signals everyone could read?

   _____

   _____

8. Where are "you" when the story begins?

   _____

   _____

9. Do you think sailors will use signal flags in the future, or will some other technology take their place?

_____

_____

10. Why did the captain in the story change course?

_____

_____

11. Write a title for the story. Use as few words as possible.

_____

_____

12. Read the story "Tramp's Code" (Reading Level 2, p. 193). How are the flag signals and the tramp's code alike? How are they different?

_____

_____

13. In your own words, tell how sailors use signal flags.

_____

_____

14. Imagine that every country had its own flag code. The United States could not read Japan's signals. Germany could not read Mexico's signals. Would this be a better system or would it be worse? Why do you think so?

_____

_____

15. The story said, "Ships talk to each other using flags of all shapes and colors." Is this statement a fact or an opinion? How can you prove your answer?

_____

_____

16.

_____

_____

Name _____   Date _____

YOUR TIME MACHINE

ABOUT THE STORY

This story tells about the distance of stars from Earth in light years. It explains that the stars give off their light many years before we see it from Earth.

PREVIEW WORDS

Earth	Dallas, Texas	New York City
constellation	Vega	Lyra
Pollux	Rigel	Orion
Sirius	Regulus	Deneb

PRIOR TO THE LESSON

Before the lesson week, prepare for a trip to the planetarium. Emphasize information about light speed, and Earth's distance from the stars and planets in our solar system.

BOOKS TO READ

Space Station, Necia H. Apfel (Franklin Watts, 1987).

Fact or Fantasy?, Neil Ardley (Franklin Watts, 1982).

Out Into Space, Neil Ardley (Franklin Watts, 1981).

Colonizing the Planets and Stars, Isaac Asimov (Gareth Stevens, 1989).

How Did We Find Out About the Speed of Light?, Isaac Asimov (Walker, 1986).

Projects in Astronomy, Isaac Asimov (Gareth Stevens, 1990).

Space Travel, Jeanne Bendick (Franklin Watts, 1982).

The Magic School Bus: Lost in the Solar System, Joanna Cole (Scholastic, 1990).

Space Travel in Fact and Fiction, Keith Deutsch (Franklin Watts, 1980).

Astronomy, Dennis B. Fradin (Childrens Press, 1987).

Skylab, A New True Book, Dennis B. Fradin (Childrens Press, 1984).

Space, Tim Furniss (Franklin Watts, 1985).

Spacey Riddles, Katy Hall (Dial Books for Young Readers, 1991).

Space Exploration, Brian Jones (Gareth Stevens Children's Books, 1989).

Regards to the Man in the Moon, Ezra Jack Keats (Aladdin Books, 1987).

E.T.: The Extra-Terrestrial Storybook, William Kotzwinkle, based on a screenplay by Melissa Mathison (Berkley Books, 1982).

Space Science, Projects for Young Scientists, David W. McKay and Bruce G. Smith (Franklin Watts, 1986).

Space, Sticky Fingers, Ting and Neil Morris (Franklin Watts, 1994).

Build Your Own Space Station, Kate Petty. Consultant: Caroline Pitcher (Franklin Watts, 1985).

Stinker's Return, Pamela F. Service (Scribner's, 1993).

VIDEOS

Tell Me Why: Space, Earth and Atmosphere, Tell Me Why series, Prism, 1987. Length: 30 minutes.

Planets of the Sun, Diamond Entertainment Corporation, 1993. Length: 30 minutes.

CDS, RECORDS, AND CASSETTES

The Planets (op. 32) (CD), Gustav Holst (Telarc, 1986).

Adventures in the Solar System: Planetron and Me, Geoffrey T. Williams and Dennis F. Regan (Price Stern Sloan, 1986).

SOFTWARE

Scholastic's The Magic School Bus Explores the Solar System: An Interactive Science Adventure, Microsoft Home. Microsoft Corporation, 1994. Based on The Magic School Bus book series by Joanna Cole and Bruce Degen. Scholastic, 1994.

INTRODUCTORY ACTIVITIES

DAY ONE

Objective: The students will visit a planetarium.
Curriculum subject: Science

Before taking the students to the planetarium, talk to the person who will be your guide. Ask him or her to cover information about the distance of the stars from Earth in light years, what light speed is, and how far away the planets in our solar system are from Earth in light years. Tell the guide that the students will pretend to travel by spaceship to the planets in our solar system. Perhaps the guide can give information that would pertain to such a trip.

DAY TWO

Story Lesson
Follow the *Presenting the Story Lesson* instructions in the Introduction. Each story lesson follows the same procedure; however, say the following in step 4:

"The title of the story we're reading today is *Your Time Machine.* What do you think the story is about?"

EXTENSION ACTIVITIES

(Note: These activities should take more than one day to complete.)

◆ The students will prepare for an imaginary trip through our solar system. Preparations will include making the spaceship, conducting research about the planets, and preparing experiments to be conducted during the flight.

1. Art: Making the Spaceship

◆ Refer to *Space* (Sticky Fingers) for ideas on how to make space equipment out of things we usually throw away. Divide the students into groups to make each piece of equipment.

2. Art: Astronaut Backpack

◆ Instructions for an astronaut backpack are on pp. 10–11 in *Space*. If you cannot find a copy of *Space,* make an astronaut backpack by covering a large cereal box with colored paper. Following the design of the students' backpacks, make shoulder straps that wrap under the arms.

3. Art: Control Panel

◆ Space shuttle astronauts fly the shuttle using controls similar to those of an airplane. To create a control panel, bring a very large cardboard box such as a wardrobe to class. Cut off one side of the box and the flaps. The opened box becomes a three-sided panel. Glue and tape three smaller, table-high boxes to each side of the panel. The students use their imaginations to make what looks like the inside controls of the space shuttle. Chairs placed in front of the panels make the seats where the pilot and copilot sit. Space posters taped to the insides of the panels represent views from the windows. Photographs of the inside of the space shuttle might help the students in their design.

4. Science: Solar Map

◆ Using a large piece of black or deep-blue bulletin board paper, the students make a solar map. They will need drawings from reference books as guides. They must include the moons around the plants, and the asteroid belt. The students write the distance of the planets from Earth in light years on the bottom corner of the map as a legend. Supply the students with the following information on the distance of each planet from the sun.

Planet	Distance From Sun in Light Years to the Nearest Minute
Mercury	3 minutes
Venus	6 minutes
Earth	8 minutes
Mars	13 minutes
Jupiter	43 minutes
Saturn	1 hour 20 minutes
Uranus	2 hours 40 minutes
Neptune	4 hours 3 minutes
Pluto	5 hours 30 minutes

5. Language Arts: The Solar System

◆ Break the students into ten groups. Assign one planet to each of the first nine groups, and the asteroid belt to the tenth group. The students will prepare a presentation about their assigned topic. They can make models, use videos approved by the teacher, or use film strips or the overhead projector. Their presentation must tell about the unique qualities of the planet or asteroid belt. Where is it located? Can it support life? Can people live on the planet or asteroid in the future? If it has moons, what are their names? The students will give their presentation during the imaginary trip through the solar system. For example, when the ship stops at Venus, the Venus group will give its presentation.

6. Science: Space Experiments

◆ Break the students into teams. Assign each team an experiment to conduct during the imaginary space flight. At this point, the students simply prepare to conduct the experiments that they will do during the imaginary space flight (Extension Activity 7). They must make a list of equipment they need to take on the trip, plan a strategy, and make a prediction of the outcome. Refer to *Space Science,* Projects for Young Scientists by David W. McKay and Bruce G. Smith for more experiments.

Include experiments in:

ANIMAL BIOLOGY: Conduct an experiment to grow fish on the space ship to become a food source on longer flights. What special modifications must they make to compensate for zero gravity? How will air circulate in the tank? How will the fish eat the food if it does not sink in the tank? How will the fish stay in the water and not float away?

HUMAN BIOLOGY: Conduct an experiment on a human body's ability to tolerate zero gravity and light speed. The students might set up an exercise bike for their fellow astronauts to use during the flight. This team will monitor the astronauts' life signs during exercise, and when at rest. This team's list of equipment might include watches with second hands to measure pulse rates and stethoscopes to listen to the strength of the astronauts' hearts.

PLANT BIOLOGY: Conduct an experiment in the growth of plants on a spaceship. Long space flights require astronauts to grow plants for food on the ship. How will the seeds, water, plants, and dirt stay in containers without gravity? How will plants grow up and the roots grow down without gravity? What type of light will the plants use without sunlight?

OTHER: Any team that would like to create their own experiments may do so. They must be able to conduct these experiments during their imaginary space flight.

7. Friday: A Trip Through the Solar System

The students will participate in an imaginary space flight through the solar system.

◆ Begin the day by listening to the cassette and book set *Adventures in the Solar System: Planetron and Me* by Geoffrey T. Williams and Dennis F. Regan. The cassette is recorded in stereo, so separate your speakers to get the best effect. The students go on an exciting ride through the solar system with Planetron, a transformer robot.

◆ Next, act out a flight through the solar system from takeoff to landing. Assign a pilot and copilot to the control panel. The rest of the students strap themselves into their seats.

◆ The flight path will take the imaginary ship from Earth to Venus, to Mercury then back to Earth, Mars, the asteroid belt, and the outer planets. As the ship travels through the solar system, students map their flight by marking the solar map made in Extension Activity 4.

◆ Set a timer for the number of minutes it will take the ship to fly from Earth to Venus at light speed (2 minutes). When the timer rings, the group assigned to Venus will give their presentation. Mark the solar map, and set the timer for 3 minutes (the time in light years needed to travel from Venus to Mercury). The pilots resume their flight and the students strap themselves into their seats.

◆ After the timer rings, the Mercury group gives their presentation. Mark the solar map, set the timer and return to Earth. The Earth group gives their presentation, then the flight continues to Mars, the asteroid belt and the outer planets. During the hours between the outer planets, the students conduct their experiments.

◆ Ask a parent or volunteer to bring lunch to class. The students imagine trying to eat in zero gravity. What problems do they encounter while eating?

◆ If a student leaves the classroom, he or she is out of the spaceship. For these trips, the student must wear the astronaut backpack.

◆ Allow the students to stretch their imaginations. They might create many activities, experiments, and equipment as they travel through space.

◆ The imaginary flight will last the entire day. During the regular classroom schedule, try to coordinate the lessons with the space flight. To close the day, calculate the time needed to travel to Pluto when not traveling at light speed.

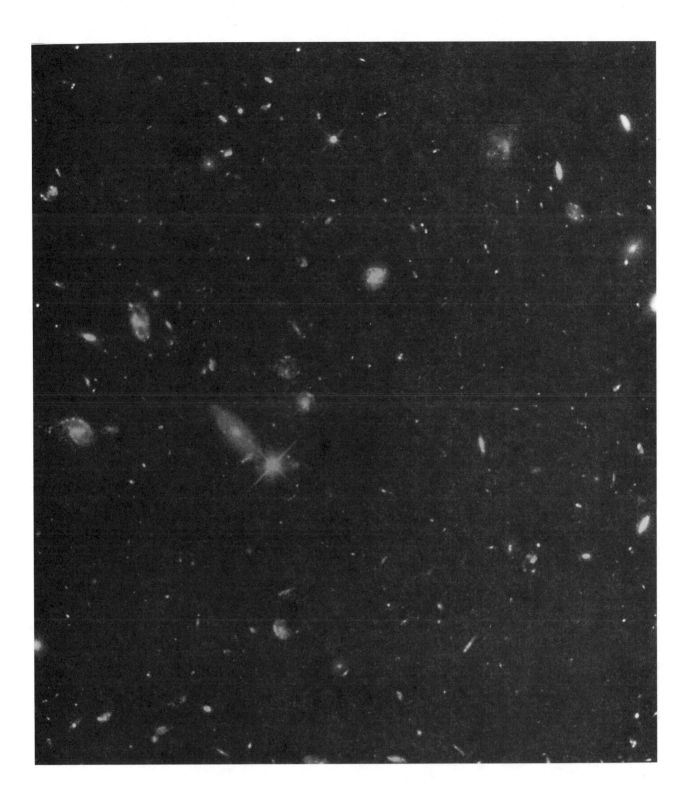

YOUR TIME MACHINE

Would you like to travel back in time and see what the stars looked like 84 to 650 years ago? You don't need a time machine. Just go outside any clear night and look up.

The light from the stars takes many years to reach Earth. Imagine this: I gave Sam a letter in Dallas, Texas. I told him to walk to New York City, and give the letter to a man there. If it takes Sam one year to walk to New York City, we can say New York is one walking year from Dallas, Texas. The man in New York will read a letter I wrote one year ago.

The light given off by the star Vega today takes 27 years to reach Earth. Vega is 27 light years away from Earth. If you look at Vega tonight, you are seeing what it looked like 27 years ago.

Try to find one of these stars tonight, then check the list. The light years tell you how long ago the star gave off the light you see tonight.

Star	In the constellation –	Light years away
Vega	Lyra	27
Pollux	Twins	35
Rigel	Orion	650
Sirius	Large Dog	9
Regulus	Lion	84
Deneb	Swan	54

Note: Light travels 6,000,000,000,000 miles a year. One light year = 6,000,000,000,000 miles.

QUESTIONS FOR YOUR TIME MACHINE

1. Where can you look to see back in time?

   _____

   _____

2. How many light years away from Earth is the star Vega?

   _____

   _____

3. When you look at the star Vega, how old is the light you are seeing?

   _____

   _____

4. In what constellation can you find the star Vega?

   _____

   _____

5. If the stars Sirius, Regulus, and Rigel all gave off their first light today, which star would be seen from Earth first?

   _____

   _____

6. If the stars Vega, Pollux, and Deneb all gave off their first light today, which star would appear in the Earth's sky last?

   _____

   _____

7. Imagine looking at the star Rigel from Earth. Suddenly, the star explodes. If you saw Rigel explode tonight, how many years ago did Rigel really explode?

   _____

   _____

8. If we were in a spaceship near the star Rigel, would the star Vega still be 27 light years away? Why do you think so?

   _____

   _____

9. Do you think people will travel to the stars? If you said yes, of the stars in the story, which one might people visit first? Why?

_____

_____

10. Astronomers study the stars. Would you like to be an astronomer? Why?

_____

_____

11. Write a title for this story. Use as few words as possible.

_____

_____

12. How are the stars Deneb and Sirius alike? How are they different?

_____

_____

13. In your own words, tell what a light year is.

_____

_____

14. After reading this story, will you look at the stars differently from the way you did before? Why do you think so?

_____

_____

15. The story says, "The light given off by the star Vega today takes 27 years to reach Earth." Is this a fact or an opinion? How can you prove your answer?

_____

_____

16.

_____

_____

Name _____   Date _____

FOR THE LOVE OF PATTY CAKE

ABOUT THE STORY

This story tells about a baby gorilla named Patty Cake. Patty Cake injured her arm in an old box cage with heavy bars. Zoo keepers debate the safety of these cages versus the need for the baby gorilla to stay with her family.

PREVIEW WORDS

gorilla	Patty Cake	Lulu
Kongo	Central Park Zoo	Bronx Zoo
dangerous	Richard D. Nadler	zoo keeper
New York		

PRIOR TO THE LESSON

◆ Make the necessary arrangements for a field trip to the zoo. If a field trip is not possible, arrange for a zoo spokesperson to visit the class.

◆ At the end of the lessons, the students donate an incomplete model zoo to a children's hospital, Ronald McDonald House, homeless shelter or related facility. Contact the institution beforehand and make the necessary arrangements.

◆ Contact a local home improvement store (building contractors might also donate), requesting one donated piece of plywood.

◆ Ask a local model railroad club or store to donate sheets of imitation grass, trees, or other landscaping. If grass is not donated, an inexpensive substitute is wood shavings. Students glue the wood shavings on the plywood, then paint the shavings green.

BOOKS TO READ

What Would You Do If You Lived at the Zoo?, Nancy White Carlstrom (Little, Brown, 1994).

Animals and the New Zoos, Patrica Curtis (Lodestar Books, 1991).

Tiger, Tiger, Growing Up, Joan Hewett (Clarion Books, 1993).

The Work of the Zoo Doctors at the San Diego Zoo, Georgeanne Irvine (Simon & Schuster Books for Young Readers, 1991).

To the Zoo: Animal Poems, selected by Lee Bennett Hopkins. Poets include Myra Cohn Livingston and Maxine W. Kumin (Little, Brown, 1992).

Patty Cake, Elizabeth Moody (Quadrangle, 1974).

A Day in the Life of a Zoo Veterinarian, David Paige (Troll Associates, 1985).

Goodnight, Gorilla, Peggy Rathmann (Putnam, 1993).

I Can Be a Zoo Keeper, James P. Rowan (Childrens Press, 1985).

Inside the Zoo Nursery, Roland Smith (Cobblehill Books, 1993).

Zoo Animals, Children's Nature Library, Eileen Spinelli (Gallery Books, 1991).

CDS, RECORDS, AND CASSETTES

A Zippity Zoo Day (cassette), Derrie Frost (Melody House, 1989).

The Gorilla (cassette and book), Paula Z. Hogan (Raintree Publishers, 1981).

Curious George Visits the Zoo (cassette and book), Margaret Rey (Houghton Mifflin and Clarion, 1988).

Lyle, Lyle, Crocodile (story kit), Bernard Waber (Lakeshore Learning Materials, 1994). Included book, cassette, puppets, zoo, and teacher's guide.

SOFTWARE

Davidson's Zoo Keeper, (Davidson and Associates, Inc., 1992).

INTRODUCTORY ACTIVITIES

DAY ONE

Objective: The students will visit the zoo. They will observe and discuss the design of the zoo. Curriculum subject: Science or Language Arts

Zoo Field Trip:

Before leaving for the zoo, ask the students to look at the design of the zoo. Does it provide a safe environment for the animals? Why do you think so? Are the animals in cages or do they wander in open areas? The students will take notebooks to write notes about the animals. They will draw pictures of the designs of the displays and the zoo itself. Tell them that they will make a model zoo in class. They will create their own zoo design.

During the field trip, point out the designs of the zoo. Point out any baby animals. Do they seem content? Are the babies kept with their families? Why do you think the animals live this way? Encourage the students to write notes and draw pictures of the designs of the displays. Which parts of the zoo will they put in their model?

After the trip, discuss what they saw. How was the zoo laid out? Would you use a similar design if you could build your own zoo?

DAY TWO

Story Lesson

Follow the *Presenting the Story Lesson* instructions in the Introduction. Each story lesson follows the same procedure; however, say the following in step 4:

"The title of the story we're reading today is *For the Love of Patty Cake.* What do you think the story is about?" If the students say a gorilla or a zoo, ask, "What do you already know about gorillas? What do you already know about zoos?"

EXTENSION ACTIVITIES

1. Discuss the students' observations of the zoo they visited on DAY ONE. How was the zoo like the zoo Patty Cake lived in? How was it different?

◆ Using a piece of bulletin board paper, work with the students to design a layout for their model zoo.

◆ Discuss the types of enclosures they will make. Will they have computers available for people to use to learn more about the zoo? What other creative ways can they make this model of a modern zoo enjoyable for all the visitors?

◆ Working as a team, the students choose the animals and area of the model zoo they wish to work on. They can work as individuals or in small groups.

2. Make the model of the students' zoo. Lay a piece of plywood on the floor. Using popsicle sticks, and materials from the "Parts Box" (see *Edwin H. Land*), work as a team to make a model zoo. The animals and other features are made of clay. If the school does not have clay, follow the clay recipe.

Salt Clay

◆ 8 cups salt

◆ 2 cups corn starch

◆ water

Stir together all the ingredients. Use enough water to make a paste. Cook over medium heat, stirring constantly. Continue until the paste becomes claylike and forms a ball. The salt prevents the clay from molding. If desired the students can add sand, pebbles, or sawdust to their clay to create the desired effect.

---

3. The students leave the zoo incomplete. Make extra clay. Take the students and the model zoo to a local children's hospital, Ronald McDonald House, homeless shelter, or other facility for children. The residents finish the zoo as a project to occupy them during a difficult time of their lives.

FOR THE LOVE OF PATTY CAKE

In 1972, a baby gorilla named Patty Cake was born at New York's Central Park Zoo. Patty Cake's parents, Lulu and Kongo, loved their baby very much. They hugged Patty Cake and played with her.

The Central Park Zoo was very old. It had old box cages with heavy bars. One day while playing with Lulu, Patty Cake broke her arm on the bars.

The arm was put in a cast. The zoo keeper called the newer Bronx Zoo. He asked them to keep Patty Cake until her arm was better. Lulu or Kongo might take off the cast, and hurt Patty Cake's arm again.

Patty Cake got better fast. When it was time to go home, the Bronx Zoo wanted to keep her. They said the old cage was dangerous.

The Central Park Zoo asked Ronald D. Nadler, who studied gorillas, for help. He told the Bronx Zoo that Patty Cake needed her family. He told the Central Park Zoo to make safer cages.

After three months, Patty Cake went home to Lulu and Kongo. The family was happy to be together at last.

QUESTIONS FOR THE LOVE OF PATTY CAKE

1. What is the name of the baby gorilla?

    _____

    _____

2. Where was Patty Cake born?

    _____

    _____

3. How did Patty Cake break her arm?

    _____

    _____

4. What did Richard D. Nadler tell the zoos to do to solve the problem?

    _____

    _____

5. What happened to Patty Cake before she was sent to the Bronx Zoo?

    _____

    _____

6. What did Ronald D. Nadler tell the Central Park Zoo to do before Patty Cake could go home?

    _____

    _____

7. What do you think might have happened to Patty Cake if the Central Park Zoo had not called Mr. Nadler for help?

    _____

    _____

8. The story says that the Central Park Zoo called Ronald D. Nadler for help. What does this tell you about Mr. Nadler's knowledge of gorillas?

    _____

    _____

9. Based on what the Central Park Zoo learned about their cages, what do you suppose will happen to cages used in other old zoos?

_____

_____

10. You read that the Central Park Zoo wanted the Bronx Zoo to return Patty Cake. One reason was to keep Patty Cake's family together. What other reason might they have?

_____

_____

11. Write a name for this story. Use as few words as possible.

_____

_____

12. Patty Cake moved to the Bronx Zoo until her arm was better. How was living at the Bronx Zoo like living at the Central Park Zoo? How was it different?

_____

_____

13. In your own words, tell why the Bronx Zoo thought Patty Cake should not go back to the Central Park Zoo.

_____

_____

14. How did Patty Cake's problem change the lives of the gorillas at the Central Park Zoo?

_____

_____

15. The story says, "He (Mr. Nadler) told the Bronx Zoo that Patty Cake needed her family." Is this a fact or Mr. Nadler's opinion? Why do you think so?

_____

_____

16. _____

_____

Name _____   Date _____

FISH FOR PETS

ABOUT THE STORY

This story tells about keeping fish for pets. It describes four types of tropical fish: neon tetra, zebra fish, guppies, and black or midnight mollies.

PREVIEW WORDS

neon tetra	zebra fish	guppies
black molly	midnight molly	nightmare
collection		

PRIOR TO THE LESSON

Obtain the materials needed to set up a small aquarium in the classroom. The schools system's science department, local pet stores, or aquarium hobby groups are good resources.

Make arrangements for a trip to pet store specializing in aquariums. Many store owners are happy to act as guides.

BOOKS TO READ

The Aquarium Book, George Ancona (Clarion Books, 1991).

Tropical Fish, Dr. Herbert R. Axelrod (T.F.H. Publications, 1988).

Fish, Mark Evans (Dorling Kindersley, 1993).

The Illustrated Encyclopedia of Aquarium Fish, Stanislav Frank (Octopus, 1980).

Fish, Junior Petkeeper's Library, Fiona Henrie (Franklin Watts, 1980).

Aquariums, John Hoke (Franklin Watts, 1975).

Play With Paper, Sara Lynn (Carolrhoda Books, 1993).

A Superguide to Aquarium Fish, Dick Mills (Gallery Books, 1989).

Know Your Pet: Aquarium Fish, Joan Palmer (Bookwright Press, 1989).

A Great Aquarium Book: The Putting-It-Together Guide for Beginners, Jane Sarnoff and Reynold Ruffins (Scribner's Sons, 1977).

What Do You Want to Know About Guppies?, Seymour Simon (Four Winds Press, 1977).

Exotic Fish As Pets, Paul Villiard (Doubleday, 1971).

VIDEOS

Starting Up and Maintaining an Aquarium: Fish, Dr. Michael Fox Animal Series (Tulchin Stuidios/The Maier Group, Inc., 1989). Length: 30 minutes.

One Fish, Two Fish, Red Fish, Blue Fish, Dr. Seuss (Random House Home Video, 1989). Video recording for the hearing impaired. Length: 30 minutes.

INTRODUCTORY ACTIVITIES

DAY ONE

Objective: Visit a local pet store specializing in aquariums. The students will take notes and make drawings of the equipment and fish.

Curriculum subject: Science

Take the students to a local pet store specializing in aquariums. Ask the shop owner to guide the students through the store. Discuss the equipment, fresh water fish, salt water fish and various types of fish available to aquarium owners.

As the students walk through the store, ask them to draw pictures of their favorite aquarium design and fish. They must label the drawings for later reference. Example:

DAY TWO

Objective: The students will set up an aquarium in the classroom.

Curriculum subject: Science

Ask a speaker to come to class to help the students set up a small aquarium. The speaker might be a local pet store owner specializing in aquarium fish or someone in the community who keeps pet fish. The students work together to set up the aquarium.

If you cannot find a speaker, show the video *Fish: Starting Up and Maintaining an Aquarium.* The video tends to move slowly, so ask students to draw pictures about setting up an aquarium as they watch the film. Following the instructions from the video, set up a small aquarium in the classroom.

DAY THREE

Story Lesson

Follow the *Presenting the Story Lesson* instructions in the Introduction. Each story lesson follows the same procedure; however, say the following in step 4:

"The title of the story we're reading today is *Fish for Pets.* What do you think the story is about? What do you already know about pet fish?"

EXTENSION ACTIVITIES

1. Write the following fish names on cards. Make one card for each student. Place the cards in a paper bag. Each student reaches in the bag and pulls out a name.

Angel fish	Sunset platy
Gourami	Gold fish
Catfish	Black molly
Barbel	Zebra danio
Pearl danio	Hatchetfish
Flame or red tetra	Platy or moonfish
Kissing gourami	Neon tetra
Guppy	Cherry barb
Siamese algae-eater	Kuhli loach
Siamese fighting fish	Swordtail
Cardinal tetra	Firemouth
Pompadour fish	White cloud
Black ruby	Epiplaty or Panchax chaperi

Materials

- large, white drawing paper
- pencils
- crayons
- blue water colors
- newspaper
- large construction paper

Procedure

- Using reference books, the students find pictures of the fish on their card.
- Imagine the large, white drawing paper as an aquarium.
- The students use pencils to draw their fish in the aquarium. They must include plants, gravel, and decorations. The students refer to the pictures they drew at the pet store.
- The students color their fish, plants, gravel and decorations with crayons. (*Do not color the water.*)
- Lay the picture on a piece of newspaper. This prevents paint from getting on the work area and makes cleanup easier.
- Using blue water color, the students paint over their pictures.
- As the pictures dry, the students write a description of their fish. For example:

Neon Tetra

Neon tetra are small fish. They have bright stripes running down their bodies. Neon tetra like to swim in groups. You need to buy more than one for your tank so they don't get lonely. Neons get sick easily, so you must watch them carefully.

◆ Mount the pictures and descriptions on construction paper. Display them in the classroom.

2. The students will make a model aquarium.

Aquarium Model
Materials

◆ any clear plastic bottle, (e.g., soda, mineral water)

◆ clay

◆ gravel

◆ construction paper

◆ magazine pictures of aquarium fish. (Some magazines specialize in pets or aquariums.)

◆ drawing paper

◆ florist wire or twist ties with paper covering removed

◆ glue

◆ large 3-pound margarine tub lid

Procedure

◆ To the teacher: Cut off the spout end of the clear bottles for the students.

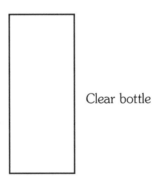

Clear bottle

◆ Lay margarine tub lid face down on the desk. Roll out ½″ layer of clay on the lid.

◆ Using the cut end of the bottle like a cookie cutter, press the cut end into the clay. Pull away excess clay from around the bottle.

◆ Raise the bottle from the clay. The circle of clay should lie on the margarine tub lid.

◆ Cut out pictures of aquarium fish from magazines, or make small drawings of fish on drawing paper and cut them out.

◆ Glue the end of a florist wire or stripped twist tie to the back of each fish. Insert the other end of the wire into the clay.

◆ Cut out plant shapes from construction paper. Set into the clay. For long shapes, crease the paper down its length. Push folded end into clay, and let the top of the plant open.

◆ If available, set small toys into the clay as aquarium decorations.

◆ Cover the top of the clay with gravel.

◆ Set the cut end of the bottle back over the edges of the clay.

FISH FOR PETS

Would you like to keep fish as pets? There are many beautiful fish you can raise at home.

Neon tetras grow to about 1½ inches long. Their bright colors of blue, green, red, and silver stripes seem to glow. Neon tetras are fast, active swimmers.

Zebra fish are also small, fast-moving fish. They grow about 1¾ inches long, and have dark stripes running from head to fin. Their markings remind you of zebras.

Guppies or rainbow fish can easily become your parents' worst nightmare. Their families grow by 30 to 60 babies every month. Guppies are about 1¼ to 2¼ inches long. Male guppies come in many colors and patterns. The females are larger, with little color.

The black, or midnight molly, is a large, elegant fish 2 to 4 inches long. The entire body is jet black. The males have a tip of orange along the top fin.

Pet stores have many other types of fish you can raise at home. Maybe you can start a collection of your own.

QUESTIONS FOR FISH FOR PETS

1. Name three kinds of fish described in the story.

   _____

   _____

2. What do neon tetras look like?

   _____

   _____

3. How many babies do guppies have every month?

   _____

   _____

4. How long is a black molly?

   _____

   _____

5. What is the first type of fish described in the story?

   _____

   _____

6. What is the third type of fish described in the story?

   _____

   _____

7. Why does the story say, "Guppies can easily become your parents' worst nightmare?"

   _____

   _____

8. Why do you think people named the one type of fish a zebra fish?

   _____

   _____

9. Will fish become more or less popular as pets? Why do you think so?

_____

_____

10. Why might someone want fish for pets?

_____

_____

11. Write a title for the story. Use as few words as possible.

_____

_____

12. How are neon tetras and zebra fish alike? How are they different?

_____

_____

13. Tell about the four kinds of fish in the story in your own words.

_____

_____

14. What would happen if you bought two guppies and had 62 guppies by the end of the month?

_____

_____

15. The story said, "There are many beautiful fish you can raise at home." Is this a fact or an opinion? How can you prove your answer?

_____

_____

16.

_____

_____

Name _____ Date _____

ROCKETS

ABOUT THE STORY

This story tells the history of rockets. The author gives several examples of inventions that relied on rocket power.

PREVIEW WORDS

rockets	gunpowder	Chinese
Greek	different	Arab
China	torpedo	Italy

THROUGHOUT THE WEEK—Read the story *Stinker From Space* by Pamela F. Service to the class. (New York: Charles Scribner's Sons, 1988). How would Stinker use rockets to travel through space? Why does our space program use rockets to launch satellites and the space shuttle?

BOOKS TO READ

Making Things Move, Action Science, Neil Ardley (Franklin Watts, 1984).

Air and Flight, Neil Ardley (Franklin Watts, 1984).

Rockets, Probes, and Satellites, Isaac Asimov (Gareth Stevens, 1988).

The Picture World of Rockets and Satellites, Norman S. Barrett (Franklin Watts, 1990).

Drawing Spaceships and Other Spacecraft, Don Bolognese (Franklin Watts, 1982).

Jet and Rocket Engines: How They Work, I.G. Edmonds (Putnam, 1973).

Model Rockets, Ed Radlauer (Childrens Press, 1983).

Finding Out About Rockets and Spaceflight, Lynn Myring (Usborne Publishing, 1982).

How to Be a Space Scientist in Your Own Home, Seymour Simon (J.B. Lippincott Junior Books, 1982).

Science at Work: Projects in Space Science, Seymour Simon (Franklin Watts, 1971).

More Mudpies to Magnets: Science for Young Children, Elizabeth A. Sherwood, Robert A. Williams and Robert E. Rockwell (Gryphon House, 1990).

More Science Activities: From the Smithsonian Institution, Megan Stine et. al. (GMG Publishing Corp., 1988).

175 Science Experiments to Amuse and Amaze Your Friends: Experiments! Tricks! Things to Make!, Brenda Walpole (Random House, 1988).

INTRODUCTORY ACTIVITIES

DAY ONE

Objective: The students will demonstrate that "every action has an equal but opposite reaction."
Curriculum subject: Science

Teacher: Can anyone tell me how people use rockets? (Examples: launching the space shut-
           tle, fireworks, military rockets.) Can you describe what a rocket launch looks like?
           Why do the space shuttle's rockets make it go up?
           Rockets prove a scientific principle: Every action has an equal but opposite reaction.
           Remember the words *action, opposite,* and *reaction.* (Write the words on the
           board.) Let's do an experiment that shows what this scientific principle means.

Materials

◆ one basketball for every two students

◆ padded floor mats

Procedure

1. Clear the desks from the center of the room.

2. Lay out the mats on one side of the floor.

3. Break the class into pairs of students.

4. One student sits on the mat holding the basketball. The other student sits off the mat, about
     three feet away. The partners face each other.

5. The students on the mats raise his or her feet and legs off the mats. They may not use their
     hands or feet for balance. (Make sure that there is enough mat behind the students so that
     they will fall back on the cushion. The students must not hit their heads on the floor.)

6. The student on the mat throws the ball to his or her partner.

     What happened to the student on the mat?

     (Answer: He or she fell backward.)

     Why did this happen?

     (Answer: Every action has an equal but opposite reaction.)

Teacher: In our experiment, what was the action? (Answer: The student threw the ball.) What
           was the reaction? (Answer: The student on the mat fell backward.) Was this an equal
           but opposite reaction? Why?

DAY TWO

Objective: The students will build balloon rockets. They will explain how these rockets prove
            the scientific principle, "Every action has an equal but opposite reaction."
Curriculum subject: Science
Teacher: What was the scientific principle we demonstrated yesterday? (Answer: Every action
            has an equal but opposite reaction.) Today we will make balloon rockets. Rockets
            move because of an action with an equal but opposite reaction. Think about this as
            we race balloon rockets.

Balloon Rocket Races
Materials

◆ balloons of various shapes about the same size

◆ sewing thread

◆ masking tape

◆ plastic straws
◆ paper lunch bags

Procedure

1. Break the class into teams of three to four students.

2. Tape one end of the sewing thread to a wall at shoulder height.

3. Draw the thread across the room. Cut the thread from the spool. This is the rocket race track. Make one race track for each team. Practice a launch before the lesson to determine the length of thread which works best for your class size and exact materials used.

4. Tape a straw to the side of a lunch bag, pointing it from the top of the bag to the bottom. Aim the bottom of the bag toward the wall. Slide the loose end of the thread through the straw.

5. Give each team a balloon. Note the balloon shape each team has.

6. Blow up the balloon. *Do not tie the neck in a knot.*

7. Keep holding the neck of the balloon tight. Slide it into the lunch bag, with the neck facing out of the bag.

8. The teacher calls, "On your mark! Get set! Go!"

9. The students release the balloons.

◆ Which balloon reached the wall first?

◆ Repeat the race. Which balloon shape repeatedly outperformed the others?

Teacher: Take out a sheet of paper. Write your name on the paper. Write a short description telling how the rocket balloons moved down the string using the scientific principle "every action has an equal but opposite reaction."

DAY THREE

Story Lesson

Follow the *Presenting the Story Lesson* instructions in the Introduction. Each story lesson follows the same procedure; however, say the following in step 4:

"The title of the story we're reading today is *Rockets*. What do you think the story is about? What do you already know about rockets?"

EXTENSION ACTIVITIES

1. Invite a hobbyist to class to talk about and demonstrate model rockets. Discuss safety, how the rockets work, and the varieties of rockets available.

◆ As a rocket is launched, the students can calculate the height the rocket reached. Using a stopwatch, time the launch from takeoff to landing. Help the students calculate the height using the following formula:

$$Height = 16 \left(\frac{time}{2} \right)^2$$

For example, if the flight from takeoff to landing is eight seconds, eight is the time. Therefore,

$$Height = 16 \left(\frac{8}{2} \right)^2$$

$$Height = 16 \, (4)^2$$

$$Height = 16 \, (16)$$

$$Height = 256 \; feet$$

2. The students will design and describe inventions requiring rockets.

◆ Teacher:

This week we looked at rockets. We learned how rockets move based on the scientific principle that states, "Every action has an equal and opposite reaction."

We read a story about inventions that used rocket power. Can you think of an invention you would like to create using rockets? (Examples: rocket-powered roller skates, school buses, lunch trays.)

Write a description of your invention. Answer the following questions: (Write the questions on the board.)

Who would use your invention?

What would your invention do?

When would people use your invention?

Where would they use your invention?

Why do people need your invention?

After you finish, draw a picture of someone using your invention. (Display the drawings and descriptions in the classroom.)

3. You can find additional activities in the many reference books about science projects. One excellent source is *How to Be a Space Scientist in Your Own Home* by Seymour Simon.

ROCKETS

We think of rockets as a new idea. How long have people used rockets? Can you guess?

Men made rockets hundreds of years ago. No one knows who made the first rocket.

A Greek man named Hero made a rocket about 2,000 years ago. His rocket engine used the power of steam.

In 1232, people in China made a rocket with black gunpowder. They called it "an arrow of flying fire."

People used the rocket in many different ways. In the 1200s, a Chinese man made a rocket-powered ski-chair. An Arab made the first torpedo using rockets at about the same time. By 1420, a man in Italy made a car using rocket power.

So you see, rockets are very old. People use rockets in many different ways. Can you think of a new way to use rockets?

QUESTIONS FOR ROCKETS

1. Who made the first rocket?

   _____

   _____

2. What did Hero use to power his rocket?

   _____

   _____

3. What did the Chinese call their rocket?

   _____

   _____

4. Name two ways people have used rockets.

   _____

   _____

5. Where did the first person known to make a rocket live, Greece or China?

   _____

   _____

6. Which was invented first: rockets made with black gunpowder, or a car using rocket power?

   _____

   _____

7. Hero made his rocket engine over 2,000 years ago, using steam. Gunpowder was not used until A.D. 1232. Give a reason why gunpowder might not have been used earlier.

   _____

   _____

8. The story tells us that no one knows who made the first rocket. What reason can you give for this?

   _____

   _____

9. What new ways might people use rockets in the future?

_____

_____

10. People make new things because there is a need for them. What reasons might the Chinese have had for making their rockets?

_____

_____

11. Write a title for the story. Use as few words as possible.

_____

_____

12. How are a rocket-powered ski-chair and a rocket-powered car alike? How are they different?

_____

_____

13. In your own words, tell about two different fuels used to power rockets.

_____

_____

14. How has the use of rockets changed our lives?

_____

_____

15. The story says, "People use rockets in many different ways." Is this a fact or an opinion? Why do you think so?

_____

_____

16.

_____

_____

Name _____   Date _____

THE SNOWSHOE RABBIT CHANGES ITS FUR

ABOUT THE STORY

This story tells how the snowshoe rabbit uses camouflage to hide from predators. The snowshoe rabbit turns white in the winter and brown in the summer.

PREVIEW WORDS

snowshoe rabbit   clothes   fur

BOOKS TO READ

We Hide, You Seek, Jose Aruego (Greenwillow Books, 1979).

Nature's Tricksters: Animals and Plants That Aren't What They Seem, Mary Batten (Sierra Club Books, 1992).

Summer Coat, Winter Coat: The Story of the Snowshoe Hare, Doe Boyle (Soundprints, 1993).

Can You Find Me?: A Book About Animal Camouflage, Jennifer Dewey (Scholastic, 1989).

Creatures of the Sea, John Christopher Fine (Atheneum, 1989).

How to Hide a Gray Treefrog and Other Amphibians, Ruth Heller (Grosset & Dunlap, 1986).

How to Hide a Crocodile and Other Reptiles, Ruth Heller (Grosset & Dunlap, 1986).

How to Hide a Polar Bear and Other Mammals, Ruth Heller (Grosset & Dunlap, 1994).

How to Hide an Octopus and Other Sea Creatures, Ruth Heller (Grosset & Dunlap, 1985).

How to Hide a Butterfly and Other Insects, Ruth Heller (Grosset & Dunlap, 1985).

Nature's Pretenders, Alice L. Hopf (Putnam's Sons, 1979).

Mistaken Identity, Joyce Pope (Steck-Vaughn, 1992).

Backyard Insects, Millicent Ellis Selsam (Four Winds Press, 1981).

Hidden Underneath, Kim Taylor (Delacorte Press, 1990).

Hidden Under Water, Kim Taylor (Delacorte Press, 1990).

Too Clever to See, Kim Taylor (Delacorte Press, 1991).

INTRODUCTORY ACTIVITIES

DAY ONE

Objective: The students will make an imaginary creature from another planet. The teacher will read a book about animal camouflage to the class.
Curriculum subject: Reading, Language Arts, Science, or Art

Art: Crazy Papier Mâché Creatures

Collect household discards and other items such as cola bottles, bleach bottles, trash bags, newspaper, and pipe cleaners. Using papier mâché (see recipe on page 294), the students will create imaginary creatures from another planet. *Papier-Mâché for Kids* by Sheila McGraw is an excellent resource for making funny creatures (Buffalo: Firefly Books, 1991).

Encourage the students to make their creatures as unique as possible. The creatures might have purple spots or gold stripes. Display the creatures and save them for use on Day Two.

Read the book *Can You Find Me? A Book About Animal Camouflage* by Jennifer Dewey. Discuss the various ways animals use camouflage.

DAY TWO

Objective: The students will create a landscape where their creatures (see Day One) can hide, using camouflage.

Curriculum subject: Science or Art

Creature Landscapes
Materials

◆ various sized cardboard boxes

◆ construction paper

◆ poster paint

◆ glue

◆ household discards such as margarine containers, cola bottles, pipe cleaners

Procedure

1. Match the boxes to the size of the creatures from another planet (DAY ONE).

2. Cut the boxes in half diagonally from corner to corner, making two landscape boxes for two creatures.

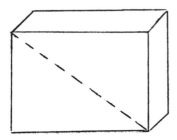

3. Set the creature in the box. Think about what the landscape around the creature would look like for it to blend into the background. For example, a purple creature with pink spots would live in a purple and pink landscape. The ground might be purple with pink stones. The sky might have pink clouds. Even the plants will match the color and shape of the creature.

4. Using whatever is available, decorate the inside of the box to make the landscape of the creature's planet.

5. After finishing the landscapes, set the landscapes without the creatures in the front of the class. Display the creatures away from the landscapes. Ask one student at a time to try to find the landscape for a creature he or she did not make. Can the students match the landscape to its creature?

DAY THREE

Story Lesson

Follow the *Presenting the Story Lesson* instructions in the Introduction. Each story lesson follows the same procedure; however, say the following in step 4:

"The title of the story we're reading today is *The Snowshoe Rabbit Changes Its Fur*. What do you think the story is about?" If the students' answers include animal camouflage, ask, "What do you already know about animal camouflage?"

EXTENSION ACTIVITIES

1. The students will write a story about their creatures who use camouflage.

◆ Teacher:

We have learned how camouflage helps animals and insects hide in their environment. We made creatures from other planets who matched their landscape. Today we'll write a story about what happens to our creatures when they leave their home planets and no longer match the landscape. Think about these questions before you write the story. (Write the questions on the board.)

◆ Who is my creature?

◆ When does my creature leave its planet?

◆ Where does my creature go?

◆ Why does my creature leave its planet?

◆ What problems does my creature encounter along the way?

2. The students will illustrate and bind the story written in Extension Activity 1.

◆ Read the picture book *Summer Coat, Winter Coat: The Story of a Snowshoe Hare* by Doe Boyle to the class. Before reading the story, tell the students to watch where the author located the page turns. Discuss the layout of the picture book after reading the story.

◆ The students will make the stories about their creatures into a picture book. They illustrate the story, choosing the best place for page turns. There might be several illustrations without text. Perhaps the students will make fold-out illustrations. Encourage them to be creative in their designs.

◆ The students write out the text in their best handwriting, matching the text pages to the illustrations. If a computer is available, the students can print out their pages.

◆ Bind the book with cardboard rectangles as covers. Punch holes along the left edge of the book. Use string or yarn to tie the pages and cardboard covers together. Cover the cardboard with shelf paper and decorate the front cover.

◆ The students trade books, and read their neighbor's story. The neighbor writes a brief critique of the book. Glue the critique to the back cover of the book.

THE SNOWSHOE RABBIT CHANGES ITS FUR

What color clothes would you wear to play hide-and-seek in a grass field? Green clothes would hide you in the grass. Your friends would easily see you if you wore black clothes.

The snowshoe rabbit needs to hide from other animals that eat it. The snowshoe rabbit lives in places that are very cold and snowy in the winter, however. In the summer, the snow melts to show the dark brown dirt. How can the snowshoe rabbit hide? It changes its clothes.

The snowshoe rabbit's fur is brown in the summer. It lies still on the dirt so other animals can't see it. In the fall, the first snows come. The snowshoe rabbit changes its clothes to hide in the brown dirt and snow. Now its fur is white with brown spots.

What do you think happens to the snowshoe rabbit's fur in the winter? It turns a beautiful, pure white. Sitting still in the white snow, the snowshoe rabbit can't be seen by other animals.

QUESTIONS FOR
THE SNOWSHOE RABBIT CHANGES ITS FUR

1. What does a snowshoe rabbit need to hide from?

   _____

   _____

2. Where do snowshoe rabbits live?

   _____

   _____

3. What color is the snowshoe rabbit's fur in the summer?

   _____

   _____

4. What color is the snowshoe rabbit's fur in the winter?

   _____

   _____

5. What color fur does the story describe first?

   _____

   _____

6. What color fur does the story describe last?

   _____

   _____

7. What one word best describes the snowshoe rabbit?

   _____

   _____

8. What might happen to a brown rabbit hiding in the snow?

   _____

   _____

9. What color is the snowshoe rabbit's fur in the spring? Why do you think so?

_____

_____

10. What happens to the weather that tells the snowshoe rabbit's fur to turn white?

_____

_____

11. Write a title for the story. Use as few words as possible.

_____

_____

12. John has a pet white rabbit. It lives in a cage in his yard. The rabbit eats carrots, lettuce, and rabbit food. John likes to play with his rabbit.

    How are John's pet rabbit and a snowshoe rabbit alike? How are they different?

_____

_____

13. In your own words, tell why the snowshoe rabbit changes its fur.

_____

_____

14. How do the changing colors of the snowshoe rabbit's fur affect the hunting animals? They depend on eating rabbits for food.

_____

_____

15. The story says, "Green clothes would hide you in the grass." Is this a fact or an opinion? How can you prove your answer?

_____

_____

16.

_____

_____

Name _____ Date _____

BEFORE THE DINOSAURS

ABOUT THE STORY

This story tells about mass extinction. Ninety-six out of every 100 sea animals died. This extinction occurred long before the development of dinosaurs.

PREVIEW WORDS

Earth	planet	dinosaurs
volcano	248 million	die-off

THROUGHOUT THE WEEK—Read *Dinotopia: A Land Apart From Time* by James Gurney to the class. (Atlanta: Turner Publishing, Inc., 1992.)

BOOKS TO READ

Did Comets Kill the Dinosaurs?, Isaac Asimov (Gareth Stevens, 1987).

Dinosaurs, Asteroids, and Superstars: Why the Dinosaurs Disappeared, Franklyn M. Branley (Crowell, 1982).

What Happened to the Dinosaurs?, Franklyn M. Branley (Crowell, 1989).

The Magic School Bus: In the Time of the Dinosaurs, Joanna Cole (Scholastic, 1994).

My Daniel, Pam Conrad (Harper & Row, 1989).

Fossils, An Easy-Read Fact Book, Neil Curtis (Franklin Watts, 1984).

What Color Is That Dinosaur?: Questions, Answers, and Mysteries, Lowell Dinqus (Millbrook Press, 1994).

What Is a Fossil?, Meish Goldish (Raintree Steck-Vaughn, 1989).

Fossils of the World, Chris Pellant (Thunder Bay Press, 1994).

Janice VanCleave's Dinosaurs for Every Kid: Easy Activities That Make Learning Science Fun, Janice Pratt VanCleave (Wiley & Sons, 1994).

Let's Go Dinosaur Tracking, Miriam Schlein (HarperCollins Publishers, 1991).

VIDEO

What Ever Happened to the Dinosaurs?, Golden Book Video, 1992. Length: 31 minutes.

INTRODUCTORY ACTIVITIES

DAY ONE

Objective: The students will identify and date fossils, using reference books as guides.
Curriculum subject: Science

Materials

◆ sets of three fossils for every three to four students in the class

◆ reference books about fossils

Teacher: What is a fossil? A fossil is an animal or plant that is so old, it has become part of a rock. Some fossils are the bones of ancient animals. Others are imprints of plants pressed into a rock. Even footprints so old that the mud turned into stone are fossils.

Today we'll look at many different fossils. You will look at the fossils and identify them.

Break into groups of three to four people. (Give each group a set of three fossils. The fossils should be common and clearly seen.) Look at your fossils. Talk about any unique features you see. Is the fossil round? Is it long? What kind of plant or animal do you think it was?

Next, look in the reference books and try to find your fossils. You will write a short description of each fossil. Write the name of your fossil at the top of the page. Answer these questions in your description. (Write the questions on the board).

1. Is the fossil from a plant or an animal?
2. Did it live on the land or in the water?
3. How old is your fossil?
4. During what period or periods of Earth's history did the plant or animal live?
5. What else did you learn about the fossil?

To help you determine the period or periods of Earth's history in which the plant or animal lived, you can use this information. (Display this chart in front of the class and read it to the students.)

Periods of Earth's History

Name of Period	Millions of Years Ago
Cambrian	600-700
Ordovician	500-440
Silurian	440-395
Devonian	395-345
Carboniferous	345-280
Permian	280-225
Triassic	225-190
Jurassic	190-136
Cretaceous	136-65
Tertiary	65-2
Quaternary	2 to present

Walk from group to group, helping the students identify their fossils. When the students finish, mount the descriptions on construction paper. Use a different color for each period of Earth's history from which the fossils came. Display the descriptions on a table next to the fossils they identify.

DAY TWO

Story Lesson

Follow the *Presenting the Story Lesson* instructions in the Introduction. Each story lesson follows the same procedure; however, say the following in step 4:

"The title of the story we're reading today is *Before the Dinosaurs.* What do you think the story is about? What do you already know about dinosaurs?

EXTENSION ACTIVITIES

1. The students will identify which fossils used on Day One came before and after the mass extinction described in the story lesson (DAY TWO).

◆ Teacher:

The story, *Before the Dinosaurs,* told us about a volcano that scientists believe caused the death of most of the plants and animals living on Earth. Scientists found the volcano in Siberia. Who can find Siberia on the map? (Locate Siberia with the students.)

Scientists call the die-off of such a large number of animals and plants *mass extinction.* The mass extinction described in the story occurred 248 million years ago. In which period of Earth's history did this mass extinction take place? (Answer: The mass extinction took place in the Permian period.)

◆ Working together, help the students divide the fossils into two groups: Pre-mass extinction and Post-mass extinction. How are these two groups alike? How are they different?

2. If possible, visit a museum displaying fossils. What creative ways did the museum use to display the fossils? Did the museum show what the ancient animals and plants looked like? Did the museum show how they lived? If so how did the museum do this? What did the museum try to teach in its displays?

3. Designate a section of the classroom as the fossil museum. Allow room for displays and murals.

◆ Teacher:

Today we will make a fossil museum. What is a fossil museum? What do you want to teach the people who come visit our museum?

In your own words, what is the objective of our museum? In other words, what do you want visitors to learn as they come through the museum? (Write the objective on a piece of chart paper and display it in the room.)

◆ The students will design and create their fossil museum based on their objective. Some suggestions are:

Display the projects from Day One.

Make models of what the fossilized animals and plants looked like when they were alive.

Include a "Fossil Petting Zoo" section. Visitors can touch the fossils and make clay imprints of them.

Paint a mural depicting the progression of life from the Cambrian Period to the Quaternary Period.

4. Invite other classes to your museum. Some of your students will act as guides. Others stand by the displays to answer questions or help the visitors in the hands-on activities.

◆ Between visits, discuss what went well and what areas of the museum need improvements. Make changes in the museum based on what the students saw. Continue with the discussions and improvements between visits.

◆ After all the classes finish their visits, discuss the whether the museum met the objective the students set out to meet. Did the changes they made between visits help make a better museum? Do you think museums watch the visitors and make improvements, too? Why do you think so?

5. In a clear container, layer colored sand. In each layer, place small fossils against the side of the container. The oldest fossils are in the bottom layer and the youngest are in the last layer. When complete, viewers look into the container and see a model of fossils imbedded in the layers of the earth.

6. An excellent source of activities for the classroom is *Fossils of the World* by Chris Pellant.

7. Some of us are fortunate to have fossil sites near our homes and schools. Read *Fossils of the World,* then take your class on a fossil-hunting field trip.

BEFORE THE DINOSAURS

What killed the dinosaurs? You have heard this question before. Something happened to Earth that changed it. Earth changed so much that the dinosaurs could not live on the planet anymore. Did you know that this was not the first time Earth changed?

Long before the time of the dinosaurs, different animals lived on Earth. Many of the animals were like snails and clams. Suddenly, most of these animals died. What killed them?

Earth changed so much that they could not live. Some people think that a volcano made Earth change. About 96 sea animals out of every 100 died. Most of the land animals died, too. The volcano killed these animals 248 million years ago. This large die-off of animals made room for the dinosaurs.

QUESTIONS FOR BEFORE THE DINOSAURS

1. Why did the dinosaurs die?

_____

_____

2. How many sea animals died from the volcano?

_____

_____

3. How many years ago did the volcano kill the animals?

_____

_____

4. What did this large die-off do for the dinosaurs?

_____

_____

5. What type of animals lived on Earth before the volcano erupted?

_____

_____

6. What happened after the volcano erupted?

_____

_____

7. Do you think dinosaurs would have lived if the volcano had not killed so many animals? Why do you think so?

_____

_____

8. The story tells us that a volcano changed Earth. How could a volcano do this?

_____

_____

9. The story tells us that Earth changed twice. Earth changed so much that many animals could not live anymore. Do you think such a change could happen again? Why do you think so?

_____

_____

10. Why do people want to learn about these changes in the earth? Is this important for us to know? Why do you think so?

_____

_____

11. Write a title for this story. Use as few words as possible.

_____

_____

12. How are the animals like snails and clams in the story also like the dinosaurs? How are they different?

_____

_____

13. In your own words, tell what happened to the animals that died before the time of the dinosaurs.

_____

_____

14. What do you think happened to the plants on Earth when the volcano erupted?

_____

_____

15. The story says, "Some people think that a volcano made Earth change." Is this a fact or an opinion? Why do you think so?

_____

_____

16.

_____

_____

Name _____   Date _____

THE PUPFISH OF DEVIL'S HOLE

ABOUT THE STORY

This story tells about a pond named Devil's Hole. Endangered pupfish live in Devil's Hole. Ranchers in the area need the water to grow their crops.

PREVIEW WORDS

pupfish	pupfishes'	Devil's Hole
Nevada	anywhere	ranchers
cover	Supreme Court	responsibility

PRIOR TO THE LESSON

Look around the school or near the school for a place that has less activity. For example, a small side yard where students do not play. Ask the principal if your class could use that area for a bird sanctuary.

THROUGHOUT THE WEEK—Read *Oliver Dibbs to the Rescue!* by Barbara Steiner to the class. (New York: Four Winds Press, 1985.)

BOOKS TO READ

Riverkeeper, George Ancona (Macmillan, 1990).

Endangered Species, Sunni Bloyd (Lucent Books, 1989).

Living Treasure: Saving Earth's Threatened Biodiversity, Laurence Pringle (Morrow Junior Books, 1991).

Keepers of the Animals: Native American Stories and Wildlife Activities for Children, Michael J. Caduto and Joseph Bruchac (Fulcrum Publishing, 1991).

The Endangered Florida Panther, Margaret Goff Clark (Cobblehill Books, 1993).

Animals in Danger: Forests of Africa, Compiled by Gill Gould (The Rourke Corporation, 1982).

Included in this series: *Animals in Danger: The Seas, Animals in Danger: North America, Animals in Danger: Europe, Animals in Danger: Asia.*

World's Endangered Wildlife, George Laycock (Grosset & Dunlap, 1973).

Wetlands, A New True Book, Emilie U. Lepthien and Joan Kalbacken (Childrens Press, 1993).

Take Action: An Environmental Book for Kids, Ann Love (Tambourine Books, 1993).

Lost Wild America: The Story of Our Extinct and Vanishing Wildlife, Robert M. McClung (Linnet Books, 1993).

Coastal Rescue: Preserving Our Seashore, Christina G. Miller and Louise A. Berry (Atheneum, 1989).

Oliver Dibbs and the Dinosaur Cause, Barbara Steiner (Four Winds Press, 1986).

Oliver Dibbs to the Rescue!, Barbara Steiner (Four Winds Press, 1985).

INTRODUCTORY ACTIVITIES

DAY ONE

Objective: The students will learn about wildlife conservation (birds) from a speaker. They will focus on how to help our wildlife.

Curriculum subject: Science

Invite a speaker who is involved in wildlife preservation (birds) to class. The speaker might be a representative of the Audubon Society or the zoo. Individuals involved in bird watching are often knowledgeable in the care of wild birds.

Ask the speaker to focus on what the students can do at school and at home to help in wildlife preservation. What activities can the students become involved in that are taking place in their neighborhood and community?

Later in the week, students will make a bird sanctuary at or near the school. Ask the speaker to give advice on how to make the sanctuary. What plants should the students grow in the sanctuary that are appropriate to your climate? Ask about plants that produce berries for winter food and foliage for spring nesting. End the lesson with a question-and-answer session.

DAY TWO

Story Lesson

Follow the *Presenting the Story Lesson* instructions in the Introduction. Each story lesson follows the same procedure; however, say the following in step 4:

"The title of the story we're reading today is *The Pupfish of Devil's Hole.* What do you think this story is about?"

EXTENSION ACTIVITIES

1. Break the students into groups. Give each group a different how-to book about making birdhouses and birdfeeders. A greater variety of houses and feeders adds to the beauty of the sanctuary. Each student makes his or her own birdhouse and feeder. A few books about making birdfeeders and birdhouses are:

   Bird Buddies, Better Homes and Gardens, Des Moines, Iowa: Meredith Corporation, 1989.

   Editors of Creative. *How to Have Fun Making Birdhouses and Birdfeeders.* Mankato, MN: Creative Education, 1974.

   Herzog, David Alan. *How to Invite Wildlife Into Your Backyard.* Matteson, Illinois: Greatlakes Living Press, 1977.

   Hiller, Ilo. *Introducing Birds to Young Naturalists: From Texas Parks & Wildlife Magazine.* College Station, TX: Texas A&M University Press, 1989.

2. Build a bird sanctuary. Before this lesson, collect the following (ask for donations or help from your PTA):

   plants, appropriate to your climate, that provide food for birds in the winter and nesting areas in the spring a birdbath

a bench

shovels, gloves, other tools

◆ Stretch a large piece of paper in front of the class.

◆ Tell the students that they will make a bird sanctuary today. Before they begin, they must make a plan or design. Working with the students, draw a layout for the bird sanctuary that will act as a map as the students make the sanctuary. Mark the bench, birdbath, trees, and plants on the layout to create a relaxing and inviting sanctuary.

◆ Assign groups of students to various parts of the sanctuary. Work as a team, following the layout. Water the plants, fill the feeders, hang the houses, and fill the bird bath.

◆ During the year, assign weekly teams as caretakers of the bird sanctuary. They will refill the feeders, clean and refill the bird bath, pull weeds and generally care for the upkeep of the sanctuary. When the sanctuary is left unattended for several days during school holidays, empty the birdbath to prevent mosquitoes.

3. The students will observe and identify birds using the sanctuary.

◆ Take the students quietly to the sanctuary. They will need one piece of drawing paper, pencils, and crayons or colored pencils. As the students sit quietly in the sanctuary, each student draws and colors one bird she or he sees.

◆ When the students return to class, they will use reference books to identify the birds. If there is a bird they cannot identify, the Audubon Society or a local wildlife preservation group might help them.

◆ The students write a brief description of the bird and its habits. Share the pictures and description with the class, then display them around the room.

◆ Later, bind the pictures and descriptions into a book entitled "Our Bird Sanctuary."

4. Invite other classes to visit your bird sanctuary. The students in your class act as guides, pointing out the various types of birds using the sanctuary.

5. The book *Take Action, An Environmental Book for Kids,* by Ann Love and Jane Drake, is an excellent source of activities involving students in wildlife preservation. (New York: A Beech Tree Paperback Book, 1993.)

THE PUPFISH OF DEVIL'S HOLE

In Nevada, there is a pond named Devil's Hole. Tiny fish called pupfish live in the water.

Pupfish are only one inch long. About 200 pupfish live in Devil's Hole. Pupfish don't live anywhere else in the world.

A rock sits just under the water in Devil's Hole. Water plants grow on this rock. The plants are the pupfishes' only food. If the water drops below this rock, the water plants will dry up and die.

Ranchers in Nevada also need the water. They use the water to grow plants.

Some people don't want the ranchers to use the water from Devil's Hole. They want to save the pupfish. Devil's Hole is the only place ranchers can get water. Who do you think is right?

In June 1976, the Supreme Court saved the water in Devil's Hole for the pupfish. However, they said the ranchers can use the water, too. It is the ranchers' responsibility to see that the water stays high enough to cover the rock where the water plants grow.

QUESTIONS FOR THE PUPFISH OF DEVIL'S HOLE

1. Where is the only place that pupfish live?

_____

_____

2. How long are pupfish?

_____

_____

3. About how many pupfish live in Devil's Hole?

_____

_____

4. How do the ranchers use the water from Devil's Hole?

_____

_____

5. What would happen to the water plants after the water drops below the rock?

_____

_____

6. Which happened last: the Supreme Court ruling, the pupfishes' need for the water, or the ranchers' need for the water?

_____

_____

7. Do you think the Supreme Court's ruling was fair to the pupfish and the ranchers? Why do you think so?

_____

_____

8. The story tells us that the pupfish eat only the water plants that grow on the rock. If the water level goes below the rock, these plants will dry out and die. What will happen to the pupfish?

_____

_____

9. The pupfish are not the only animals having trouble living with people. Many animals and plants die when people use the land. People need the land for food and houses. How can people use the land for food and houses without hurting the animals?

_____

_____

10. Why do you think the Supreme Court thought it was important to save the pupfish?

_____

_____

11. Write a title that best describes this story. Use as few words as possible.

_____

_____

12. How are the needs of the ranchers like the needs of the pupfish? How are they different?

_____

_____

13. In your own words, tell what the Supreme Court said about the use of the water in Devil's Hole.

_____

_____

14. If the water of Devil's Hole drops too far, the pupfish will die. Will this change your life? Why do you think so?

_____

_____

15. The story says, "Ranchers in Nevada also need the water." Is this a fact or an opinion? Why do you think so?

_____

_____

16. _____

_____

Name _____   Date _____

THE FIRST ASTRONAUT

ABOUT THE STORY

This story tells about the first "astronaut." NASA trained a monkey named Ham to ride in the first space ship.

PREVIEW WORDS

astronaut	Alan Shepard	chimpanzee
gravity	levers	

THROUGHOUT THE WEEK—Decorate the classroom with photographs of astronauts and space ships from the NASA programs. If available, display pictures of space programs from other countries.

Coordinate this week's lesson with the P.E. teacher's lessons on physical endurance. This is an excellent time to teach the students how astronauts also develop their endurance. The first astronauts, particularly, went through rigorous tests of physical endurance.

Read the following book to the class.

Service, Pamela F., *Stinker's Return*. New York: Charles Scribner's Sons, 1993.

BOOKS TO READ

I Want to Be an Astronaut, Byron Barton (Crowell, 1988).

I Can Be an Astronaut, June Behrens (Childrens Press, 1984).

On the Shuttle: Eight Days in Space, Barbara Bondar (Greey De Pencier Books, 1993).

Women in Space: Reaching the Last Frontier, Carole S. Briggs (Lerner Publications, 1988).

Bluebonnet at Johnson Space Center, Mary Brooke Casad (Pelican Publishing Company, 1993).

Space Travel in Fact and Fiction, Keith Deutsch (Franklin Watts, 1980).

The Dream Is Alive: A Flight of Discovery Aboard the Space Shuttle, Barbara Embury (Harper & Row, 1990).

NASA Visions of Space: Capturing the History of NASA, Robin Kerrod (Courage Books, 1990).

The Astronaut Training Book for Kids, Kim Long (Lodestar Books, 1990).

Astronaut Critter, Mercer Mayer (Simon & Schuster, 1986).

Christa McAuliffe, Teacher in Space, Corinne J. Naden and Rose Blue (Millbrook Press, 1991).

What's It Like to Be an Astronaut, Susan Cornell Poskanzer (Troll Associates, 1990).

I Know an Astronaut, Michael Rubinger (Putnam, 1972).

The Day We Walked on the Moon: A Photo History of Space Exploration, George Sullivan (Scholastic, 1990).

A Twenty-Fifth Anniversary Album of NASA, Gregory Vogt (Franklin Watts, 1983).

The Explorer Through History, Julia Waterlow (Thomson Learning, 1994).

VIDEO

America's Space Adventure: To Be an Astronaut, Indianapolis, IN, KVC Home Video, 1988.
      Length: 45 minutes.

INTRODUCTORY ACTIVITIES

DAY ONE

Objective: The students will watch a film about becoming an astronaut. They will discuss what
             an astronaut must know before going into space.
             The students will make an astronaut picture, using a photograph of themselves.
Curriculum subject: Science
Teacher: This week we'll learn about becoming astronauts. All astronauts go through training.
             You too will train for a mission. In your P.E. class, you'll work on building your phys-
             ical endurance. During the week, you'll prepare for next week's mission to travel by
             space ship to the planets of our solar system.
             Before we begin, let's learn about what it takes to become an astronaut.

             Show the movie *Americas' Space Adventure: To Be an Astronaut.*
             After the film, discuss what the students learned about becoming an astronaut.

Astronaut Picture
Materials

◆ copies of the black-line drawing of an astronaut in this section

◆ photographs of the students

◆ blue construction paper

◆ glue sticks

◆ crayons

Procedure

1. Give each student a copy of the black-line drawing of an astronaut.

2. Looking at a photograph of an astronaut in a space suit, the students color the picture.

3. Cut out the astronaut drawing along the wide black line.

4. Glue the picture onto blue construction paper, leaving space at the top.

5. The students cut out their faces in their photographs.

6. Using the glue stick, glue the faces into the face mask of the astronaut drawing.

7. Using a black crayon or marker, the students write their names at the top of the blue construction paper (e.g., Astronaut Susan Jones).

8. Display the pictures around the room.

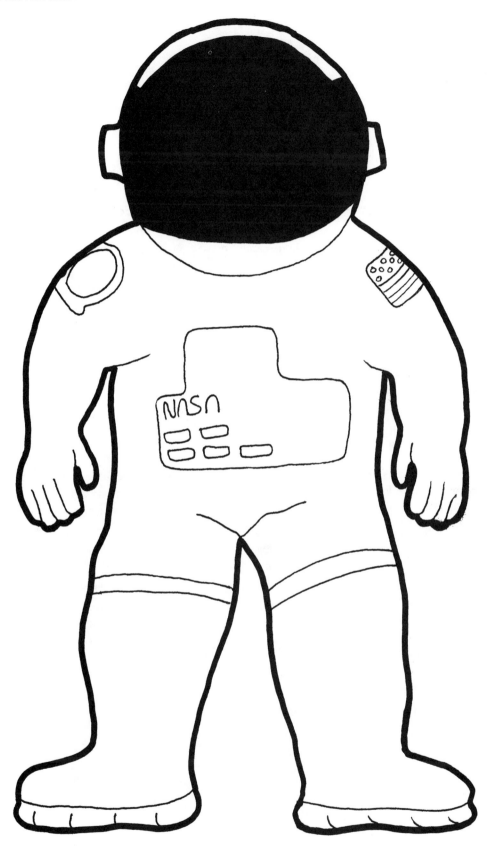

DAY TWO

Story Lesson

Follow the *Presenting the Story Lesson* instructions in the Introduction. Each story lesson follows the same procedure; however, say the following in step 4:

"The title of the story we're reading today is *The First Astronaut*. What do you think the story is about? What do you already know about astronauts?"

EXTENSION ACTIVITIES

1. Working in groups, the students will research and write a short report about assigned NASA programs.

◆ Using one name per card, write the following on index cards. Divide the class into groups of two to four students. Give one card to each group.

Apollo missions	Mercury program
Mariner program	Viking mission
The Pioneers	The Voyagers
Skylab	Apollo-Soyuz
Space shuttles	Magellan spacecraft
Galileo spacecraft	Hubble Space Telescope

◆ Teacher:

Astronauts must know the history of space exploration. Today, we'll break into groups of two to four people. I will give each group a card with a name written on it. Using reference books, videos, the computer, and other library resources, learn about the name on your card.

Write a report describing the subject. You'll tell me (write the following on the board as you read it to the students): What was it? Who was involved in it? When did it happen? Where did it happen? Why is it important to the history of space exploration?

2. The students will make a shadowbox depicting the spacecraft written about in Extension Activity 1. They will share the shadowbox and report with the class in historical order.

Spacecraft Shadowboxes
Materials

◆ medium-sized boxes

◆ black paper (preferably bulletin board paper)

◆ clear thread

◆ glue

◆ glitter and sequins

◆ drawing paper

◆ thin cardboard

◆ crayons, markers, paint

Procedure

◆ Each group uses one box. Line the box with black paper.

◆ Decorate the inside of the box, showing the destination of the spacecraft. For example, the group who wrote about the Magellan spacecraft would show a scene overlooking Venus. *The students do not include a picture of the spacecraft at this time.*

◆ Using drawing paper, the students cut out and color the appropriate planet or scenery. They glue the picture into the box. To give the appearance of stars, glue sequins and glitter on the black paper.

◆ The students draw pictures of their spacecrafts on drawing paper. Emphasize that the picture must be large enough to be seen in the box, but not so large as to overwhelm the background.

◆ The students color and decorate their pictures.

◆ Using a glue stick, glue the picture onto a piece of thin cardboard to make it rigid. Cut out the picture with the cardboard.

◆ Attach clear thread to the top of the drawing on the cardboard. Attach threads in more than one place on the spacecraft, if needed for balance.

◆ Punch small holes in the top of the box. Thread the ends of the clear threads through the holes. Tape the threads to the top of the box.

◆ The shadowbox shows the place where the spacecraft went. The spacecraft dangles on the clear threads in the foreground of the shadow box.

◆ The students read their reports to the class as they display their shadowboxes. The students present their spacecrafts in their chronological order. For example, the students who wrote about the Mercury program are the first to present their reports.

THE FIRST ASTRONAUT

Alan Shepard was the first person in space, but someone else went into space before him. On January 31, 1961, a little chimpanzee named Ham became the first "astronaut."

Ham trained for his flight months before his trip into space. Like human astronauts, Ham learned what it was like to fly at very fast speeds. Astronauts float in their space ships when they leave Earth's gravity. Ham learned what it felt like to float.

To be a good astronaut, Ham learned to drive his spaceship. He pulled special levers when bright lights flashed.

If Ham was to fly in a spaceship, he had to be able to sit a long time by himself. Ham liked to be close to people, so he learned to be alone.

Finally, Ham was ready for his flight. He learned his lessons well. When the lights flashed, he pulled the levers. Ham flew 5,000 miles. After his ship landed, doctors looked him over carefully, just as they do human astronauts. Ham's flight taught us that people could fly safely into space.

QUESTIONS FOR THE FIRST ASTRONAUT

1. Who was the first person in space?

   _____

   _____

2. On what day did the chimpanzee named Ham become the first "astronaut?"

   _____

   _____

3. What did Ham do when bright lights flashed?

   _____

   _____

4. How many miles did Ham fly?

   _____

   _____

5. Name two things Ham had to learn before his flight.

   _____

   _____

6. What did the doctors do to Ham after his ship landed?

   _____

   _____

7. Was Ham a smart chimpanzee? Why do you think so?

   _____

   _____

8. How did Ham's flight teach us that people could fly safely into space?

   _____

   _____

THE FIRST ASTRONAUT

Alan Shepard was the first person in space, but someone else went into space before him. On January 31, 1961, a little chimpanzee named Ham became the first "astronaut."

Ham trained for his flight months before his trip into space. Like human astronauts, Ham learned what it was like to fly at very fast speeds. Astronauts float in their space ships when they leave Earth's gravity. Ham learned what it felt like to float.

To be a good astronaut, Ham learned to drive his spaceship. He pulled special levers when bright lights flashed.

If Ham was to fly in a spaceship, he had to be able to sit a long time by himself. Ham liked to be close to people, so he learned to be alone.

Finally, Ham was ready for his flight. He learned his lessons well. When the lights flashed, he pulled the levers. Ham flew 5,000 miles. After his ship landed, doctors looked him over carefully, just as they do human astronauts. Ham's flight taught us that people could fly safely into space.

QUESTIONS FOR THE FIRST ASTRONAUT

1. Who was the first person in space?

   _____

   _____

2. On what day did the chimpanzee named Ham become the first "astronaut?"

   _____

   _____

3. What did Ham do when bright lights flashed?

   _____

   _____

4. How many miles did Ham fly?

   _____

   _____

5. Name two things Ham had to learn before his flight.

   _____

   _____

6. What did the doctors do to Ham after his ship landed?

   _____

   _____

7. Was Ham a smart chimpanzee? Why do you think so?

   _____

   _____

8. How did Ham's flight teach us that people could fly safely into space?

   _____

   _____

9. Some people want to go to Mars. No one knows if it would be too dangerous. How might NASA test the trip to see if humans can go safely?

_____

_____

10. Why do doctors check astronauts after their flight?

_____

_____

11. Write a title for the story. Use as few words as possible.

_____

_____

12. How is sending a chimp into space like sending a person? How is it different?

_____

_____

13. In your own words, tell about what Ham learned before he went into space.

_____

_____

14. How did Ham's flight help start America's space program?

_____

_____

15. The story says, "He (Ham) learned his lessons well." Is this a fact or an opinion? How can you prove your answer?

_____

_____

16.

_____

_____

Name _____   Date _____

READING LEVEL 3
BIBLIOGRAPHY

Ancona, George, *The Aquarium Book.* New York: Clarion Books, 1991.

Andersen, Yvonne, *Make Your Own Animated Movies and Videotapes: Film and Video Techniques from the Yellow Ball Workshop.* Boston: Little, Brown, 1991.

Angelucci, Enzo, and Attilio Cucari, *Ships,* pp. 808–809. New York: Greenwich House, 1983, c1977.

Aust, Siegfried, *Communication!: News Travels Fast.* Minneapolis: Lerner Publications, 1991.

"The Battle for Patty Cake," *Nature/Science Annual,* 1974, Alexandria, Virgina: Time/Life Books, pp. 162–165.

Boyle, Doe, *Summer Coat, Winter Coat: The Story of the Showshoe Hare.* Norwalk, CT: Soundprints, 1993.

Bunting, Edward, *The Ancient Music of Ireland: An Edition Comprising the Three Collections by Edward Bunting Originally Published in 1796, 1809, and 1840,* pp. 23–28. Dublin, Ireland: Waltons' Piano and Musical Instrument Galleries (Publications Dept.) Ltd., 1969.

Crampton, William, *Flag.* New York: Alfred A. Knopf, 1989.

d'Agapeyeff, Alexander, *Codes and Ciphers.* New York: Oxford University Press, 1949.

Dewaard, E. John, and Nancy Dewaard, *History of NASA: America's Voyage to the Stars,* p. 20. New York: Exeter Books, 1984.

Fox, Charlotte Milligan, *Annals of the Irish Harpers.* London: John Murray, 1911.

"Humpback Whale," *Encyclopedia Americana,* (1963), 14, 495.

Kahn, David, *The Code Breakers: The Story of Secret Writing.* New York: Macmillan, 1972.

Lobron, Barbara, " The Legacy of Edwin H. Land," *The Americana Annual: 1992,* p. 428.

Monastersky, Richard, "Geology," *The Americana Annual: 1991,* p. 248; *1992* p. 250.

Patent, Dorothy Hinshaw, *All About Whales,* p. 12. New York: Holiday House, 1987.

"Peck, Annie S.," *Pictorial Encyclopedia: People Who Made America,* Vol. 13, p. 1019. Skokie, IL: United States History Society, Inc., 1973.

Rey, H.A., *The Stars.* Boston, Mass.: Houghton Mifflin, 1962.

Robertson, Patrick, *The Book of Firsts.* New York: Clarkson Potter, Inc., 1974.

Sanders, Dennis, *The First of Everything: A Compendium of Important, Eventful, and Just-Plain-Fun Facts About All Kinds of Firsts.* New York: Dell Publishing, 1981.

"Saving the Pupfish," *Nature/Science Annual* (1978), Alexandria, Virgina: Time/Life Books, p. 174.

Stephenson, Ralph, *The Animated Film,* p. 29. New York: A.S. Barnes & Company, 1973.

"The Story of the Rocket," *Our Wonderful World: An Encyclopedia Anthology for the Entire Family,* (1962), 2, 247–251.

Williams, Heathcote, *Whale Nation,* p. 28. New York: Harmony Books, 1988.

Teacher Notes

Teacher Notes

Teacher Notes

Teacher Notes

Teacher Notes

Teacher Notes